Ancient Grains *for* Modern Meals

Mediterranean Whole Grain Recipes for Barley, Farro, Kamut, Polenta, Wheat Berries, & More

MARIA SPECK

PHOTOGRAPHY BY **SARA REMINGTON**

Ancient Grains
for Modern Meals

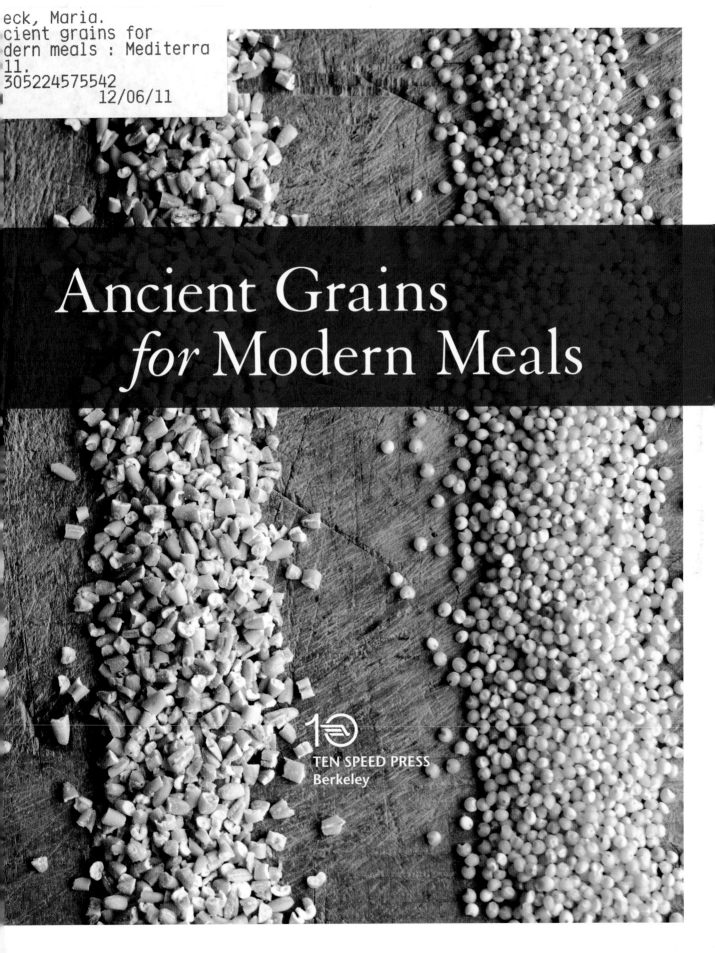

TEN SPEED PRESS
Berkeley

Ten Speed Press and the Ten Speed Press colophon are
registered trademarks of Random House, Inc.

Excerpt from *The Philosophy of Andy Warhol: From A to B and Back Again* copyright © 1975
by Andy Warhol, reprinted in the United States and its territories by permission of Houghton
Mifflin Harcourt, outside of the United States by permission of Penguin Books Ltd., and reprinted
electronically by permission of The Wylie Agency LLC.

Library of Congress Cataloging-in-Publication Data

Speck, Maria.
 Ancient grains for modern meals : Mediterranean whole grain recipes for barley, farro, kamut,
polenta, wheat berries & more / Maria Speck.
   p. cm.
 Summary: "A whole-grain cookbook featuring well-balanced and wholesome recipes inspired by
the Mediterranean cuisines of Greece, southern France, Italy, and Turkey"— Provided by publisher.
 Includes bibliographical references and index.
 ISBN 978-1-58008-354-6 (hardback)
 1. Cooking (Cereals) 2. Grain. 3. Cooking, Mediterranean. 4. Cookbooks. I. Title.
 TX808.S665 2011
 641.59822—dc22
                        2010045867

ISBN 978-1-58008-354-6

Printed in China

Cover and text design by Nancy Austin
Food styling by Katie Christ
Prop styling by Nyssa Quanstrom

10 9 8 7 6 5 4 3 2 1

First Edition

CONTENTS

AMARANTH

ACKNOWLEDGMENTS

THIS BOOK GREW OUT OF A BRIOCHE. Actually, it was a plate of butter-rich whole wheat brioches, ever so slightly sweet and risen slowly overnight. I had baked these soft, chewy beauties for Sunday brunch with friends almost exactly ten years ago, another one of my many efforts to transform the world into one planet of whole grain lovers. Our friend Isabel Bradburn soon raved about James Beard, the American icon and a name I had never heard before, and popped the life-changing question: "Why don't you write a cookbook?" To which I replied, "What?"

At the time, I was a foreign journalist, covering technology and society stories for German magazines. English was my third language, after my native German and Greek. And I had never published in the United States. Forget about any expertise in food writing. Well, little did I know that indeed I would write a cookbook one day, and how hard it would be.

Professionally, many people helped along the way. First, my editor at Germany's *Stern* magazine, Bert Gamerschlag, who supported my midcareer change to a budding food writer from the day I started pitching stories to him. In the United States, Darra Goldstein gave me the opportunity to write about my lifelong passion for whole grains in a piece for *Gastronomica*. Equally, Jim Oseland, in his unpretentious way, welcomed a piece on whole wheat German *Pfeffernüsse* cookies in *Saveur*. Both stories paved the way to a newfound love of writing in English that surprised even me. And Toni Allegra invited me to speak at, and later to occasionally host, the IACP-Teleforum, a national phone conference for food writers.

For this book, Rachel Laudan shared her knowledge on polenta's historical uses, and introduced me to the unforgettable term *nixtamalization*. Anne Willan answered questions about whole grains with her signature friendliness—despite the fact that we had never met before. Elizabeth Andoh helped with thoughtful advice on recipe testing. For lively exchanges on many matters of food, I thank Paula Wolfert, Grace Young, CiCi Williamson, and food writer extraordinaire David Leite. Roberta Dowling, founder of the Cambridge School of Culinary Arts, and Sean Leonard supported my teaching throughout.

I would like to thank Lisa Ekus-Saffer, who connected me, a first-time author, with my dynamo of an agent, Jenni Ferrari-Adler. Jenni not only grasped my vision for this book in an instant, but she also pushed my proposal out the door at lightning speed—while I honed my French cooking skills at the Culinary Institute of America. Jenni patiently helped me understand the U.S. publishing world and provided support whenever a crisis hit. To top it all off, she made the time in her busy schedule to try and test some of my whole grain recipes.

My passion for food I owe to my Greek mom, Theochanthi, who has always cooked for us, regardless of how difficult life would turn at times. And she continues to do so. Her single-minded obsession with the beauty and simplicity of good food ignited my own love affair with all things edible. As I'm writing this, I miss my German dad, Paul, who was one of the very few dedicated carnivores I know who embraced whole grains for what they are—delicious. Last but not least, my late Greek grandma, who, for lack of space, covered the furniture in her elegant living room with her own handmade made phyllo dough, and whose craft is my inspiration.

As a first-time book author, I am especially grateful to my testers, who provided their feedback on many of the recipes, first and foremost the tireless Karen Levendusky. Karen and her husband, Joe, have literally eaten through this book with a curiosity and openness to whole grains that I will never forget. From the moment she learned of this project, Karen said in her understated way, "Send me whatever you have and I'll try it." With an editor's eye, she pointed out missing teaspoons, ingredients, or any other matters that inevitably got jumbled during the endless testing, retesting, and tweaking of recipes. And she worked with the precision of Sherlock Holmes, measuring the size of bulgur kernels, timing the seconds for grinding sesame seeds, and providing uplifting feedback throughout. Thank you.

My thanks go also to Vivian Liu, whose critical palate challenged me more than once to go back to the drawing board. Many more people lent a hand in the process: my sister-in-law Yasmin Dharamsi, Dharni Vasudevan, Diane Asadorian, Myrna Greenfield, Lindsay Haugland, and—who knew—even our own amazing real estate agent, Marsha Price, who, along with her daughter Gabrielle Rosenfeld, kept my spirits up.

Personal support came from people who believed in this book—even as the rejection letters from agents kept streaming in: my friends Bea Giersig, Lucia Glahn-Kussel, and Jutta Werner. Edward and Lisabeth Weisband were convinced that my whole grain passion would ride out the tough years when the nation went low-carb. My friend Katrina Heron intently listened to all the obstacles and always came up with new ideas on how to move on. I thank my Italian friend Alessandra Campana for her fun-loving approach to making pasta and immensely good cheer throughout, and Thomas Peattie, who kept the wine coming (one with violet notes!) for our dinners together. And Hildegard Eisenmann who brought the whole grains of my childhood back into my life—little did she know at the time what a profound transformation would follow.

I will be forever grateful to master baker Greg Patent, whose late career change inspired my own. He saw a first draft of my proposal, joyously prodded me along, and provided support throughout; and to my colleague and super-talented pastry chef, Julie Usher, for her friendship.

More than anything, a cookbook writer needs eaters: thank you to enthusiastic dining companions and friends Marion Fremont-Smith, Oonagh Breen, Jane Nelson, Vera Coelho, Michelle Johnson, Golnaz Tabatabai and her son Hassan, Kate Scott and her daughter Jiao Jiao, and the Khwaja family with Sehr, Asim, Aman, and Nuriya; and to Ali Asani and Bapa, who always picked at his dinner plate like a bird until he died at the age of eighty-one, but ate every whole grain dish I put in front of him, surprising even himself. And the homeless men of the Cambridge First Church Shelter who graciously accepted any overflow from my kitchen, the good, the mediocre, and the less-than-perfect.

A generous thank-you also goes to the friendly and helpful staff at Bob's Red Mill and at the King Arthur Flour Company, who not only shipped boxes of whole grain flours and grains to my door for endless rounds of testing, but also answered many questions along the way. And I'm grateful that I live around the corner from Evergood Market in Cambridge, which is somehow always open when I need one more ingredient for last-minute testing.

This book would not have come to life without the support of my publisher, Ten Speed Press. Three editors accompanied me along the way to bring it to fruition: Melissa Moore, Dawn Yanagihara, and Jenny

Wapner, who took over late in the process but nevertheless provided encouragement and positive feedback until the end. Editorial director Julie Bennett provided backing at a crucial moment. I would like to extend a special thank-you to creative director, Nancy Austin, who helped translate my passion to the pages of this book, and to photographer Sara Remington, who teamed with food stylist Katie Christ to fill it with delectable food and the fresh, modern look I believe whole grains deserve. Copy editor Abigail Bok polished my words even further, and I also benefited from the clear-eyed proofreader Jean Blomquist. When I signed my contract with Ten Speed Press, a personal dream came full circle: this was the publisher I always wanted, and little did I know how many turns and twists life would throw my way before I finally could write for them.

While I was working on this book, America's own Julia Child was often on my mind. She once sat nearby at a conference, surrounded by fans, while I was rather clueless. I learned much about her life later, last but not least when I moved into her Cambridge neighborhood and started shopping at her butcher, Savenor's Market, which provided meat and fish for this book. Her much-quoted wisdom, "If you're afraid of butter, use cream" has been an inspiration, reminding me how important good ingredients are to good cooking whenever the health police in the back of my head started screaming.

And to my husband, Alnoor, whose fine palate and unwavering appetite is a food writer's dream, and who never relented.

"Progress is very important and exciting in everything except food."
—ANDY WARHOL

POLENTA

INTRODUCTION:
The Glamour of Whole Grains

WHOLE GRAINS HAVE CAST A SPELL ON ME—from the first sweetened wheat berries I chewed on during my grandfather's funeral to the comforting corn polenta my Greek mother makes to this day. I crave the tender chewiness of brown rice, the soft, translucent pearls of quinoa, and the warming lightness of millet. I love the subtle sweetness of whole oats, the slight sourness of rye, and the pleasing nuttiness of wheat berries. But I don't eat whole grains because they are healthy, or wholesome, or to reap their nutritional benefits. To me, whole grains carry luxurious qualities: lively textures, vivid colors, and rich flavors.

My passion is rooted in my upbringing. I was raised by a Greek mom, a fervent home cook, and a gluttonous food-loving father from Germany. I spent parts of my childhood in Greece, where my grandmother and my aunt would rise at 4:00 a.m. on holidays to prepare food for the extended family, from elaborately stuffed grape leaves with currants and pine nuts to oven-roasted kid lamb and bulgur pilaf. And I spent my formative years in Germany, where whole grains are part of the culinary fabric to this day, most famously in the country's rustic loaves of dark bread.

Our family table reflected these two contrasting cultures: my mom's tomato omelet with feta cheese was served with huge slices of my dad's favorite whole grain bread, cut from a traditional loaf almost the size of a bicycle tire. One week we indulged on German pork roast with homemade gravy, the next we spooned into tangy Greek *stifadho*, a wine-infused beef stew. My dad couldn't imagine life without liverwurst; my mom suffered when she couldn't find oranges or lemons.

This heritage is at the heart of this book. In it, I combine my mom's Mediterranean cuisine—its simplicity, its mesmerizing aromas, and its use of fresh ingredients—with the centuries-old traditions of preparing whole grain foods in northern Europe. In a nutshell, this whole grain cookbook brings you the bounty of the Mediterranean in tandem with the vast universe of ancient whole grains. It will take you on a journey from Greece to Turkey, from the south of France to Italy, and to Lebanon, adding tempting and delicious meals to your table with innovative flavors and new textures, some tender and some toothsome.

The recipes in this book will show you how to transform these ancient staples into fresh modern meals for breakfast, lunch, dinner, and even dessert—while adding health benefits all along. Whole grains were,

Bittersweet Koliva

In memory of my Greek papous *and my German father*

On one of the saddest days of my early childhood, I chewed on the best whole grain berries of my life. I was six years old, and my family had gathered at a cemetery in Thessaloniki to commemorate the recent death of my Greek grandfather, my *papous.* As is customary, everyone was handed a little white paper bag containing a traditional wheat berry concoction called *koliva.*

   I completely forgot myself and the occasion, and blissfully dug into the mixture of cinnamon and cumin-scented grains, chewing on their succulent, starchy centers, interspersed with chunks of roasted walnuts and sugarcoated almonds—until the wailing of my mom and my grandma reached my ears. It was then that I realized that I shouldn't show too much exhilaration over this celestial confection in the midst of such aching sadness. Yet my wheat berries became even sweeter.

   I created this simple version of *koliva*, similar to my childhood treat, many years later, after my father died. SERVES 8

WHEAT BERRIES

2 cups water

1 cup soft whole wheat berries,
   soaked overnight and drained

KOLIVA

1 teaspoon ground cinnamon

1/2 teaspoon ground cumin

Pinch of fine sea salt

1/2 cup coarsely chopped walnuts

1 tablespoon whole wheat flour

1/2 cup dark raisins

2 tablespoons silver dragées (optional)

TO FINISH

2 tablespoons toasted sesame seeds (see page 37)

1/4 to 1/2 cup confectioners' sugar

1/2 cup Jordan almonds, for garnish

1   To prepare the wheat berries, bring the water and the wheat berries to a boil in a medium saucepan. Decrease the heat to maintain a simmer, cover, and cook until the wheat berries are tender but still slightly chewy, 40 to 50 minutes. Drain in a sieve and allow to cool for 10 minutes.

2   Place a large dishcloth on a work surface. Spread the wheat berries across the middle section. Fold the sides over to cover the kernels and press lightly to remove any remaining moisture. Let sit for at least 1 hour to dry, and then transfer the wheat berries to a medium bowl.

3   To make the koliva, combine the cinnamon, cumin, and salt in a small bowl. Heat a heavy skillet, preferably cast-iron, over medium to medium-high heat for 1 to 2 minutes. Add the walnuts and toast them, stirring frequently, until fragrant, about 3 minutes. Transfer the walnuts to a plate.

4   Add the whole wheat flour to the hot skillet and cook, stirring, for 30 seconds. Add the wheat berries and cook, stirring, until the kernels turn dry, about 2 minutes. Add the walnuts, raisins, and combined spices; cook until the mixture becomes fragrant, about 1 minute. Remove the pan from the heat and transfer the mixture to a large bowl. Allow to cool for 1 hour, and then stir in the silver dragées.

5   When ready to serve, place a paper doily on a round decorative plate or a silver tray. Cut out a piece of waxed paper to cover the center of the doily and place it on top. Transfer the wheat berry mixture to the plate and pat into a mound with your hands.

6   To finish, sprinkle the mound with sesame seeds and sift a thick layer of confectioners' sugar on top. Using the Jordan almonds, decorate it with a cross or with the initials of the deceased. Garnish the rim of the plate with the remaining Jordan almonds. To serve, spoon the mixture into small bowls.

after all, the building blocks of our diet through the millennia. But do not expect me to lecture about them, or remind you to eat them regularly. I'd much rather have you try many of them and discover their remarkable textures and stunning variety—because eating is about pleasure first, and dieting last. I believe food has to be mouthwatering and seductive to stay in our meal plan for good. This is why I use rich natural ingredients like butter, cream and bacon, though in moderation. To me, whole grains are the ultimate comfort food. Chewy, sensual, and immensely satisfying, they are homey and nourishing in an old-fashioned way. And economical to boot.

In this book you will learn how to utilize quick-cooking grains like polenta, buckwheat, couscous, and millet as well as how to prepare "slower" whole grain berries in advance for a busy workweek. Whether you are a novice in the kitchen or an experienced home cook, you will find many short cuts and practical advice.

This book is not a whole grain bible, or the definitive guide to the grains of this planet. It is, rather, a personal selection of the whole grains I like to eat, inspired by the flavors and ingredients on which I was raised. And while most of these recipes draw from the rich food culture of the Mediterranean, they are typically not traditional dishes. Just like humans, traditions in food are always in flux. Today, in posh bakeries in Thessaloniki in northern Greece where my extended family lives, you find traditional olive oil cakes right next to, yes, American muffins. But these muffins are flavored with distinct local flavors and ingredients for their Greek customers, as are the anise-flavored muffins in this book, with dates and dried apricots and pistachios. Or indulge in saffron-scented waffles, topped with a creamy, rich yogurt topping with oranges—these are the flavors of my childhood, yet waffles, to my knowledge, have not yet arrived in the Mediterranean. Or have they?

Other recipes will transport you to the Mediterranean in an instant: enrich dinner with a wine-infused mussel stew with tomatoes and farro, an artichoke-rosemary tart with polenta crust, or an easy pasta with ground lamb and minted yogurt. Or feast on a stunning Moroccan-inspired salad with Kamut berries, carrots, cinnamon, and pomegranate seeds. For dessert, choose from an intensely fruity olive oil cake, bursting with figs plumped in orange-scented liqueur, or a purple rice pudding with rose water–infused dates.

While almost all of the recipes are Mediterranean-inspired, I couldn't hide my German roots. They bring you a luxurious chocolate-hazelnut muesli with dark chocolate and a crusty aromatic loaf of whole grain bread, flavored with coriander and fennel. And let's not forget an olive bread with bacon and thyme. Bacon, as an ingredient, has re-entered my cooking only in recent years. After all, my last name, Speck, means "bacon" in German. Having faced relentless teasing as a kid in school, I shunned this ancient ingredient for way too long—this bread brought it back, with a Mediterranean twist.

I believe the glamorous qualities of whole grains are vastly underrated. With this book, I would like to invite you to explore their star power. I hope you will learn more about matching and pairing their unique flavors and splendid textures, adding culinary highlights to your everyday life. Give these ancient staples a try—never have they been so ready for our modern tables.

Musings on Health, Dieting, and Good Eating

Almost every conversation about my passion for whole grains evokes this well-meaning remark: "Your diet must be very healthy." This comment always leaves me speechless, because health is the last thing on my mind when I eat. Of course, we all want to eat and live in a healthy way. But the reality is that good intentions rarely last, even a day.

ABOUT THE RECIPES

I have written this book for anyone who wants to eat well. It's for people who look for deliciously tempting food on their plate every day. Many recipes in this book can be on the dinner table fast; others require a bit of time and an openness to learning about new ingredients. None are truly difficult, as you will always find detailed instructions to guide you along.

Many stories are also woven into the fabric of this book. In essays, I introduce grains that I believe to be underappreciated despite their intriguing textures and flavors. Other essays provide a glimpse into my lifelong passion for food and cooking.

I call all chewy, slow-cooking whole grain kernels such as wheat, rye, hulled barley, or whole oats "berries." While this expression is commonly used only for whole wheat, I simply like how this word beautifully describes a single grain, lusciously plump and cooked to perfection.

In my baking, I always use 100 percent whole grain flours. In some baked goods you might not notice it because the whole grain flours are discreetly woven into a scone or cookie. In certain breads or muffins, however, I let the distinct texture and appealing chew shine for what they are. If you are not accustomed to eating baked goods made with whole grains, you will notice this difference. Baked goods will not be as light and fluffy, but a bit denser—I believe, deliciously so. Give yourself time to explore and appreciate these new textures and flavors, and enjoy the character whole grain flours bring to your table.

Nothing is as individual as portion sizes. My husband and I sometimes devour four servings of a soup or salad, because it tastes so good or simply because we are hungry. All recipe yields are my best estimates. Similarly, you might find the sweet treats in this book more modest in size than what you might be used to. They resemble the sweets of my childhood in Germany and Greece. Cookies, cakes, and dessert were special, and servings were small—I have my mom's crystal dessert bowls to

prove it. I can't imagine life without sweet endings, but I do serve them in modest amounts. Recent research makes the point as well: the bigger our plates are, the more we eat. Not surprisingly, our waists have grown with our plate sizes. So hunt down a beautiful set of smaller plates and dessert bowls at an antiques market. And enjoy everything, including dessert.

I have included a few recipes without any whole grains. These are recipes I fall back on because they pair splendidly with whole grain dishes. And I snuck a few of my favorite decadent delights into the dessert chapter. Last but not least, a Mediterranean recipe for roast chicken awaits you in the center of the book.

Almost all of the recipes include instructions on how to cook the whole grain being used, and you can also refer to the two tables that follow the section "Kitchen Basics for Whole Grains." At the bottom of each recipe I provide various helpful suggestions:

- "To get a head start" gives advice for busy people. It points out the parts of a recipe that you can make ahead, and gives storage recommendations.

- "To lighten it up" gives instructions on ways you can cut down on fat if you must.

- "To make it a feast" adds real richness for the days you simply want to celebrate the bounty of the table.

- "To make it vegetarian" tells you how to omit meat, poultry, and fish in a recipe, and replace them with complementing ingredients for a nourishing meal.

- "To vary it" gives you ideas on how to change the flavor in certain dishes. But you can always go much further and be creative on your own.

- "To time it" provides tips on how to fit an involved recipe such as a slow-rising bread into your schedule.

Today, I don't try anymore. I have stopped dieting for good. Like most women and many men, I have dieted many times, and from a young age. But I never had much stamina. Dieting exhausted me—not because I was weakened by a lack of food (I was a reasonable dieter), but simply because I ended up fantasizing about food all the time. Especially about all the food I was *not* allowed to eat. I soon found myself thinking about chocolate truffles every ten seconds, about a piece of German cream torte one minute, and about lamb chops or deep-fried calamari the next. This soon became unbearable, and distracting. So I did what every reasonable person would do: I drifted toward my dreams and broke my diet, again and again—until whole grains came along.

I'm not telling you that whole grains will make you lose twenty pounds in one month. But in my case, they succeeded in doing what no diet had done before. They brought me, a fast-food lover at the time, back into the kitchen. Whole grains and their tantalizing textures and fantastic flavors made me so curious about food that I started to cook. Soon I was on the best diet I have ever been on. And I stayed on it, for good. Most important, it included all food—cream, butter, bacon, and cookies—can you see where I'm going? I soon started to familiarize myself with unknown fruits and vegetables, and later with fish and meats of all kinds. Cooking made me appreciate food. It made me slow down and enjoy. Today we call this "mindful eating." I believe this happens naturally—when you cook.

I admit I was very lucky. Unlike many of us today, I was never introduced to whole grains as a health food. No one lectured me to add them to my diet, or reprimanded me to eat them because they are "oh so good for you." When I was growing up in Greece and Germany, some whole grains were still part of everyday life. In Greece, as a kid, I excitedly chewed on wheat berries, barley rusk, and bulgur. In Germany I spooned into warm oatmeal and indulged on whole grain breads, from crusty chewy wheat loaves to deliciously dense rye breads. But that changed when I moved away from home. Frozen pizza and ready-made chocolate pudding with whipped cream became my main food groups, accompanied by coffee, cigarettes, and wine—I was a journalist at a news agency, after all.

That all changed when a German friend of mine brought the whole grains of my childhood back to my table. Without uttering a line about health, she just put plate after plate of lip-smacking, tasty whole grain dishes in front of me—soups, salads, pies, and tarts, all with a distinct chew and impressive yet understated flavor. Hildegard, a single mom and my neighbor at the time, served whole grains with the fervor of a chef. She didn't skimp on cream or butter. Her meals were beautifully simple, and while German, they were Mediterranean in spirit. She successfully paired the unique flavor of each grain with fish or cheese, fruits and vegetables, herbs and spices, marrying them to perfection. She was always hunting for the best ingredients. Her fruit and vegetables were fresh from the farmers' market, her cream and butter organic when possible. Today we would call someone like her a locavore. I think all she wanted was to eat well. To me, this passion was contagious. She opened up a gustatory universe. And made me curious about whole grains—so much so that it changed my life.

What are whole grains, anyway? They are exactly what the name implies, the whole kernels or seeds of a grain with only the inedible outer husk removed, while the nutritious bran and germ are retained. The germ contains natural oils that can go rancid when exposed to air. In refined all-purpose flour, rice, or wheat, the bran and germ are removed for longer shelf life. Unfortunately, much of the nutrients are thrown out as well—you are left with the starchy endosperm, the center of the grain, containing largely "empty calories."

Whole grains, on the other hand, contain beneficial minerals such as iron and magnesium, B vitamins, vitamin E, antioxidants, and fiber. On average, Americans eat only 15 grams of fiber per day, about half of what is recommended. While fiber is not digested, it helps your digestion and it keeps you feeling full longer. This is great news for anyone trying to shed those extra pounds. No magic diet pill needed. Last but not least, it never hurts to know a few hard-nosed facts about adding more whole grains to your diet:

- Repeated studies have shown that a diet rich in whole grains significantly reduces the risk of major chronic diseases, such as heart disease, type 2 diabetes, and stroke.

- Eating three servings of whole grains per day can reduce the risk of certain cancers.

- People who eat whole grains regularly have a lower risk of obesity. They also have lower cholesterol levels.

This is all I want to say about the health benefits of whole grains. Much has been written on the topic, and one quick search on the Internet will bring you up to date. But mainly I don't want to tout the health benefits of whole grains because I don't believe this will actually make us eat them. After all, experts have been trumpeting these messages for years—yet so many of us still don't know what most whole grains look like.

So why don't we eat more whole grains? For one, I believe, it's because we don't know how to cook them. Fair enough. But I believe the real reason is that when it comes to whole grains, we are constantly reminded that we *have* to eat them because they are good for us. And that is also how they are still often served. Go to a bakery and you will find an assortment of beautiful breads with nuts and seeds, olives and sun-dried tomatoes, and then the one, oh-so-plain, whole wheat loaf. Or try a whole grain salad at a lunch buffet. Healthy it might be, with all the right ingredients, with lowfat this and no-fat that. I have chewed through many of those well-intentioned bowls. The thought makes me cringe. Because everyone else on the table is having a really good meal. Thank you very much.

I believe the only way to eat well for good is to eat all good food, within reason. Renowned journalist Michael Pollan puts it this way: "Don't eat anything your great-grandmother wouldn't recognize as food." Cookbook author and food writer Mark Bittman from the *New York Times* calls it a "moderate diet of wholesome foods." I believe whole grains have to be a significant part of our everyday meals to make us eat and live better, and perhaps even to lose a few pounds along the way. But first and foremost, they have to be deliriously delicious. Why else would we try them?

THE TRUFFLE THEORY

My eating philosophy can be summed up in what I call the truffle theory. It is based on my own experience, and it derives from one of my deluxe culinary pleasures: eating a homemade chocolate truffle.

When I buy a box of truffles, I often devour the whole box in, say, one day. Not so if I make my own. When one of my homemade dark chocolate truffles with cream, butter, and a fleeting hint of Grand Marnier starts to melt on my tongue, I go quiet fast. Not only is its sensational freshness positively overwhelming; I am also reminded of its creation. I remember the effort that went into making these unevenly shaped pieces of bliss. The wait for the silky ganache to cool. The brisk rolling between my palms so as not to melt the chocolate. And the good ingredients I bought to make them in the first place. So to my own surprise, one or two truffles will be all I eat. I don't have to tell myself to stop. It just happens because each truffle is simply so good.

I admit this is an indulgent start to an eating philosophy in a whole grain cookbook, yet it best encompasses my four principles of eating well:

- Cook as often you can.
- Eat everything, with pleasure and not in a rush.
- Buy whole ingredients, close to home.
- Strive for imperfection; no need to be a four-star chef.

This, in essence, also sums up the pleasures of the Mediterranean table and how I was raised. From Greece, to Turkey and Tunisia, from Italy to Israel, from Spain to France—eating across the Mediterranean is a soulful combination of cooking from scratch and preparing mouthwatering meals with whatever is on hand. Tables can be bursting with plates as if there is no tomorrow, or just have a few luscious appetizers. Ingredients are farm-fresh and simple. Most important, everyone comes together, takes their time to eat, and relishes the food.

The Whole Grains on My Table

This section is a brief introduction to the grains used in this book. It is not a reference guide to all whole grains. My aim is to give you a basic understanding of the grains I love, and to pique your curiosity so you seek them out and try them. Grains have been a staple of mankind for thousands of years. Early humans, the so-called hunter-gatherers, needed food to help them through the lean, cold winter months because fresh meat, fruit, and leaves could not be stored. Growing grains enabled them to collect and store seeds for later consumption, and thus became an essential tool for survival.

I have included a number of seeds such as amaranth, buckwheat, or quinoa that are commonly referred to as "pseudograins" or "pseudocereals," as they have a nutritional value similar to and are eaten like grains. Then there are staples such as couscous and bulgur, which are derived from grains but are not technically grains themselves.

This section also includes information on the varying temperaments of the whole grain flours used in this book. As you start using them in baking, this information will give you a better understanding of their different characters and qualities. Flour is not a consistent product. Its texture depends, for example, on the mill it was ground in, or the fineness of the grind. These differences affect the outcome of your baked goods. Try different brands of whole grain flours and see if you have a preference.

Last but not least, I provide guidance for when you shop. I have done this for a few select grains and flours that might cause confusion (or a headache, depending on your perspective) when you look for them in the grocery store, or when you cook them at home. But don't despair. There is nothing mysterious about whole grains, and you will soon become an expert.

AMARANTH

Minuscule amaranth is a nutritional powerhouse. It is often referred to as a pseudocereal because it is not part of the same plant family as so-called true cereals such as wheat or oats. A staple of the Aztecs, it has been cultivated in Central America for an estimated five thousand to eight thousand years. It is considered a "super grain" because its seeds contain all of the essential amino acids, providing high-quality protein.

Amaranth's tiny seeds, as small as poppy seeds, are part of a tall plant of which there are about sixty different species. The name *amaranth* stems from the Greek *amaranthos*, "one who does not wither." Most amaranth varieties grow as an annual weed, commonly known as pigweed. Certain kinds are cherished for their delicious dark green leaves. These amaranth greens, also called Chinese spinach, are part of the diet in Africa, Indonesia, China, and Greece.

The grain amaranth is high in minerals such as calcium and iron and has a subtle grassy flavor that some call earthy. Others detect a lively pepperiness. In many parts of South America, it is sold popped like corn rather than as a cooked grain. In parts of India, the popped grains are eaten in a traditional energy-rich sweet called *laddu*. Amaranth is gluten-free.

AMARANTH FLOUR Whole grain amaranth flour has a delicious concentrated nuttiness. But it is also an unusual flour, to say the least. Some say it makes baked goods gummy. I prefer to say that amaranth flour can yield intensely dense textures, and that only with trial and error will you learn how to compensate for this characteristic. Try the Amaranth-Walnut Cookies with Brandy (page 208) and judge for yourself. To get there, I baked a truckload of cookies, but it was well worth it—and the botched creations were almost as good.

BARLEY

Barley was likely the most important grain of ancient civilizations, from the Chinese to the Egyptians, from the Greeks to the Romans. Celebrated in Homer's *Iliad*, it was cultivated as early as 8000 BC. Pliny (AD 23–79) called barley "the oldest of food" and describes a common barley mush. Hippocrates praised the grain's healthful properties—in times of illness, he prescribed a diet of cereals and breads made solely from barley.

Highly adaptable, barley can grow from the hot, dry plains of northern India to the Arctic Circle, from Ethiopia to South America. So it comes as no surprise that it is baked into flat breads around the world. Barley is also at the heart of the English measurement system. In 1324, King Edward II of England standardized the inch as equal to "three grains of barley, dry and round, placed end to end lengthwise." While Columbus brought barley to the New World, it was cultivated only later by settlers from England and Scandinavia—to make beer. Bars and pubs would suffer without it: germinated into malt, barley is a crucial ingredient in beer (and whiskey) production (see also "Barley: Mild and Adventurous," page 129).

Barley has a faint earthy aroma, slightly sweet, and stands out among grains for its low glycemic index. Of all the whole grains, barley has the highest fiber content. It contains high levels of the soluble fiber beta-glucan, which can reduce cholesterol and help control blood sugar.

BARLEY FLOUR Barley flour adds delicious character to baked goods. It has a mild sweetness; some detect a hint of maltiness. I always use whole grain barley flour, which should be noted on the package. You can use barley flour in many recipes. However, since barley is low in gluten, it cannot stand in for wheat flour on a one-to-one basis. It is best not to replace more than about a third of your flour with nutty-sweet barley flour, otherwise your baked goods will not rise well.

WHEN YOU SHOP Pearl (or pearled) barley is the processed version of whole grain (hulled) barley, as the germ and much of the bran have been removed. I have used it in a few recipes in this book despite the fact that is not a whole grain. For one, it is a great introduction to the distinct flavor and character of barley. In addition, unlike most grains, barley's fiber is not concentrated in the outer bran but distributed throughout the kernel, so refined barley still adds nutritional benefits to your plate. According to the National Barley Foods Council, even heavily pearled barley typically retains at least 8 percent fiber. Look for pearl barley in the Latino sections of supermarkets, where it is often sold in a less refined form. Here is how you can tell: The more the grain kernels are coated with darker skin patches from the bran, the better. The reverse is also true: the whiter the grain looks, the more polished it probably is.

BUCKWHEAT

Buckwheat, despite its name, is not related to wheat. Technically, it is not a grain, but yet another pseudocereal from a herbaceous plant belonging to the rhubarb and sorrel family. First documented in China and Japan, where it is believed to have originated, the staple was brought to the United States by early European settlers. Its name is derived from the Dutch *bockweit*, literally, "beechwheat," and refers to beechnuts, which are larger but have a similar triangular shape (see also "Buckwheat: Bold and Almost Instant," page 145).

Buckwheat grows in poor soil conditions, which makes it ideally suited to cold climates. Thus, in eastern Europe and Russia, the cereal has been a staple for centuries. In English, the term *kasha* often refers to buckwheat, while in Slavic languages the term includes any porridge also made from wheat, barley, or rye. Japan also has a long history of eating buckwheat as porridge or dumplings. Highly esteemed soba noodles, made from buckwheat flour, date back to the seventeenth century and are a fairly recent addition to the Japanese diet.

Gluten-free buckwheat kernels (or groats) stand out for their high levels of rutin, an antioxidant that can improve blood circulation. When shopping for buckwheat, you have two options: already roasted kasha, which is brownish red in color and has an assertive earthy flavor; or grayish green raw buckwheat groats, which are milder and therefore a more appealing introduction. White-blooming buckwheat is attractive to bees and makes for an intensely aromatic dark-colored honey.

BULGUR

Bulgur (also bulgar, or burghul) is a godsend for busy cooks. You could call it the perfect ancient fast food—it transforms slow-cooking whole wheat into a quick everyday staple. In a traditional technique used for centuries, bulgur is made by first boiling wheat, and then drying, cracking, and sorting it by size. The outer layers of the bran are removed—still, bulgur retains a considerable amount of fiber, more than quinoa, oats, or corn.

This traditional convenience food is vital to many cuisines of the former Ottoman Empire, including those of Armenia, Turkey, Greece, Syria, and Iraq. For its versatility and countless preparations, some refer to it as Middle Eastern pasta. Bulgur has an appealing mild wheat flavor and pleasing texture. One of its best-known uses is in tabouli, the famous Middle Eastern salad, made with lots of parsley, mint, and tomatoes. It is also added to soups and meatballs, and cooked into nutritious pilafs.

Bulgur is most often made from durum wheat, but other kinds of wheat can be used as well. Bulgur is often confused with cracked wheat, which is exactly what the name says: cracked but uncooked wheat.

WHEN YOU SHOP Bulgur comes in fine, medium, and coarse varieties. All kinds are great for a speedy dinner, as precooked bulgur can be on the table in 10 to 20 minutes, depending on the size of the grain. Some cooks just reconstitute bulgur by soaking it in cold or hot water for as little as 10 minutes, or up to 1 hour. I prefer the chew of coarse or medium-coarse bulgur, but fine varieties are an interesting starting point. Middle Eastern stores often sell bulgur in packages that label the different grinds with numbers from 1 to 4, fine to coarse. Now, here is the puzzling part: You might have a batch of bulgur that a company identifies as "fine to medium," but whose kernels resemble a "coarse" grain to a *T*. In addition, those two kernels, which look absolutely alike, might cook up differently, in anything between 10 to 25 minutes. What is a cook to do? It's easy. Just check your grain after 10 minutes or so. If it is still slightly chewy, add a little more water to your pot if needed, and cook it a bit longer. Done!

CORN, GRITS, AND POLENTA

Corn, more accurately called maize or *mahiz* for its indigenous roots, is a kind of grass native to the Americas. According to recent DNA profiles, the "cradle of maize evolution" has been located in a river valley in southern Mexico. In this region, archaeologists also found milling tools with maize residue that date back almost nine thousand years. Corn grows in many colors, from white and yellow to bluish gray, purple, and red.

Columbus brought maize to the Old World from which it spread rapidly around the globe. While delicious as a staple, its protein is of lesser quality because it lacks two essential amino acids. Serving corn together with beans, dairy, or meat compensates for this shortfall.

The Aztec, Maya, and North American Indians treated corn with an alkali, a process called *nixtamalization*, which makes an important amino acid available to the human body. However, this traditional knowledge never made it across the Atlantic. As a result, impoverished southern Europeans who relied on a diet of cheap corn became sick with pellagra (from Italian *pelle agra*, literally, "sour skin"), a deficiency of vitamin B, or niacin. The disease, still common in Africa and China, also reached epidemic proportions in parts of the American South in the late nineteenth century.

Today corn is eaten around the globe, in countless variations from freshly grilled sweet corn on the cob to cornbreads and porridge—be it as southern grits, Italian polenta, Romanian *mamaliga*, or Greek *katsamaki* (see also "Corn: Comforting and Uplifting," page 107).

CORNMEAL For baking, I always choose stone-ground whole grain cornmeal, which comes in different grinds. Look for the term "whole grain" on the package. Stone milling grinds grains more slowly and at a lower temperature than large-scale commercial steel milling, and produces delicious, more textured flours. Supermarket products are typically degerminated. This means that the nutritious germ and the fiber-rich bran have been removed for longer shelf life. Not all companies put the grind—fine, medium, or coarse—on the package. Sometimes you have to play a guessing game, looking closely at the meal or running it through your fingers.

WHEN YOU SHOP Polenta, grits, and cornmeal cause a lot of confusion. First, on a light note, when a recipe in this book calls for polenta, don't go out and buy the plastic-wrapped tubes filled with a firm yellow mush. This is a ready-made product for last-minute preparations. Once you have tried real polenta, you will leave these tubes on the supermarket shelf. Italian polenta, now a trendy food, is essentially coarsely ground cornmeal, each little granule about the size of couscous. For the recipes in this book, look for packages labeled "polenta" or "corn grits" (but not the instant or quick-cooking kind). They will provide you with a pleasant introduction to the grain and will deliver consistent results. However, polenta and grits sold in the United States are often refined, which makes them not a whole grain. As a nutritious alternative, my recipes also give instructions for coarse stone-ground whole grain cornmeal from widely available Bob's Red Mill. This and other brands of more perishable whole grain cornmeal (with varying cooking times) are worth seeking out for their rich natural sweetness and toothsome texture (for sources, see page 219).

In the recipe testing for this book, we have also successfully used medium-coarse stone-ground cornmeal (see also "cornmeal" above), which will give you a softer, less textured mush, but will still be delicious.

COUSCOUS

A thirteenth-century cookery book contains one of the first written references to the tiny flour pellets called couscous. At the time, the anonymous author described it as "known all over the world," according to Mediterranean food expert Clifford A. Wright. Today, couscous remains a staple across North Africa. It is

neither a grain nor a pasta, but it is included here as it is commonly eaten like a grain and served in countless preparations—for breakfast, lunch, and dinner.

Traditionally couscous is made in a labor-intensive process from coarsely ground durum wheat. Women sprinkle salted water onto a bowl of flour while at the same time raking through it, causing tiny pellets of dough to form. Arab cookery expert Charles Perry notes that couscous has customarily been made from freshly ground whole grain. He describes the minuscule granules as "in effect a grain turned inside out" because the perishable bran and germ particles are coated with an envelope of starch, thus protecting them from the air, which allows couscous to last for months or years. Couscous is often steamed at least twice to achieve its characteristic ethereal fluffiness. The cookware used for steaming resembles a double boiler and is known by its French name, *couscoussière*.

Couscous is both simple and elegant. Infinitely adaptable to the flavors and sauces that infuse it, it is a most versatile side dish. Whole wheat couscous is more nutritious and richer in fiber than refined couscous. It is made from whole wheat durum flour and is precooked, like any modern-day factory-produced couscous, which makes for a fast everyday staple. In West Africa, couscous is also made from millet, and in parts of Morocco and Algeria aromatic barley couscous is common.

MILLET

Recent research has identified millet as among the oldest staples of mankind, tracing its cultivation in East Asia back ten thousand years. Part of a larger family of grasses, this small-seeded cereal spread across the globe because it grows well in drought-prone areas. To this day, millet is a staple in Africa, India, and northern China (see also "Millet: Sweet, and Waiting to Be Served," page 216).

In 2005, archaeologists discovered the world's most ancient noodles in China. They were made from millet and were four thousand years old. The pasta was found in twenty-inch-long strings and was surprisingly well preserved. This spectacular find may finally settle the debate on who first invented pasta: the Chinese, the Italians, or the Arabs.

From antiquity through the Middle Ages, millet was an important staple in central Europe before it was replaced by potatoes and corn from the New World. Millet porridge was widely eaten by the poor, from Greece to Italy to the Balkans. The significance of the grain as a major staple is also documented in language use. For example, the German term for millet, *Hirse*, derives from an old Germanic term for "nourishment."

Millet is a gluten-free grain. It is high in B vitamins, iron, magnesium, and zinc. And while this nutritious staple is derided by many in the West as "bird food," it is a deliciously mild whole grain, quick-cooking and almost endlessly versatile, much like polenta and couscous.

OATS

Comforting oats are the one whole grain Americans love to eat. Whether in a soothing bowl of warm oatmeal or in a chewy oatmeal cookie, the delicate natural sweetness and appealing texture of oats have wide appeal. The ancient Greeks and Romans, on the other hand, were less excited about the grain. They considered it barbarian fare, good enough only for their animals: Alexander the Great fed oats to his legendary horse, Bucephalus.

Oats are considered a relative latecomer to the human diet. The grain was cultivated in Europe only from about 1000 BC. The plant thrives in moist and cooler weather, which explains its popularity in northern Europe, especially in Scotland but also in parts of Germany, Scandinavia, and Russia (see also "Oats: Sweet and Sturdy," page 79). Scottish haggis combines oatmeal with sheep's heart, liver, and lungs, packaged in a sheep's stomach, for a favorite national dish.

In processing oats, the germ and the bran are hardly ever removed. As a result, this whole grain is widely available and can be easily added to your diet. There are different kinds of oatmeal to chose from: precooked instant oats, quick-cooking oats, and old-fashioned rolled oats. I enjoy chewy steel-cut oats for breakfast, and for other meals whole oat berries (groats). Compared to other grains, oats are high in protein and in beneficial fat. If processed correctly, they are gluten-free. And just in case you have always wondered: there are about 26,000 rolled oats in a 500-gram (1.1 pound) package. Start counting!

QUINOA

Nutrient-rich quinoa (pronounced KEEN-wa) was revered by the Incas, who called it *chisaya mama*, the mother of all grains. In pre-Columbian civilizations in the Andes, it was more important than corn and second only to the potato as a major food crop. The Spanish conquistadors banned its cultivation because of its ceremonial significance among indigenous peoples, but it survived in the wild.

Cultivated at least five thousand years ago, quinoa is another so-called pseudograin. While it has a similar nutritional profile and is eaten like a grain, botanically it is part of the goosefoot family, which includes spinach, chard, and lamb's quarters. The United Nations has named drought-resistant and undemanding quinoa a "supercrop" for its potential to feed the poor.

Quinoa is gluten-free and has an appealing, faintly grassy sweetness. The seeds contain all the essential amino acids, which makes them an excellent source of protein. They come in a rainbow of colors: black, purple, red, ivory, orange, and yellow. Quinoa seeds are about the size of sesame and have the shape of small disks. More than one hundred varieties of quinoa are grown in the Andes.

WHEN YOU SHOP Quinoa naturally has a bitter-tasting saponin layer around each kernel that protects the grain against insects. Thorough washing removes this bitter residue. However, most quinoa sold in the United States has undergone an abrasion process that also shaves off some of the beneficial bran and germ. Still, quinoa is a nutritious, quick, and delicious dinner staple worth exploring.

RICE

Rice is the staple for about half the world's population, especially across large parts of Asia, but also in Latin America.

A descendent of a wild grass, rice grows best submerged in water. Until fairly recently it was the accepted view that the Chinese Yangtze River Valley was the birthplace of rice, with cultivation reaching about ten thousand years back. However, in 2003 a handful of burned rice grains was discovered by archaeologists in Korea. This rice was dated back fifteen thousand years. In medieval Europe, rice was so precious that it was locked away in spice cabinets and its quantity diligently recorded, according to the *Oxford Companion to Food*.

About 120,000 rice varieties are known to exist, according to the International Rice Research Institute. In the United States, more than one hundred different kinds of rice are commercially grown, with Arkansas and California the top producers. Rice can come in many varieties and colors, ranging from black and purple to brownish red or red. The grain is easy to digest and available in short-, medium-, and long-grain varieties—with short-grain and medium-grain releasing more of the starch amylopectin during cooking and thus becoming stickier. Long-grain varieties, by contrast, contain more of the starch amylose and turn out fluffy with distinct separate kernels. While some kinds of rice are called glutinous, this term is confusing, as rice does not contain any gluten.

Brown rice, ever so slightly chewy and more aromatic than refined white rice, is a whole grain with the bran and the germ intact. Other rice varieties are available today in their whole unrefined state, such as Bhutanese red rice or Chinese black rice. Indian brown basmati rice with its mesmerizing aroma is another delicious example (the word *basmati* does mean fragrant). Brown kalijira, a rice from Bangladesh, is an interesting variety for whole grain lovers as its small grains cook up relatively fast. Don't hesitate to try the various kinds in your cooking (for sources, see page 219).

RYE

Rye is another latecomer to mankind's nutrition compared to other major grains, such as wheat or barley. It was probably first cultivated about 3000 BC. Pliny describes the growth of rye in the Alps in the first century BC, and calls it "unpleasant to the stomach," fit only for the very hungry. A disease in rye called ergot can cause hallucinations in those who consume grains infected with the highly toxic fungus. Some historians blame rye ergot for triggering hallucinations leading to the Salem witch trials in Massachusetts in 1692. Today in industrialized countries, the swollen black or purple lumps of diseased rye are sieved out after threshing.

Because rye can grow in cold, wet climates, it was the major bread-making grain in northern Europe for centuries, and it remains popular to this day also in eastern Europe and Russia (see also "Rye: Tangy and Surprisingly Sweet," page 188). Germans have long enjoyed dense, dark whole grain rye loaves and the Russians their black bread, while in Poland and Sweden lighter, paler rye breads are preferred.

Slender whole rye kernels have a distinct grayish-green hue and an appealing subtle tanginess, a terrific grain to add to your table. Rye also contains a type of fiber that makes you feel full fast—great for anyone hoping to lose a few pounds.

PUMPERNICKEL FLOUR AND DARK RYE FLOUR Both of these are whole grain flours milled from whole rye berries, with pumpernickel flour typically being a coarser grind, perfect for traditional pumpernickel bread (for a recipe, see page 77). Light rye flour is processed, with the bran and the germ removed. Rye flour does not contain much gluten, the protein that helps wheat bread rise and contributes to its fine elastic texture. To help rye bread rise, it has traditionally been leavened with sourdough, because yeast alone doesn't produce desirable results. Rye flour adds a slight stickiness to bread, which comes from a natural gum in the grain—it also keeps rye bread moist longer.

WHEAT AND ITS FAMILY

Wheat is one of the oldest domesticated grains, along with barley, millet, and rice. It is now the most widely cultivated cereal around the globe, exceeding even rice. Domestic cultivation of wheat has been documented at least since 9000 BC. The popularity of wheat has to do with its high content of gluten—a protein—which helps bread rise and is responsible for its elastic texture. Throughout history, wheat was highly cherished and used by the rich, while the poor subsisted on lowlier grains such as barley and millet. According to the *Oxford Companion to Food*, the name *wheat* even refers to the valued "whiteness" of its flour. In the New World, wheat was first grown in 1529 by Spanish explorers in Mexico, with the American Midwest and Canada eventually becoming major growing regions.

While some ancient wheat varieties survive, two kinds of wheat are most commonly cultivated today. Durum wheat is a very hard grain that is best suited for making pasta (for which it has probably been used as far back as the first century BC). When durum kernels are ground, they splinter into fragments that are called semolina—which are also the basis for making couscous. The other main wheat is "hard" bread wheat. Here the hardness refers to the protein content—bread wheat has a large proportion of glutenin, the main protein forming the gluten that gives nice elasticity to wheat bread. Wheat is also distinguished by color (red and white) and by the growing season (winter and spring).

In cooking and baking, you might also encounter "soft" wheat, which has a lower protein content and is typically milled into cake flour. Ancient wheat varieties such as farro, spelt, and Kamut have seen a comeback in recent years and have found new appreciation with food lovers. Some people who are sensitive to wheat can tolerate these ancient grains and products made from them (see also "Farro: Ancient and Ambrosial," page 163). I discuss each one separately below.

WHOLE WHEAT FLOUR AND "WHITE" WHOLE WHEAT FLOUR Regular whole wheat flour is milled from hard red wheat berries and has a hearty flavor and texture. Some people perceive it as slightly bitter, though I think one reason could be that the flour was old (and thus rancid). However, if your family is not very experimental, try using "white" whole wheat flour in your baking and no one will be able to tell. *White* here does not mean that the flour has been refined, but rather that it has been milled from a different kind of hard wheat. White whole wheat is lighter in color and naturally slightly sweet (it has less tannin), but it retains the same beneficial nutrients and fiber as regular whole wheat. It has become much more widely available in the past decade.

While you can use regular and white whole wheat flour interchangeably, I suggest that you use the flour I recommend in each recipe, as their flavors are unique. I use regular whole wheat flour for baked goods when I look for heartiness and a more savory aroma, as in rustic breads and certain pizzas for example. In sweet baked goods, I typically choose white whole wheat flour. But try for yourself and see.

WHOLE WHEAT PASTRY FLOUR This flour is ground from soft whole wheat berries and is best used for more delicate baked goods such as cakes. It has a lower protein content similar to that of refined cake flour, which is also milled from soft wheat. I often combine it with protein-rich white whole wheat flour, which adds structure and texture to baked goods.

WHEN YOU SHOP Whole wheat berries are sold as *hard* or *soft* wheat berries. While soft wheat berries are harder to track down, they are an appealing choice, especially if you are new to whole grains. For one, they cook faster. But they are also less chewy, which makes them an attractive addition to stews, pilaf, and salads.

FARRO Popular farro is not one kind of wheat; rather, the term is commonly used when referring to three ancient wheat varieties still cultivated in Italy: *farro piccolo* (also known by the German einkorn), *farro medio* (also known as emmer, the Hebrew word for mother) and *farro grande* (also known as spelt, see below). Ancient wheat varieties such as these grow well in poor soil but are less amenable to modern farming methods and have thus fallen by the wayside.

Emmer was first domesticated in the Fertile Crescent, almost ten thousand years ago. It has survived to this day in mountainous regions of Morocco, Spain, and Turkey, and it is likely the most common ancient wheat still cultivated in parts of Italy, especially in Tuscany. In Ethiopia, emmer also still plays a significant role as a traditional food. Einkorn was grown by the ancient Egyptians and was discovered in four-thousand-year-old tombs of the pharaohs. After languishing in obscurity for centuries, these ancient grains have become trendy and have seen a comeback in the United States and in Europe. Restaurant chefs cherish their nutty sweetness and delicate chew.

WHEN YOU SHOP Farro sold in the United States is typically of the emmer variety and often semi-pearled, retaining some but not all of the bran and nutrients (on packages imported from Italy, you might read *semi-perlato*). Thus, my recipes have been written for this type of farro: it cooks up fast, in 20 to 25 minutes, and it enables you to enjoy the grain's alluring texture and aroma with hints of cinnamon. Once you appreciate this new grain on your plate, feel free to "upgrade" to the real deal, deliciously plump and chewy whole grain farro. Farmers have started to grow this ancient grain in the United States, and it is worth your time and effort to track it down. There are different kinds of whole grain farro available; some cook up fast, such as *farro piccolo*, while others are best soaked ahead, and simmered from anything between 35 to 70 minutes (for sources, see page 219). If you can't tell from the package whether you have refined or whole grain farro in front of you, fiber content, a close look at the kernels, and some experience will help you distinguish whether you have a whole or a pearled kernel in front of you (see also above, the "When you shop" section under "Barley," page 8).

KAMUT Kamut has stunningly large, almost bronze-colored grain kernels and a rich, buttery flavor. This ancient wheat variety is properly called *khorasan* and is commercially sold under the trademarked name Kamut. In the United States, it was first cultivated in Montana about sixty years ago, and has become more widely available only in the past twenty years. The grain, which is still grown in Egypt and in small plots in Turkey, has never been hybridized. Its trademark certifies that all Kamut is grown organically.

Compared to modern-day wheat, Kamut is higher in protein and certain minerals such as selenium. Stories abound that Kamut was found in an ancient Egyptian tomb, and that its seeds were miraculously replanted in modern days—these stories are, well, just good stories.

SPELT The ancient wheat species spelt, probably a hybrid of emmer and bread wheat, was widely cultivated in parts of Europe during the Bronze Age. With its tough outer hull, it has a natural resistance to pests, but it is not easy to harvest—and hence was replaced by higher-yielding wheat varieties in the twentieth century. Until that time, spelt was a popular staple in Switzerland, Austria, and Germany, as well as in France and Spain. In Germany, spelt is called *Dinkel*—the town of Dinkelsbühl is named after the grain.

The German mystic and Benedictine abbess Hildegard von Bingen (1098–1179) considered spelt the best of all grains and recommended it for its healing properties. Germans also cultivate *Grünkern*, literally, "green kernel." This is spelt harvested early, before it is fully ripened, then roasted. It has a strong and brothy, almost meaty, flavor which is cherished by many. It is traditionally used in grain cakes, soups, and pasta.

Spelt, a high-protein grain with a reddish hue, has a mild natural sweetness and is thus a great introduction to the wheat family.

SPELT FLOUR Spelt flour has seen a revival across many parts of Europe. Lately, it has also become more widely available in the United States. Always look for whole grain spelt flour for the recipes in this book. The flour has an attractive mildness and is very easy to work with. I like using it not only in pizzas and flatbreads, but also in cakes and cookies.

WILD RICE

Wild rice is the seed of an aquatic grass native to North America. While the plant is not a grain, it is closely related to true rice, which is also a grass. Varieties of wild rice grow naturally in isolated lakes and riverbeds, especially in the Great Lakes region and southern-central Canada, as well as in Texas and Florida. Most of the wild rice sold in the United States today is cultivated in Minnesota and California.

The term *wild rice* comes from *riz sauvage*, coined by early French explorers. Native Americans revered wild rice as a "gift from the Great Spirit." The Ojibwe people referred to it as *manoomin*, which translates as "the good berry." Harvesting of wild rice is regulated in Minnesota and Canada to protect the way of life of Native American communities and to preserve the wild rice beds.

Commercial cultivation started in the early 1960s when demand outgrew the traditional labor-intensive harvest. Cultivated seeds are generally shiny and more uniformly dark, while "wild" wild rice has a mottled brownish look with an intense smoky aroma, the result of traditional parching over an open fire.

The intense nuttiness of wild rice and its distinct chewy texture are its main appeal. It is also higher in fiber and protein than brown rice. While it is always a pricey addition to your dinner table, you can enjoy it on occasion—or combine it with less expensive varieties to create your own blend.

Kitchen Basics for Whole Grains

Cooking whole grains is no more difficult than boiling pasta. There is nothing truly challenging about it. In fact, many can be prepared so easily that you will probably ask yourself why you've never tried before. It is just a matter of getting used to their different characters.

Over the years, I have found it most useful to divide whole grains into two groups. Quick-cooking whole grains can be on the table without much effort, in anywhere from 5 to 30 minutes at most. Slow-cooking whole grains, on the other hand, are easiest when prepared ahead on a leisurely weekend or the night before. And while ready-made whole grain products such as instant brown rice never match the flavor and texture of home-cooked, by all means use them when in a hurry. Most important, enjoy exploring the vast variety, colors, and textures of whole grains.

In the book, I provide cooking instructions for whole grains in almost every recipe. However, I have also included two tables at the end of this section that provide cooking methods and times for different grains at a glance so you can venture on your own and use whole grains in many more dishes.

BUYING

I buy organic whole grains and flours whenever possible (see also "Musings on Health, Dieting, and Good Eating," page 3). While pesticide residue on whole grains and flours might be negligible, my diet is built on whole grains. It is my staple food. Eating whole grains means exactly that, it includes the outer skin or bran of the grain—so buying organic is important to me. Plus, I like supporting farmers who try to keep the soil healthy.

STORING

I transfer all grains from their packages into individual tight-sealing glass jars such as inexpensive Ball or Mason jars. This keeps my grains handy when I need to add them in a rush—no fiddling with clamps, clips, and rubber bands, no grains strewn all over the kitchen counter. Plus, lining up my grains in glass jars on a pantry shelf allows me to survey my options at a glance, and it looks beautiful. To make it easier, I keep quick-cooking grains on one side of the shelf and slow-cooking grains on the other, or I separate them on different shelves.

I suggest keeping all your grains in a cool, dry pantry. I do not store my grains in the fridge—I find it impractical and simply don't have the space for it. Yes, whole grains can go rancid faster than their refined cousins, but they don't go bad overnight. In a cool pantry, grains can last for many months without problems. If it makes you feel better and you have the space (or if you live in hot humid climate), by all means put your whole grains in the fridge.

Storing grains in glass jars has other advantages. It allows me to visually inspect my grains on a regular basis. And it enables me to my shake my grains. Why on earth would I do that? I have learned the hard way that flour moths tend to grow in undisturbed environments. Thus about once a month, whenever I remember really, I will pick up a few of my jars and give them a good shaking to prevent problems. Storing the grains in individual jars keeps my other grains protected too: I can detect any potential infestation right away. If I see clumped grain clusters in a jar, I throw out the contents of the affected jar without having to worry about all my other grains being contaminated.

RINSING

Most whole grains sold in the United States today, either domestic or imported, are very clean—unlike in the past. Rarely will you find a package with dusty, sandy, or otherwise dirty grain full of chaff, tiny stones, and other minuscule things. Some people insist that you rinse all grains; others say to refrain from it. I have often tested rinsed and unrinsed grains side by side, and frankly, I could not tell the difference. As a result, I just take a quick glance and, most of the time, save myself the additional step of rinsing.

There are two exceptions: One grain that I always rinse is quinoa, because of the natural bitter saponin layer around each kernel—and while this layer is mechanically shaved off in most quinoa on the market, producers continue to recommend rinsing the grain. On the other hand, you should *never* rinse short-grain brown rice if you want to make risotto: rinsing removes what makes risotto so deliciously creamy, the starch.

But by all means, rinse quick-cooking grains such as buckwheat, millet, or quinoa in a fine-mesh sieve if you like, or if they don't seem clean, or if it makes you feel better. Exceptions are amaranth and teff: their seeds are so tiny that you will wash them down the drain.

In the rare case of a dirty batch of whole grain berries (such as wheat, rye, or hulled barley), you can rinse them in a sieve, or else place the kernels in a bowl, fill the bowl with cold water, and swish the grains around with your hands until chaff and broken pieces float to the top. Carefully pour out the water and floating residue. Repeat if needed, and then drain the grain berries in a sieve.

SOAKING

Quick-cooking grains such as buckwheat, millet, and quinoa do not need to be soaked. Some grains like brown rice or whole oats can but do not have to be soaked. Slow-cooking whole grains such as rye and wheat berries benefit from soaking, for two reasons. As a rule of thumb, soaking decreases their cooking time and makes, in my opinion, for plumper, more appealing and tender kernels. I also find that the grain becomes easier to digest. This is even more important if you are new to eating whole grains.

Hence, I recommend that you always soak chewy whole grain berries for at least 8 hours or overnight. Tough-skinned berries such as rye and hard wheat can soak for up to 24 hours. If you can't cook the soaked grains right away, drain and store them in the fridge until you are ready to cook. For cooking times and other details see the table below (pages 24–25). To preserve nutrients, some people prefer to cook their whole grains in the water used for soaking. Feel free to do this, following the same water amounts recommended in the table.

If you forget to soak your slow-cooking whole grains such as wheat or rye, you have two options: Just cook them longer, adding more water if needed, until they are tender with a slight chewiness. Or use a quick-soak method that you might know from dried beans. Put the grains in a pot, cover with an inch of water, and bring to a boil. Cook for 2 minutes, remove from the heat, cover, and let stand for 1 hour. Drain and cook as directed in the recipe.

With the growing interest in whole grains, I have seen recipes that recommend cooking hard wheat berries in just 25 to 45 minutes without previous soaking. Frankly, this will require a lot of chewing by the humble eater. I also worry about his or her digestive system. Anyone who has eaten undercooked beans knows what I'm talking about. Most important, give whole grains the time they need to cook up nicely so you will actually enjoy them more than once. And when you have no time to do that, enjoy one of the many quick-cooking grains.

TOASTING

Some cooks toast small grains such as buckwheat or millet before cooking them. This adds nice aroma, and it allows the kernels to cook up more distinctly. To me, this is a personal choice. I often prefer the comforting softness and mild flavor of each grain. But I suggest you try it and see what you like better. You can toast the grains in a dry saucepan over medium-low to medium heat until they crackle and become aromatic, and then carefully add water (it will splatter!) and cook as directed.

COOKING METHODS

My technique for cooking most grains is easy and no-nonsense: bring the grains to a boil in water, cover, and simmer until they are tender but still slightly chewy (for more, see also "Simmering," below, and the grain cooking tables (pages 24–25). A heavy-bottomed pot with a tight-fitting lid will make your life easier (see "Equipment," page 29). Add salt towards the end of cooking.

Furthermore, all grains benefit from steaming after cooking, if you have the time. Here is how it works: remove the pot from the heat, cover, and let steam for 5 to 10 minutes for tender grains such as brown rice, quinoa, or millet. Drain any liquid that remains. Fluff and serve. Allow 10 to 15 minutes (or up to 1 hour) of steaming time for tougher grains such as rye, wheat, spelt, Kamut, and hulled barley. When making these grains ahead, I typically just "forget" about them after cooking, leaving them to steam and cool before I refrigerate or freeze them. During steaming, grains continue to absorb any remaining traces of cooking liquid and thus plump up beautifully.

I have written the majority of the recipes in this book to allow for much of the water to be absorbed during cooking and steaming. However, no two grain kernels are alike so use common sense and watch your grains.

Don't be concerned about burst grain kernels. I like to cook my grains long enough to make them more easily digestible, so I often end up with 10 percent to 15 percent of wheat or barley bursting in the pot. I cherish the succulence these berries add to a dish.

For cooking polenta, please see the actual recipes in the book and page 106).

SIMMERING is a crucial technique in cooking many a dish, including grains. It is equally important in cooking soups and stews and in poaching. To simmer grains, bring them to a boil and reduce the heat until only tiny bubbles poke through to the surface of your cooking liquid. This is the heat level you should try to maintain. You will most often reach this point with the lid closed over a low flame. But it varies with

different stoves and pots, so keep an eye out for this perfect gentle bubble. It is magic, and it will truly create a superior grain, or anything else that should not cook over too high a heat. I used to be a pretty carefree cook, paying little attention to all matters of technique—but perpetually wondering why my beans always burst. Well, I was cooking them at bursting high temperatures. Lesson learned. Simmering also helps retain the water level in your pot so you don't scorch your grains (a heavy-bottomed pot helps too).

STEAMING FINE GRAINS Some grains such as couscous or fine bulgur require no cooking at all, but just a brief steaming period (see the table on page 24). Here is how you do it: add the required amount of water to a pot and bring to a boil; stir in the grain, cover, and remove from the heat. Set aside to steam for 5 to 10 minutes, depending on the grain or the recipe.

REHYDRATING is an easy common technique used for bulgur that is already parboiled. To do this, place the bulgur in a bowl and cover it with water (warm or hot water will speed up the process a bit). Wait until the bulgur has the desired consistency (this depends on the grind), and then drain and enjoy it in soups or salads. For more details on varieties of bulgur, see page 10.

COOKING TIMES Just like with beans, the different varieties and the freshness of your whole grains affect cooking time (for details see the grain tables that follow this section). I have had soft whole wheat berries that cooked to a lovely plumpness in 30 minutes, and batches that still retained quite a chew after more than an hour of cooking. Same with millet or quinoa. Sometimes it takes 12 minutes, sometimes 25 minutes. Since your grocer will not tell you how old the grain on the store shelf is, allow for some flexibility. Check occasionally and cook a bit longer, adding a little more water to your pot if necessary.

MAKING AHEAD

Many grains can be cooked ahead. To ease your busy schedule, you will find this information in notes labeled "to get a head start" throughout this book. After cooking and steaming the grains, uncover the pot to allow them to cool, and then transfer them to a lidded container and refrigerate. Cooked grains will keep in the fridge for five days.

Chilling can harden the starch in many grains so they will clump together, and others such as millet can become a lumpy, hard mass. This is not a problem. Just separate the grains before using them in cooking, either with a wooden spoon or with your fingers. The grains will soften nicely when reheated (see below).

If you don't anticipate using your grains within several days, freeze them, either in ziplock bags or in plastic or glass containers. All grains freeze well for at least three months. You can defrost grains in the microwave straight from the freezer (if they are in a microwave-safe container), or defrost them in the fridge overnight and reheat as described below.

REHEATING

If you want to reheat grains, place them in a saucepan with about $1/4$ inch of water, cover, and heat over medium-low until they are softened and warmed through. Or use the microwave to reheat them. Place the grain in a microwave-safe bowl, cover with a paper towel (no need to add water), and microwave on high until the grain is steaming hot, stirring once or twice in between.

QUICK-COOKING WHOLE GRAINS

The grains below are my go-to grains for busy weeknights. Some, like whole wheat couscous, can be on the table in 5 to 10 minutes; others simmer for up to half an hour while the rest of dinner gets prepared. More details are provided on the preceding pages.

GRAIN	AMOUNT (CUPS)	WATER/LIQUID (CUPS)	COOKING TIME (MINUTES)	APPROXIMATE YIELD (CUPS)
buckwheat groats (not kasha)	1	1 3/4	15	3
bulgur, fine	1	1	10, steaming time	3
bulgur, medium and coarse	1	1 3/4	10–20	3
cornmeal, coarse	1	3 1/2	30	4
couscous, whole wheat	1	1 1/4	5–10, steaming time	3
farro, semipearled	1	2	20–25	3
millet	1	1 3/4	15–20	3 1/2
oats, steel-cut	1	3 1/2	25–30	3 1/2
polenta/grits, instant or quick-cooking	1	3 3/4	1–3, or per package instructions	4
polenta, corn grits	1	4	20–25	4
quinoa	1	1 3/4	10–20	3

SLOW-COOKING WHOLE GRAINS

This table lists all the grains that cook up best when soaked ahead. It also includes grains for which soaking is optional but that typically require 30 to 60 minutes of simmering. More details can be found on the preceding pages.

I have laid out this cookbook using just enough grains for each recipe. Often these are relatively small amounts. I have done this to entice you to try these grains in many different ways. The more familiar you get with whole grains, the more likely it is that you will experiment with them in your day-to-day cooking, preparing larger amounts. This is where the table below will come in handy.

GRAIN	AMOUNT (CUPS)	WATER (CUPS)	COOK TIME (MINUTES)	APPROXIMATE YIELD (CUPS)	TO SOAK?	SOAKING TIME (HOURS)
barley, pearl	1	2$1/2$	30–40	3$1/2$	optional	2–3
barley, hulled	1	2$1/2$	40–50	3	yes	overnight
brown rice, long-grain	1	1$1/2$	35–45	3	optional	2–3
brown rice, short-grain	1	1$3/4$	40–50	3	optional	2–3
farro, whole grain	1	3	25–70 dep. on type	3	yes	overnight
Kamut berries	1	1$3/4$	50–60	2$1/2$	yes	overnight
oat berries (whole oat groats)	1	1$3/4$	30–40	2$1/2$	optional	2–3
rye berries	1	1$1/2$	50–60	3	yes	overnight, up to 24
spelt berries	1	1$3/4$	45–55	2$1/2$	yes	overnight
wheat berries, hard	1	1$1/2$	50–60	3	yes	overnight, up to 24
wheat berries, soft	1	1$3/4$	40–50	3	yes	overnight
wild rice	1	2	40–50	3	optional	overnight

To include delicious "slow" whole grains into your busy life, you can do what I do:
- Cook your grains ahead on the weekend.
- Make more than you need and chill or freeze (see "Making Ahead," page 23).
- Soak your whole grains in the morning before you leave for work, and start cooking them the moment you step in the door. By the time you wash up and take a deep breath, your grains will be halfway there.

PARBOILED BROWN RICE

While I sometimes passionately pursue time-consuming kitchen projects with infinite patience, I'm also a busy person who often wants to eat fast and well. Brown rice, a versatile staple, never cooks fast enough for me. Depending on the freshness and the kind, it can set you back up to fifty minutes. Inspired by store-bought parboiled rice, I have tested a number of different parboiling methods for brown rice. I find this one easy and delicious.

I keep parboiled rice on hand pretty much at all times, either in the fridge or in the freezer for last-minute dinners. I find it tastes much better than any of the commercial instant or quick-cooking varieties. If you want to make large amounts, you can multiply the recipe as needed. It's dead easy. Try the parboiled brown rice in dishes such as the Greek Egg and Lemon Soup with Chicken and Brown Rice (page 123), or the Spring Pilaf with Artichokes and Green Peas (page 101). Do not rinse short-grain brown rice if you want to use it in any risotto recipe, such as the Saffron Risotto with White-Wine Clams and Peas (page 182).

MAKES ABOUT 3 CUPS PARBOILED LONG-GRAIN BROWN RICE OR ABOUT 2 1/2 CUPS PARBOILED SHORT-GRAIN BROWN RICE

1 cup long-grain or short-grain brown rice
1 cup water

Place the brown rice and the water in a small heavy-bottomed saucepan with a tight-fitting lid and bring to a boil over medium-high heat. Stir once, and then decrease the heat to maintain a simmer, cover, and cook for 15 minutes. Remove from the heat, cover, and let sit for 15 minutes. There should be no liquid left.

If you are not using the rice within 1 to 2 hours, allow to cool and then chill, covered, up to 5 days, or freeze up to 3 months. Defrost in the fridge overnight, or—if the rice is in a microwave-safe container—you can defrost it in the microwave straight from the freezer.

In case you want to use the parboiled brown rice in your own recipes, here is what you need to do to finish cooking it: Place 3/4 cup stock or water, salt to taste, and the parboiled rice in a small heavy-bottomed saucepan and bring just to a boil over medium-high heat. Reduce the heat to maintain a simmer, cover, and cook until no liquid is left and the rice is tender with a slight chewiness, about 15 minutes. (As for all rice, do not stir during this time, or it will become mushy.) Remove from the heat, cover, and allow to steam for 5 minutes. Fluff with a fork and serve.

You will have about 3 1/2 cups fully cooked long-grain brown rice and about 3 cups fully cooked short-grain brown rice, enough to serve 4.

Baking Basics for Whole Grain Flours

Here you will find a few suggestions to help you succeed if you are new to baking with whole grain flours. While their character is indeed quite different from all-purpose flour, they are not at all difficult to use. As with all cooking, you just have to master the basics, after which everything else is fun.

Cookies, cakes, muffins, scones, and breads baked with whole grain flours have a pleasing texture— sometimes just a slight toothiness, and sometimes a delicious chew. But they need not be dry or overly chewy. If you have to steel yourself to eat a whole grain treat, it is often because the baker has not adjusted for the unique properties of whole grain flours. These are easy to learn. Most important, whole grain flours generally need more liquid compared to refined white flour, and often they also benefit from a resting period. The extra liquid and the additional time allow the bran to soften which makes for more appealing results.

I have found that a short resting period of 15 to 20, sometimes 30 minutes does not add to my time spent in the kitchen. I usually clean up in the meantime and preheat the oven. Many whole grain baked goods made with yeast or baking powder can also go into the fridge overnight without problems. I do this often to take the stress out of the mornings when I long for freshly baked goods.

PURCHASING AND STORING WHOLE GRAIN FLOUR

Buy whole grain flours from reputed companies and suppliers. When shopping from bulk bins, go to stores that quickly turn over their stock. You will find out if they do by always smelling or tasting flour before you use it.

As with whole grains, I store whole grain flours in a cool, dark pantry, not in the refrigerator. I keep the different flours in tall Mason jars, which can be closed tightly. While it is correct that whole grain flours go rancid faster than all-purpose flour (this is one reason they vanished from our diet in the first place), they don't go bad in an instant. Fresh whole grain flours typically last months if stored properly in sealed containers in a cool dark place. In any case, I always smell or taste flour if I haven't used it in a while. It should not taste bitter or have a musty or otherwise "off" smell; if it does, discard it.

If you love baking bread and bake a lot, consider buying a grain mill, which will allow you to grind fresh flour on the spot when you need it (see also the essay "My Life with Two Grain Mills," page 148). And if you find yourself with way too much whole grain flour on hand, just hold a bread-baking party. Invite your friends and bake until you drop; freeze the bounty and enjoy the loaves of your labor weeks later.

MEASURING WHOLE GRAIN FLOUR

A simple digital scale (see "Equipment," page 29) is a worthwhile investment for any baker, regardless whether you use whole grain or regular flour. Using a scale in baking will give you more consistent results than cup measures, which can be packed differently by different methods and by different people. Furthermore, very humid or dry cold winter weather can significantly alter the amount of flour in your measuring cup, enough at times to throw off your favorite recipes. Using too much flour is particularly challenging with whole grains, as the baked goods can become heavy and dense. A scale will provide a more accurate measurement. Hence, I provide the weight of flour for all the baking recipes used in this book. If you don't have a scale, I recommend using the "spoon and level" method for measuring whole grains. Unlike when you dig your cup into your flour jar, this method results in less flour in the measuring cup and thus lighter results.

Here is how you do it:

- Fluff or stir the flour with a fork to aerate slightly.
- Spoon flour into your cup until it is overflowing. Do not pat down, shake, or bang the measuring cup on the counter, as this will compress the flour.
- Using a knife or a slim metal spatula, sweep across the top to level the cup.

BAKING AND HUMIDITY

The humidity in the air affects your baking, whole grains or not. Biscotti dough may require gentle handling on a dry day, and be as malleable as the proverbial wet noodle on a day heavy with rain. A recipe for delicate scones may require up to 1/4 cup less liquid when the clouds hang low in a thunderstorm. Same for icy-cold winter days, when humidity levels in a heated apartment can drop to an arid 10 to 20 percent— your dough will be "thirsty" and need more liquid as a result.

If a recipe says the dough should be moist but yours is more than that, just sprinkle on a bit of flour or add it by the tablespoonful. Alternatively, if your dough is very dry instead of malleable, add a tad more liquid. With time and experience, you will get a good understanding of this balance.

PREHEATING OVENS

I suggest you give your oven at least 20 minutes to preheat. I sometimes allow for 30 minutes—this is especially important when baking "wet" bread dough, which needs the initial heat blast for rapid expansion (see also "The Magic of Wet Dough," page 73). Here is why: I have tested the oven temperature in my new and perfectly calibrated American oven many times. I have noticed that the preheat indicator consistently beeps "ready" a fair bit before the temperature inside the oven has reached the desired setting. So give your oven a little extra time to heat up. And if you want to know your oven even better, buy an oven thermometer!

Equipment

I have always admired home cooks all around the world, be it in Germany, India, Greece, or Tunisia, who create the most amazing lineup of dishes in tiny low-tech kitchens, with just the most basic of tools. Not that I don't fancy shiny new kitchen gadgets. But all too often, my new tools clutter up valuable work surface without contributing much else. Below, I list the tools and equipment I find helpful for cooking and baking with whole grains. Most of these will not set you back much. After all, cooking is not about fancy high-tech gadgets, but about enjoying the firestorm of flavors you create on your stove.

BENCH SCRAPER

Also called a dough scraper or a bench knife, this tool is immensely useful if you like to bake or make pasta. It enables you to lift and turn dough with ease on your work surface. Bakers use it also to portion dough for individual bread rolls. To me, its best use comes after the work is done: you can effortlessly remove any dried-on pieces of dough from your work surface. I like an old-fashioned stainless steel bench scraper with a wooden handle.

CAST-IRON SKILLET

A timeless piece of cookware is a medium-size cast-iron skillet. These affordable workhorses last a lifetime and will never let you down. I have used and abused my fair share of nonstick skillets. Some were quite pricey and came highly recommended, others were cheap. Yet I was not able, even with the greatest care, to avoid scratching their nonstick surfaces, even on high-end models. Cast-iron skillets, on the other hand, become essentially nonstick with seasoning and use. You can now buy them preseasoned—or just enjoy the campfire charm old-fashioned seasoning brings into your kitchen. Another beauty of these traditional pans is that they can go from the stove top to the oven. And I love the beautiful crusts that form at the bottom of foods cooked in cast-iron. Take cornbread, for example—out of this world!

DIGITAL SCALE

Any passionate baker should have a digital scale. It should include a "tare" feature to enable you to zero the scale between weighing different ingredients. Place your mixing bowl on the scale and measure your ingredients right into the bowl. Nothing could be easier! No more fiddling with cup measures, trying to fill them properly, and spilling the contents everywhere. No more cleaning your kitchen counter from overflowing flour or other ingredients. A digital scale is the one piece of equipment I can't live without.

DOUGH WHISK

This ingeniously simple tool is nothing but two thick stainless steel wire loops on a wooden handle. Invented in Denmark, it helps to stir dough together more efficiently than a wooden spoon or a silicone spatula. No more clumps while mixing, either. The result is less gluten development in the batter, and thus more tender cakes and muffins.

DUTCH OVEN

For stews and slow-simmering braises, a large Dutch oven is invaluable for home cooks, as it distributes heat beautifully. There are a number of good-quality models on the market. No need to buy a high-end one if you are on a budget. Many cooks, myself included, cherish their enamel-coated cast-iron Dutch ovens.

FINE-MESH SIEVE

A fine-mesh sieve (or strainer) to drain grains, small and large, is a must if you don't want to pour half your dinner staple down the drain. And it is essential when kernels are tiny, such as millet and quinoa.

HANDS

My hands are my most important kitchen tool. No electrical appliance, no kitchen gadget can replace the feeling in my fingertips when testing the silkiness of homemade pasta, the shaggy moistness of dough for tender scones, the heavy mixture that will eventually become a whole grain bread. I consider hands the most underrated tool in the American kitchen. Learning to use and trust your senses, especially the sense of touch, in cooking is one of the most rewarding experiences in the kitchen. When you pat the bottom of a bread loaf and detect the perfect hollow sound of "ready," or when cookies yield to your touch just right—that's a baker's heaven, and only your hands can tell.

SAUCEPANS

Good quality heavy-bottomed pots with tight-fitting lids are essential for easy cooking with whole grains. I still use my very first set of first-class saucepans from Germany. I have set them on fire, and unwittingly tried to destroy them many times—to no avail. Money well spent! If your budget is small, get at least one 2-quart pot. If you can afford it, buy a set of three (small, medium, and large) that will serve your kitchen needs for life. Grains, and any other food for that matter, will simmer in them without losing much cooking liquid (no scorched grains anymore). Plus their energy-efficient bottoms retain the heat when steaming grains after cooking, which will result in beautiful plump kernels.

VEGETABLE BRUSH

To clean potatoes, carrots, turnips, and other root vegetables, I use an old-fashioned vegetable brush. I have a simple brush made from coir (coconut fiber) that fits nicely into the palm of my hand. Thoroughly scrubbing vegetables with a brush removes dirt and can make peeling them with a knife unnecessary. Plus, it preserves valuable nutrients, which are often found in the skin.

ZESTER

If you like to cook and bake, you will inevitably need a good tool for zesting. Having tried a few, I now always recommend a handheld Microplane zester because nothing beats its ease of use and its speed: you just grate the orange or lemon across the long super-sharp blade and a little mound of zest accumulates on your work surface in an instant. Of course, you can also use the tiny holes of a box grater.

Ingredients

CITRUS AND DRIED FRUITS

Oranges and lemons are the backbone of many Mediterranean flavor compositions. Today's supermarkets offer a wide selection of citrus to choose from, especially during the winter months, blood oranges, satsumas, kumquats, pomelos, and clementines. Use the recipes in this book as inspiration, and start experimenting with their various bright aromas. The flavorful oil in citrus zest will elevate many of your recipes, be it a simple rice pilaf or a breakfast cake. When I plan on using the zest of citrus, I choose organic fruit. To learn how to keep organic zest on hand for future use, see "Always Fresh Citrus Zest on Hand," page 55.

Traditionally, fruits such as plums, apples, and figs were dried to preserve the bounty of summer for the lean winter months. I cherish these concentrated flavor packages because they can effortlessly spruce up a meal, from Chicken Stew with Artichokes and Dried Apricots over Brown Rice (page 118) to Lemon-Scented Olive Oil Cake with Plumped Figs (page 210). In most of my cooking and baking, I look for dried figs from Greece and Turkey for their soft sweetness and alluring flavor. However, by all means use Calimyrna figs or dark Mission figs if this is all you can find. If possible, gently press on the fruit through the packaging to test for softness. Avoid buying figs that are dried-out and old. Soft dried Turkish apricots are sweeter than tangy Blenheim apricots. Both have a place in different recipes.

CREAM AND BUTTER

Yes, I love cream—heavy whipping cream, that is. And real butter, preferably the fattier kind from Europe on which I was raised. These ingredients transform the food we cook into the food we love. Hence, I will not ban them from my kitchen.

For heavy cream, I typically choose a pasteurized (organic) brand as it has a fuller taste and whips up so much better than ultrapasteurized cream. And while I use olive oil in much of my cooking, butter's unsurpassed delicious richness still has a place in my kitchen. I continue to finish certain dishes with a dab of it. And sometimes I choose butter over oil in baking because it contributes deep flavor and a distinct crispness like no other ingredient. For more thoughts on all things fat, see also "Musings on Health, Dieting, and Good Eating," page 3.

In the past few years, a number of rich European-style butters have appeared on store shelves, some imported, some by American producers. The USDA requires American butters to contain 80 percent butterfat, European-style butters typically have a higher fat content, up to 86 percent—and while this might not sound like much, you can taste it, believe me. Some are sweet, others are cultured and have a distinct tang. Just as with any good food, I suggest you try different kinds of butter and pick your favorite. I often reach for Irish butter because its luscious creaminess and deep flavor remind me of the local butter I slathered on slices of whole grain bread as a kid in Bavaria. Plus, it has become more widely available, and I love convenience as much as anyone.

I always opt for unsalted butter. For one, I bake a lot and like to be able to determine the exact amount of salt I add to a recipe (different salted butters have different salt content). And I prefer to salt my *Butterbrot* myself, a hearty open-faced sandwich a German can eat any time of the day—because there is nothing like the distinct crunch of salt crystals fusing into golden butter.

HERBS AND SPICES

Fresh and dried herbs play a central role in many cuisines around the Mediterranean. From rosemary to sage, mint to oregano, a handful of herbs takes a simple meal from pedestrian to ambrosial.

I will never forget the timid participant in one of the first cooking classes I taught. She asked whether to measure 1/4 cup dill for *tzatziki*, the Greek yogurt appetizer, *before* or *after* chopping. Well, in my opinion, it simply doesn't matter. It's just a matter of personal taste. Furthermore, herbs such as rosemary, sage, and oregano can have varying potency—a dry summer, for example, will concentrate the oils in the leaves, resulting in a stronger aroma. There is no right or wrong here; you learn through experimentation and tasting what you like and enjoy.

Fresh herbs are also the culinary foundation of my mom's cooking, and—no surprise there—the more I cook, the more I try to imitate her. My mom will dash into her garden, while a sauce bubbles away in a pot, and chop down a handful of this and a fistful of that to add to her pot. Somehow, it always turns out addictively good. I have since come up with a formula for this use of herbs: the more you use, the less can go wrong.

Herbs and spices can also enhance the flavor of whole grains. I learned this while traveling in Sri Lanka years ago. The intense spicing of the local cuisine had a profound impact on my own cooking. When I returned to Germany, I started adding whole cinnamon sticks, coriander, cloves, and whole peppercorns to my whole grains. Soon, I also started to drop herbs into the cooking water, such as a twig of rosemary or whole bay leaves. The latter are in a class of their own, worth seeking out and using often. Bay leaves impart a potent unique fragrance, floral yet a bit pungent, to simmering grains, but also enhance soups and stews. I was raised on Mediterranean bay leaf (often labeled as Turkish), so my choice is biased, and in the recipes in this book I always use Mediterranean bay leaf. California bay leaf has about double the strength. Quality and freshness really matter here, so you must try a few different brands or kinds until you find the one you like.

HONEY

In my native Germany and Greece, honey has been used for centuries as a traditional sweetener. Sugar was expensive and hard to come by until fairly recently in history. As a child in Greece, I poured delectable and highly aromatic thyme or pine honey over thick yogurt and freshly harvested walnuts, a classic combination and an addictive treat. In parts of Greece, we also savor fruity orange blossom honey. The French love their intoxicating lavender honey. And more recently, in Boston, I have been introduced to the delicate scent of local blueberry and cranberry honey.

Unfortunately, the quality of honey is hard to judge by the label. And regulations and controls are insufficient. Some say the most reliable source for good-quality honey is a beekeeper, if you know one. Hence, in my own baking, where the honey is heated and other ingredients may overpower the delicate scent, I typically buy a basic and affordable honey. Only when the honey is not heated, say, to sweeten a bowl of fruit or a cold dessert, do I choose one of the fine specialty honeys, or more precious and pricey raw honey—and hope for the best.

MEAT AND POULTRY

I was a vegetarian for many years because I was appalled by factory farming in Germany and in the United States. Much has changed in the past decade as some farmers are striving to raise animals more naturally and humanely. Many are producing healthier chickens, and older breeds of pigs and turkeys with tastier meat have become more readily available. This has made me downright ecstatic, as it has allowed me to enjoy meat again on occasion. I buy the best-quality meat I can afford. Organic is my first choice. Yes, good-quality meat is pricey. But in food, as in anything else, the simple truth holds: you get what you pay for. The simple answer to that dilemma is to eat less meat—which is my preference, anyway.

OLIVE OIL

Over the past decade or so, heart-healthy olive oil has become a household staple in the United States—that wasn't the case when I arrived in 1993. Today there are hundreds of brands on the market, with wide-ranging aromas, textures, and hues. Some are unfiltered or filtered, some are stone-pressed or from a single variety, and some are sold with the passion of a good wine. In fact, there are now so many varieties available from so many parts of the world—including Spain, Italy, France, Greece, California, Australia, New Zealand, Israel, and Morocco—that it can be a challenge to pick one.

Here is what I do: For everyday cooking and for much of my baking in which the oil is heated, I buy a good-quality but not-too-costly extra-virgin olive oil. For all the other times when the oil is a featured ingredient, I buy the best-quality extra-virgin olive oil I can afford. I use this oil in salads, to drizzle on appetizers, or for dipping bread. I love olive oils that are highly aromatic and I enjoy exploring their different flavors, from buttery to fruity and peppery. I do not buy so-called light olive oils, as they are usually processed and contain only small amounts of virgin or extra-virgin oil. As a result, they lack olive oil's rich natural flavor.

Unfortunately, most producers won't describe the aroma of their olive oil on the label, so shopping for it is often a guessing game. Sometimes stores offer olive oil tastings; if not, don't be shy about asking a store clerk for help. If you do not already have a favorite extra-virgin olive oil, you simply have to purchase with an open mind and be prepared to appreciate the differences in flavor. Certain olive oils can be quite pungent and can be an acquired taste for some, but learning which oils you like is fun to do.

In the Mediterranean, olive oil has always been used by homemakers not only for cooking, but also for baking. I have rediscovered baking with olive oil over the past ten years, finding that it adds a sublime fruitiness and makes for a beautiful crumb in many baked goods. No need to worry that your treats will taste like, well, salad. Just try it and see!

Oh, and if a bit of olive oil drops onto the counter or ends up on your hands, don't forget to use it as a natural ointment to "cream" your most valuable work tool. Your skin will thank you for it.

SALT

The salt content in our diet has been a contentious issue for many years. Many experts recommend that we cut down on our use of salt. This is not a diet cookbook, but a book that I hope will make you enjoy all food more, and take you into the kitchen more often.

My passion is to make whole grains thoroughly delicious. As a result, I do specify a relatively modest amount of salt to bring out flavors, while giving you the opportunity to adjust it later to your liking. My recipe testers asked for this information as basic guidance. In much of my day-to-day cooking I use fine sea salt, which is a bit coarser than regular table salt.

I never provide an amount for salting pasta water, as opinions of pasta connoisseurs differ on this topic. During testing I ran into another hair-raising issue: salt content in broth can vary considerably, even in the low-sodium kind. Low-sodium chicken broth can have 70 milligrams per cup, and low-sodium vegetable broth or stock can have up to 440 milligrams. So please use common sense when following my recipes and increase or decrease salt as you see fit.

SEAFOOD

From the Mediterranean to the Pacific, all over the world the oceans are being depleted by overfishing faster than we can blink an eye. As I'm finishing this manuscript, the oil has been gushing for weeks into the Gulf of Mexico from a BP oil well, endangering local fishing grounds and so much more. Making the right choice has become increasingly difficult, and I have struggled with these questions as I was developing the recipes for this book. Generally, I try not to serve more than 3 to 4 ounces of fish per person. Whenever possible, I choose fish that has been certified by the Marine Stewardship Council. For more information, see www.msc.org/. A great resource on how to make ocean-friendly seafood choices is the Seafood Watch at the Monterey Bay Aquarium: www.montereybayaquarium.org/cr/seafoodwatch.aspx. The site also offers a pocket guide you can download to have on hand when shopping for fish.

STOCK OR BROTH

If you don't make your own stock or broth (I rarely do), finding a good-quality product with appealing flavor is not easy. You have to try different brands to choose a favorite. Plus, certain store-bought products can slow down the cooking of grains because of their high salt content. As a result, I either cook grains in water, sometimes combined with herbs and spices, or I use half broth and half water, which has the additional advantage of not overpowering the subtle flavors of the grains.

SUGAR

Despite my passion for natural and unrefined ingredients, I continue to use regular granulated sugar, especially in baked goods. It lends an irresistible crispness to certain treats such as whole grain cookies, which I don't want to miss. I use it when sweeteners such as honey or agave syrup don't produce a desirable outcome.

In baking, I often add turbinado sugar, also called raw sugar, which has become more widely available in recent years. Less refined than regular granulated sugar, it yields from pressing sugarcane to extract its juice. The juice is then heated and spun to retain the characteristic coarse crystals. Turbinado's distinct caramel aroma pairs especially well with the nutty flavors of whole grain flours; plus turbinado sugar adds moisture, which is a benefit when baking with whole grain flours.

YOGURT AND GREEK YOGURT

In this book, Greek yogurt, sometimes also called Greek-style yogurt, always refers to strained yogurt. To my infinite joy, it has become widely available across the United States. Some markets now even offer organic versions. For best flavor, I prefer rich and creamy, plain whole-milk Greek yogurt. In my recipes, I almost always offer you ways to lighten up the recipe by using lower-fat versions.

If you can't find Greek yogurt, make your own. It's easy: line a sieve with a double layer of paper towels and set it over a bowl. Spoon 1 quart plain yogurt into the sieve. Cover with plastic wrap and place in the fridge to drain for at least 4 hours and up to 24 hours. Spoon the strained yogurt into a bowl, carefully removing the paper towels, and beat with a fork until smooth. You will have a scant 2 1/2 cups.

As for regular yogurt, my first choice is a creamy plain whole-milk yogurt, which can be spooned over many a dish. This is how yogurt is often served in Turkey and the Middle East. It brings cool creaminess to hot meals in hot climates. Trader Joe's carries my favorite, its own plain European-style whole-milk yogurt, which is finger-licking good. And if your travel ever takes you to Greece, be sure to look for rich sheep's milk yogurt sold in old-fashioned clay containers like in the days of yore. This, of course, is the best yogurt in the whole wide world.

HOW TO TOAST NUTS

I toast small amounts of nuts in a medium or large skillet, depending on the quantity. For large amounts (more than 1 cup for most nuts, $1/2$ cup for sesame seeds) I prefer to use the oven. To save energy, I try to do this on days when I'm already heating the oven for baking.

You can toast your nuts lightly, just to enhance flavor, or to a lively golden brown. This is a personal choice. Do as you like, but always keep a close eye because nuts can burn *fast*.

To toast whole nuts and seeds on the **stove top**, place a heavy skillet with the nuts over medium heat. Cook the nuts until fragrant, stirring or shaking the skillet a few times and following the times given below as a guideline. Watch closely and move the nuts more often as the skillet gets hotter, so they don't burn. With the exception of hazelnuts, immediately transfer the toasted nuts to a plate to cool before using them in a recipe.

- **Almonds:** 6 to 8 minutes.
- **Hazelnuts:** 5 to 7 minutes, until they become fragrant and the skin is charred in spots. Immediately transfer to a clean dish towel, fold the towel over the nuts, and rub until the loose skin comes off. Discard the skin, and allow the nuts to cool.
- **Pine nuts:** about 3 minutes.
- **Pistachios:** about 3 minutes.
- **Sesame seeds:** about 7 minutes for unhulled, 3 minutes for hulled.
- **Walnuts:** 5 to 7 minutes.

To toast whole nuts and seeds in the **oven**, position a rack in the center and preheat to 350°F. Spread the nuts or the seeds on a large rimmed baking sheet. Toast until fragrant, turning or shaking the sheet once or twice in between, depending on the length of baking time. Watch closely as oven temperatures can vary. With the exception of hazelnuts, immediately transfer the toasted nuts to a different baking sheet or a large plate to cool before using them in a recipe.

- **Almonds:** 7 to 9 minutes (5 to 6 minutes for slivered or sliced almonds).
- **Hazelnuts:** 10 to 12 minutes, until they become fragrant and the skin is charred in places. Immediately transfer the nuts to a clean dish towel, fold the towel over, and rub the nuts until the loose skin comes off. Discard the skin, and allow the nuts to cool.
- **Pine nuts:** 5 to 7 minutes.
- **Pistachios:** 5 to 7 minutes.
- **Sesame seeds:** about 10 minutes for unhulled, 3 to 5 minutes for hulled.
- **Walnuts:** about 7 minutes.

CHAPTER 1

BREAKFAST, BRUNCH, & BREADS

For years, my breakfast routine sounded all the alarm bells of nutritional experts: a minimum of two cups of coffee before I started my long days as an ambitious young journalist and, well, nothing else. I was following in the tradition of my mother's Greek compatriots, who to this day love to inhale a strong *kafedhaki* before heading to work. These tiny cups of intensely dense black liquid, and often way too much sugar, are "breakfast on the go" for many Greeks, similar to the espresso culture in Italy.

It took my Canadian husband to change my stubborn ways. With his Indian and East African heritage and my own European culture mix, we connected through food from the day we met. I devoured his warm homemade whole wheat *chapatis* and he savored my slow-rising dark German bread. Over time, his quiet prodding transformed my breakfast routine. It also helped that I had noticed that my zero-calorie breakfast habit affected my blood sugar, often leaving me drained at my desk by lunchtime.

Whole grain breakfasts have staying power. They can be delicate and light or nourishing and hearty. They have even more appeal when fused with a Mediterranean touch. You will find some unusual breakfast creations here, from warm anise-scented muesli with pistachios and figs, to an aromatic 100 percent whole wheat bread with coriander and fennel, to an orange-infused *polentina*, sweetened with honey and topped with a dollop of rich mascarpone. And don't forget to make chocolate hazelnut butter on your day off.

Never Give up Baguette, with Butter

I have a lifelong obsession with whole grains. My friends would say it is almost fanatical. But as you already know, I do not eat whole grains because they add so many nutritional benefits to my diet. Like all of the food spread out on my table, I eat whole grains simply because they taste amazingly good.

So I have to make a confession right now, early on in this book. Actually, more like two confessions. For one, I continue to fancy foods prepared from refined grains and flours. Yes, I refer to the now much-maligned all-purpose flour, white rice, and pasta. This confession always comes as a surprise to friends and acquaintances who don't know me well. After all, how can a such an ardent advocate for whole grains continue to rejoice in foods made from processed grains? The answer is easy. Because I believe, in the right hands and with good ingredients, any food can be a delicacy.

So don't be surprised to find this whole grain lover hungrily breaking off a piece of crusty French baguette from a local bakery. Or indulging in an intensely decadent über-brownie on a sunny day in the park. I will be equally in culinary heaven when biting into a perfectly charred pizza crust when my friends take me out to their favorite joint—instead of lamenting the fact that it was made from processed flour. Same when I go to an Indian wedding with my extended family, and an exquisite *biriyani* is plated high, perfumed with saffron, married to perfection with cardamom, cloves, and cinnamon, full of raisins and cashews—how could I possibly not pile it on my plate, just because the rice is not brown?

Which leads, straight down a buttery path, to my second food sin. You might already have guessed it: fat, in all its incarnations, including the long-bedeviled egg. To this day, I love to eat naturally rich dairy products such as heavy cream, plain whole milk yogurt, butter, cheese, and full-fat sour cream. I add eggs to my cooking, yolks and all. And occasionally when a dish cries for it, I will render bacon and pancetta, allowing them to unleash their mighty aromas onto my dinner plate.

Now I'm a bit anxious—because I have made these confessions before, over dinner, at my house, where whole grains always play a starring role. I have seen the stunned looks on the faces of my guests, the barely hidden disbelief when I fess up to the fact that there was lard in the whole wheat crust of the quiche. That a wee bit of butter and cream have been stirred into the saffron-scented brown rice risotto to make it so lush. Or that the lemon-scented millet dessert has been refined by heavy cream. Yes, not half and half, or light cream, but good heavy whipping cream.

All of this comes down to a simple culinary equation: I cook what I like to eat. Yet for much of my life, my obsession with whole grains has collided with the notion that whole grains are perceived merely as a health food, to be eaten only when one is on a diet. To my great dismay, we have succeeded in tainting whole grains with this "healthy" label, which takes the pleasure away from eating. Whole grains are part of a rich culinary tradition that spans the globe. I like to enjoy them for what they are, an amazing and still overlooked group of flavorful textured staples, worthy of being cooked into marvelous meals. But more than anything, I appreciate food prepared with care, from good ingredients, be it processed flour, fat, or whole grains. Here's to the celebration of all things edible! Just be sure to pick up a crisp golden loaf of baguette once in a while. And serve it with butter.

Orange Polentina *with Honey-Mascarpone Topping*

Italians enjoy humble polenta in countless preparations. *Polentina* is a creamier version, often served for breakfast. I enjoy this warming bowl of simple honey-sweetened cornmeal whenever I need a pick-me-up—the moment my spoon dives into the rich, creamy topping, I know the day will be good. This recipe uses instant polenta for hurried mornings. For a more nutritious breakfast, choose whole grain stone-ground medium-coarse or coarse cornmeal. It will need to cook longer, 20 to 30 minutes, but it will also reward you with sweeter flavor and rich texture (for more on types of cornmeal and polenta, see page 11). On Sundays, try adding a dash of citrus liqueur such as Grand Marnier or limoncello to the topping to make your breakfast sing. SERVES 4

POLENTINA

2 cups water

1¹/₂ cups whole milk

¹/₄ teaspoon fine sea salt

1 cup instant or quick-cooking polenta or grits

MASCARPONE TOPPING, AND TO FINISH

1 large orange

¹/₂ cup mascarpone

¹/₂ cup Greek yogurt

¹/₄ cup plus 2 tablespoons honey

2 teaspoons finely chopped fresh tarragon or ³/₄ teaspoon dried (optional)

1 To prepare the *polentina*, bring the water, milk, and salt to a boil in a large, heavy-bottomed saucepan over medium-high heat. Using a large whisk, gradually stir in the polenta in a thin stream. Decrease the heat to maintain a gentle bubble and whisk continuously until the polenta thickens, 1 to 3 minutes, or according to the package directions. Remove from the heat, cover, and let sit for 5 minutes.

2 Meanwhile, make the mascarpone topping. Finely grate the orange until you have 2 teaspoons zest. Peel the fruit, removing the pith if you like, and cut the segments into ¹/₂-inch pieces. Set aside. Using a fork, beat the mascarpone, yogurt, 2 tablespoons of the honey, and 1 teaspoon of the orange zest in a small bowl until smooth.

3 To finish, whisk the remaining ¹/₄ cup honey and the remaining 1 teaspoon zest into the polentina. Spoon into bowls, crowning each serving with ¹/₄ cup of the mascarpone topping, and a few pieces of orange. Sprinkle with the tarragon and serve right away.

TO GET A HEAD START: The mascarpone topping, as in step 2, can be prepared 1 day ahead. Chill the orange pieces and the topping in separate containers.

TO VARY IT: This makes a semifirm *polentina*. For a more porridge-like consistency, increase the milk to 2 cups.

TO LIGHTEN IT UP: Feel free to use lowfat milk here, as well as lowfat or nonfat Greek yogurt. In the topping, replace rich mascarpone, an unripened Italian cow's milk cheese, with ¹/₂ cup more yogurt, and add a bit more honey to adjust the sweetness.

Warm Muesli with Figs, Pistachios, and Anise

Muesli is to the Germans and the Swiss what cornflakes and breakfast cereals are to Americans. Countless variations exist of this classic breakfast with grain flakes, nuts, and dried fruit. This is a Mediterranean riff on traditional muesli with figs, pistachios, dates, and hints of cinnamon and anise. I like to serve this muesli warm, especially in the winter, allowing the oats to soften. Many Germans, who like a good chew, eat their muesli straight from the jar with milk, yogurt, or orange juice and topped with fresh fruit. Muesli lasts for weeks, so double the quantities and you'll always have a quick breakfast mix at hand.

MAKES 3 CUPS, TO SERVE 6

MUESLI

2 cups old-fashioned rolled oats (not quick-cooking)

1/4 cup whole pistachios

1/4 cup chopped pitted dates

1/4 cup chopped dried figs, preferably Turkish or Greek

2 tablespoons dark raisins

2 tablespoons sesame seeds

1/2 teaspoon ground cinnamon

1/2 teaspoon anise seeds

TO FINISH

3 cups whole or lowfat milk

Light brown or maple sugar, for sprinkling

1 To prepare the muesli mixture, combine all ingredients in a medium bowl, separating any sticky pieces of dates or figs with your fingers. Transfer the muesli to a tall Mason jar (or an airtight container), and store on an open kitchen shelf—it's beautiful to look at.

2 **MICROWAVE METHOD:** For each serving, combine 1/2 cup milk and 1/2 cup muesli mixture in a small microwave-safe bowl and heat on high for 1 minute. Let sit for 3 to 5 minutes to allow the oats to soften. Sprinkle with the sugar. **STOVETOP METHOD:** For each serving, place 1/2 cup milk and 1/2 cup muesli mixture in a small heavy-bottomed saucepan and heat over medium-high until almost boiling (it will steam, and the small bubbles around the rim will become lively). Immediately remove from the heat, cover, and let sit for 3 to 5 minutes to allow the oats to soften. Sprinkle with the sugar.

TO VARY IT: Feel free to combine any dried fruits and nuts you have at home. Here are two more Mediterranean-inspired variations. Replace the pistachios, dates, and figs in the recipe with a 1/4 cup each of walnuts, apricots, and golden raisins, or chopped or slivered almonds, dried sweet red cherries, and currants.

TO MAKE IT A FEAST: Heat your muesli in half-and-half instead of milk, or on Sundays, top each serving with a generous dollop of whipped cream to melt into the warm muesli.

Dark Chocolate Muesli with Hazelnuts

Chocolate and nuts almost always hit the spot for me. Here, I combine both of these luxurious ingredients with sweet dates and dried blueberries into a richly nourishing wake-up feast. Inspired by traditional Swiss-style muesli, this is the deluxe version! Make sure you have it on hand for those dark and rainy November days, or almost any other day. . . . Oh, before I forget: don't chop the chocolate too finely if you'd like to encounter semimelted chocolate morsels in your bowl.

Buy the best-quality chocolate you can afford, regardless of the percentage of cocoa solids. Depending on my mood, I fluctuate between old-fashioned milk chocolate for childhood comfort and the pitch-dark adult decadence of 70 percent cocoa content. This mixture will last for about 4 weeks, stored in an airtight container at room temperature. MAKES ABOUT 3 CUPS, TO SERVE 6

....

MUESLI

1/4 cup chopped dried dates

1 tablespoon packed light or dark brown sugar

2 cups old-fashioned rolled oats (not quick-cooking)

1/4 cup chopped toasted hazelnuts (see page 37)

1/4 cup dried blueberries or raisins

2 1/2 ounces chocolate with 70 percent cocoa content, cut into 1/2-inch pieces

2 tablespoons cocoa powder, preferably Dutch-process

1 teaspoon ground cinnamon

Pinch of fine sea salt

TO FINISH

3 cups whole or lowfat milk

1   To prepare the muesli, place the dates and brown sugar in a small bowl and stir to coat the pieces. Combine all the other ingredients in a large bowl, and stir in the sugared dates.

2   MICROWAVE METHOD: For each serving, combine 1/2 cup milk and 1/2 cup muesli in a small bowl. Heat on high power for 45 seconds, or until it is warmed through but melted drops of chocolate remain. STOVETOP METHOD: For each serving, heat 1/2 cup milk in a small heavy saucepan until small bubbles appear around the rim. Turn off the heat; add 1/2 cup of the muesli, cover, and let sit for not more than 1 minute so that melted drops of chocolate remain.

THE ORIGINS OF MUESLI

Swiss physician Maximilian Bircher-Benner introduced the world to this high-fiber food in the early twentieth century. Muesli literally means "little mush." Originally, muesli was a mixture of rolled oats, grated apple, and nuts combined with condensed milk and lemon juice. Condensed milk was used instead of fresh milk at the time because of hygiene concerns. Bircher-Benner served this breakfast to patients at his Vital Force (*Lebende Kraft*) sanatorium in Zurich. Contrary to the general view of his compatriots, the dietary reformer was convinced of the healing properties of raw fruits and vegetables. He was inspired by shepherds in the Alps, who mixed oats with raisins, apples, and sometimes nuts for breakfast.

Creamy Farro with Honey-Roasted Grapes

This supremely comforting breakfast is perfect for a chilly morning in the fall, especially if you can get your hands on freshly picked grapes from a farmer's market. Red grapes are the most stunning, but a mixture of red and white works as well. This recipe was inspired by a brunch item served at Inoteca restaurant in New York, and published in *Gourmet* magazine. The original called for grapes, plums, and Bartlett pears. I prefer it with grapes alone, and I scent my farro with anise seeds, which lend an ambrosial quality to this peasant grain (for more on varieties of farro, see page 16). If you have a strongly flavored Mediterranean honey at hand, such as thyme or chestnut, this is the place to use it. And if you're feeling lavish, crown your bowl with a dollop of softly whipped cream. **SERVES 4**

FARRO

2 cups water

1 cup farro

1 teaspoon anise seeds

1 (1-inch) piece cinnamon stick

Pinch of fine sea salt

ROASTED GRAPES, AND TO FINISH

3 cups seedless red grapes (1 1/4 pounds)

1 teaspoon extra-virgin olive oil

4 tablespoons honey, plus extra for serving

1/2 cup heavy whipping cream or half-and-half

1/2 teaspoon vanilla extract

Ground cinnamon, for sprinkling

1   To prepare the farro, bring the water, farro, anise seeds, cinnamon stick, and salt to a boil in a heavy-bottomed 4-quart saucepan. Decrease the heat to maintain a simmer, cover, and cook until the farro is tender but still slightly chewy, 20 to 25 minutes. Remove the cinnamon stick, drain any remaining liquid, and return the farro to the saucepan.

2   Meanwhile, prepare the roasted grapes. Position a rack 6 inches from the heat source and preheat the broiler for 5 minutes. Spread the grapes on a large rimmed baking sheet. Drizzle with the olive oil and 2 tablespoons of the honey and toss to combine. Broil until the grapes just start to shrivel and release some juices as they burst, 5 to 7 minutes. Immediately transfer the grapes with their juices to a heatproof bowl.

3   To finish, add the cream and vanilla extract to the farro and bring to a boil over medium heat, stirring frequently. Cook until the cream thickens slightly, 3 to 5 minutes. Stir in the remaining 2 tablespoons honey, add the grapes with their juices and cook just long enough to reheat the fruit, about 2 minutes. Divide among bowls, sprinkle with cinnamon, and serve warm with more honey on the side.

TO GET A HEAD START: Make the farro, as in step 1, ahead (see page 25). The grapes can also be roasted 1 day ahead. Chill, covered.

TO VARY IT: If you like a bit more chewiness, try other berries from the wheat family such as spelt, Kamut, or soft whole wheat. You will need a scant 3 cups (for cooking instructions, see page 25).

Citrus Oatmeal with Apricots and Golden Raisins

Cooking perfectly creamy steel-cut oats is time–consuming—plus I never seem to be able to get the temperature right. The oats boil over and I'm left with a veritable mess on the stove. One day, I tried to speed up the process by parboiling the grain the night before, and the next morning my oatmeal was ready in minutes. No nerve-wracking cleanup, either. Best of all, I believe that this method truly brings out the best in steel-cut oats, resulting in tender grains with a nice chewiness. I add the dried fruit in two stages. First, I mix in the raisins to let them release their sweetness, adding the apricots later so they don't become mushy and retain their fragrance. SERVES 4 TO 6

STEEL-CUT OATS

2 cups water

1 cup steel-cut oats

1/4 cup golden raisins

1 (2-inch) piece cinnamon stick

OATMEAL

1 cup water

1 cup whole or lowfat milk

1/4 cup chopped dried apricots, preferably Blenheim

Pinch of fine sea salt

1 teaspoon finely grated orange zest

Turbinado or brown sugar, for sprinkling

1 Prepare the steel-cut oats the night before: Bring the water, oats, raisins, and cinnamon stick to a boil in a heavy-bottomed 4-quart saucepan. Cook, uncovered, for 2 minutes over medium to medium-low heat, stirring a few times. Remove from the heat, cover, and let sit at room temperature until the water is absorbed, about 1 hour. Allow to cool, cover, and refrigerate until ready to use.

2 The next morning, finish the oatmeal: Add the water, milk, dried apricots, and salt to the pot with the oats. Bring to a boil over medium-high heat, stirring and breaking up any lumps of grain. Decrease the heat to maintain a simmer, cover, and cook, stirring once or twice, for 5 to 8 minutes, or until the oats are creamy but still slightly chewy. (Or, for a thicker oatmeal, cook uncovered at a gentle bubble, stirring a few times.) Remove the cinnamon stick and stir in the orange zest. Divide the oatmeal among bowls and serve, sprinkled with the turbinado sugar.

TO GET A HEAD START: The steel-cut oats, as in step 1, can be prepared up to 5 days ahead. Chill, covered.

TO VARY IT: I like tangy Blenheim apricots here, to contrast with the sweet golden raisins; but you can use any combination of dried fruit you enjoy. Replace the orange zest with lemon zest to add zing.

TO MAKE IT A FEAST: Use cream or half-and-half instead of milk to splurge on a Sunday.

Honey-Nut Granola with Olive Oil

A mild extra-virgin olive oil gives this crisp granola a subtle fragrance that you will be hard-pressed to pinpoint—so don't hesitate to use it instead of common vegetable oil. Do I need to say that this is way better than any granola you've ever had? Try it for yourself, in a bowl with milk or yogurt, or just grab a handful for a snack. This blend will keep for a week, stored in an airtight container at room temperature.
MAKES 20 (1/2-CUP) SERVINGS

....

3 cups old-fashioned rolled oats (not quick-cooking)

1/2 cup coarsely chopped almonds

1/2 cup unsweetened shredded coconut

1/2 cup sunflower seeds

1/2 cup flax seeds, preferably golden

1/2 cup sesame seeds

1/2 cup honey

6 tablespoons extra-virgin olive oil

1/4 cup packed light brown sugar

1 teaspoon vanilla extract

1/4 teaspoon fine sea salt

2/3 cup dried cranberries

2/3 cup golden raisins

2/3 cup chopped dried apricots

1 Position a rack in the center of the oven and preheat to 350°F. Line a large rimmed baking sheet with parchment paper. Place the oats, almonds, coconut, and the sunflower, flax, and sesame seeds in a large bowl and stir to combine.

2 Combine the honey, olive oil, sugar, vanilla extract, and salt in a small heavy-bottomed saucepan. Warm over medium-low to medium heat, stirring occasionally, until the sugar has melted and the mixture is well blended, about 5 minutes.

3 Add the honey mixture to the oat mixture and stir with a spatula until no dry spots remain. Spread the cereal evenly over the prepared baking sheet. Bake until light golden brown, 18 to 20 minutes, stirring once halfway through baking. Transfer the baking sheet to a wire rack and leave the granola on the sheet to cool completely, about 1 hour. It will crisp as it cools. Break into bite-size chunks and stir in the cranberries, raisins, and apricots.

Chewy Almond Butter Bars

The concentrated richness of nut butters is a boon in cooking and baking. Before I learned to appreciate American peanut butter in all its glory (I'm a fan of crunchy), I slathered intensely aromatic hazelnut and almond butters on countless sandwiches to keep me going through long workdays in Germany. In these delectably chewy, no-fuss energy bars, almond butter plays in the background to bring all the flavors together. Unrefined turbinado sugar (see page 35) adds a caramel undertone. Oh yes, they are sweet, for a treat—and great for breakfast on the go. For the best flavor, look for unsalted and dry-roasted creamy almond butter. Use leftover nut butter to spread on breads just like peanut butter. **MAKES 8 BARS**

1 cup old-fashioned rolled oats (not quick-cooking)

1/4 cup slivered almonds

1/4 cup sunflower seeds

1 tablespoon flax seeds, preferably golden

1 tablespoon sesame seeds

1 cup unsweetened puffed whole grain cereal

1/3 cup currants

1/3 cup chopped dried apricots

1/3 cup chopped golden raisins

1/4 cup creamy almond butter

1/4 cup turbinado or light brown sugar

1/4 cup honey

1/2 teaspoon vanilla extract

1/4 teaspoon fine sea salt

1 Position a rack in the center of the oven and preheat to 350°F. Butter an 8-inch or 9-inch square baking pan.

2 Spread the oats, almonds, sunflower seeds, flax seeds, and sesame seeds evenly over a large rimmed baking sheet. Bake until the oats are lightly toasted and the nuts are fragrant, shaking the pan halfway, 8 to 10 minutes total. Transfer to a large bowl and let cool. Add the cereal, currants, apricots, and raisins; toss to combine.

3 Combine the almond butter, sugar, honey, vanilla extract, and salt in a small heavy-bottomed saucepan. Heat over medium-low, stirring frequently, until the mixture bubbles slightly, about 5 minutes.

4 Immediately pour the almond butter mixture over the dry ingredients and mix with a spoon or spatula until no dry spots remain. Transfer to the prepared pan. Coat your hands with a thin film of oil and press the mixture down firmly, creating an even layer (wait until the mixture cools slightly if necessary). Chill, uncovered, until firm, about 30 minutes, and then cut into 8 bars.

TO GET A HEAD START: The bars can be made ahead and stored for up to 1 week in an airtight container at room temperature, or in the refrigerator (they will be firmer). They can also be frozen for up to 1 month. Thaw at room temperature.

TO LIGHTEN IT UP: When this recipe was first published in *Eating Well* magazine, some readers with less of a sweet tooth omitted the turbinado sugar altogether. The only caveat: the bars will be a little stickier. And, of course, you can cut smaller bars and enjoy one together with a bowl of yogurt.

Apricot-Lemon Bars with Cherries

Whenever we traveled through Greece during my childhood, I marveled at the sight of fruit drying in the hot midday sun. Farmers would spread huge canvases on rooftops, covering every available spot with figs, plums, and apricots, thus preserving the bounty of their harvest. Their soft texture and supreme fruitiness explains my ongoing infatuation with the nutrient-rich bites to this day. To give these bars an extra boost of citrus, I like to plump the dried apricots in lemon juice for half an hour as I prep the ingredients, stirring once or twice. But you can use orange juice instead to mellow the tang, especially if you can find only tart Blenheim apricots. Look for 100 percent whole wheat honey graham crackers in health foods or specialty stores, or substitute with 1¹/₃ cups regular graham cracker crumbs (9 whole pieces). **MAKES 8 BARS, OR 16 BITE-SIZE SQUARES**

....

CRUST

18 whole wheat graham crackers (5 ounces)

3 tablespoons extra-virgin olive oil

2 teaspoons finely grated lemon zest

2 tablespoons packed light brown sugar

¹/₈ teaspoon fine sea salt

TOPPING

¹/₄ cup whole wheat pastry or whole wheat flour (1 ounce)

¹/₄ teaspoon baking powder

¹/₈ teaspoon fine sea salt

3 large eggs, at room temperature

¹/₄ cup packed light brown sugar

2 teaspoons finely grated lemon zest

³/₄ cup chopped dried apricots, preferably Turkish

¹/₄ cup freshly squeezed lemon juice (2 lemons)

¹/₂ heaped cup sweet pitted cherries (about 20; thawed and drained if using frozen)

¹/₄ cup toasted slivered almonds (see page 37)

1 Position a rack in the center of the oven and preheat to 350°F. Butter and flour an 8-inch square baking pan, tapping out the excess, or coat with cooking spray.

2 To make the crust, break the graham crackers into the bowl of a food processor and process until finely ground, about 30 seconds. Add the remaining crust ingredients and pulse until just combined, 5 to 7 pulses. Press the crumb mixture evenly into the bottom of the prepared pan and bake for 8 minutes, or until set. Transfer to a wire rack to cool for a few minutes. Leave the oven on.

3 Meanwhile, make the topping. Whisk the whole wheat pastry flour, baking powder, and salt in a small bowl. In a large bowl, whisk the eggs with the sugar and lemon zest until the mixture is frothy and the sugar has dissolved, about 1 minute. Briefly whisk in the flour mixture until just blended. Stir in the dried apricots and lemon juice. Pour the filling evenly over the crust. Distribute the cherries on top and sprinkle with the almonds.

4 Bake until the top turns golden and the edges are browned, 25 to 30 minutes. Transfer the pan to a wire rack to cool. After about 30 minutes, loosen the edges and cut into bars or squares using a sharp knife. Leave to cool completely in the pan, about 1 hour total.

TO GET A HEAD START: The bars can be made 1 day ahead. Chill, covered. Bring to room temperature before serving.

TO VARY IT: Replace the cherries with raspberries, or peaches cut into ¹/₂-inch pieces.

Saffron Waffles with Orange Cream

Becoming a reasonably mature adult has not diminished the intense pleasure I get from making crisp waffles on a lazy morning. After my Iranian friend Golnaz brought me what I soon declared to be the best saffron ever (see also "Precious Saffron," page 91), I started adding a pinch of the strands to everything, including this waffle batter. Don't pass up the scrumptious cream topping which will kiss awake any prince out of *The Thousand and One Nights*. Still, it is barely sweet—so everyone can add a drizzle of maple syrup. Double the amount of topping if you have very hungry royalty descending upon you.

These waffles have a gentle toothiness, which you can lighten if you like; for a smoother texture, use 1 cup (4 1/2 ounces) white whole wheat and 1 cup (4 ounces) whole wheat pastry flour. You will need to adjust the preheating and cooking times as well as the amount of batter needed according to the manufacturer's instructions for your waffle iron. **MAKES ABOUT 4 (7-INCH) BELGIAN-STYLE WAFFLES, TO SERVE 6**

....

ORANGE CREAM TOPPING

1 cup plain whole-milk Greek yogurt

1 large orange

1/2 cup heavy whipping cream, chilled

1 to 2 tablespoons honey

WAFFLES

2 cups whole milk

1/4 teaspoon saffron threads

2 cups white whole wheat flour (8 1/2 ounces)

2 tablespoons sugar

2 1/2 teaspoons baking powder

1/2 teaspoon fine sea salt

2 large eggs, lightly beaten

6 tablespoons extra-virgin olive oil

Maple syrup, for drizzling

> **SEE MEASURING WHOLE GRAIN FLOUR, PAGE 28**

1 To make the orange cream topping, beat the yogurt in a medium bowl with a wooden spoon until smooth. Finely grate the orange until you have 1 tablespoon zest. Set the zest aside. Peel the fruit, cut the segments into 1/2-inch pieces, removing as much of the pith as you like (see "The Joy of Pith," below), and gently stir into the yogurt. In a second medium bowl, using a hand mixer, whip the cream, honey, and zest until firm peaks form. Using a spatula, scrape the cream into the bowl with the yogurt-orange mixture, and fold until just combined. Chill, covered, until ready to use.

2 Place a wire rack on a baking sheet and transfer the sheet to the center shelf of the oven. The wire rack will keep the waffles from getting soggy. Preheat the oven to 200°F.

3 To make the waffles, place 1/4 cup of the milk and the saffron in a small heavy-bottomed saucepan and heat over medium-high heat until steaming. (Or combine the milk and saffron in a small microwave-safe bowl and microwave on high until steaming, 15 to 20 seconds). Let sit for 5 to 10 minutes.

4 In a large bowl, whisk together the whole wheat flour, sugar, baking powder, and salt. In a medium bowl, whisk the eggs with the remaining 1 3/4 cups milk, saffron milk, and oil until blended. Make a well in the center of the dry ingredients. Add the wet ingredients and whisk together with a few swift strokes. Do not overmix; the batter should have a pebbled look, with many lumps. Allow the batter to sit for 5 minutes while preheating the waffle iron (or chill the batter for up to 1 hour).

CONTINUED, PAGE 52

THE JOY OF PITH

When professional chefs serve citrus, they typically remove any remnants of white pith and even cut the fruit segments out of their silky skins, the so-called membranes. My Greek mom just peels, chops, and eats the fruit, pith and all, and so do I—because I am too busy to bother, and I enjoy the slight chew with its wee bit of bitterness. And more recently we learned that pith contains beneficial nutrients. Well, even better!

5 Lightly grease the waffle iron with oil or coat it with cooking spray. When a drop of water sizzles and briskly evaporates on the surface, add 1 scant cup batter to the center and level with a spatula to distribute (or as specified in the manufacturer's instructions). Close the lid and cook until the waffles are golden and can be removed easily using tongs, 3 1/2 to 4 minutes. Transfer the waffles to the baking sheet until ready to serve. Do not stack them, as the waffles will become soggy. Continue until all the batter is used, lightly greasing the waffle iron in between as necessary.

TO GET A HEAD START: The orange cream topping can be prepared 1 day ahead. Chill, covered.

TO LIGHTEN IT UP: You can use lowfat or nonfat Greek yogurt in the topping. Or omit the heavy cream, double the amount of yogurt, and add a bit more honey to taste. In the batter, 1 percent or 2 percent milk will work fine.

Cornmeal Pancakes with Warm Cherry Sauce

These tangy buttermilk pancakes owe their appealing texture to two kinds of flour: medium-coarse cornmeal and white whole wheat. No one in your family will even notice that this is a whole grain treat. Of course, you may use regular whole wheat flour for a heartier flavor. The warm cherry sauce is addictive, but I sometimes just serve these pancakes with a dab of good-quality butter and a double dose of maple syrup. And in case you are wondering, I never bother removing the cloves from the sauce because I can never find them. . . . MAKES 12 PANCAKES, TO SERVE 4

....

PANCAKES

1 cup medium-coarse stone ground whole grain cornmeal (4 ounces)

1/2 cup white whole wheat flour (2 1/4 ounces)

2 tablespoons sugar

1 1/2 teaspoons baking powder

1/2 teaspoon baking soda

1/2 teaspoon fine sea salt

1 1/2 cups lowfat buttermilk

2 large eggs, lightly beaten

2 tablespoons extra-virgin olive oil

CHERRY SAUCE, AND TO FINISH

2 cups sweet pitted cherries (about 10 ounces; do not thaw if using frozen)

1/4 cup plus 1 tablespoon water

1/4 cup honey

2 teaspoons finely grated orange zest

3 whole cloves

2 teaspoons cornstarch

SEE MEASURING
WHOLE GRAIN FLOUR,
PAGE 28

1 To prepare the pancakes, whisk together the cornmeal, whole wheat flour, sugar, baking powder, baking soda, and salt in a large bowl. In a medium bowl, whisk the buttermilk, eggs, and olive oil to blend. Pour the buttermilk mixture over the dry ingredients and stir with a spatula or wooden spoon until just combined. Do not overmix; a number of small lumps should remain. Allow the batter to sit for 10 minutes.

2 Place a large baking sheet on the center rack of the oven and preheat to 200°F.

3 Meanwhile, prepare the cherry sauce. Combine the cherries, 1/4 cup of the water, and the honey, orange zest, and cloves in a small saucepan. Bring to a boil over medium heat, stirring occasionally. Turn off the heat, cover partially, and set aside for flavors to meld.

4 To make the pancakes, heat a large cast-iron skillet or a griddle over medium heat. Lightly grease the pan. When a drop of water sizzles and briskly evaporates on the surface, add 1/4 cup batter per pancake, leaving some space in between so you can flip them. Cook until the edges of the pancakes start to look dry and the bottoms turn golden brown, about 2 minutes. Flip and cook until golden, about 1 minute. Decrease the heat a tad if the pancakes brown too quickly. Transfer to the baking sheet in the oven to keep warm. Do not stack. Continue until all the batter is used, greasing the pan lightly in between as necessary.

5 To finish the cherry sauce, combine the cornstarch and the remaining 1 tablespoon water in a small bowl. Add to the saucepan with the cherries and return to a boil over medium-high, stirring gently so you don't crush the fruit. Cook until the mixture thickens slightly, 1 to 2 minutes. Serve right away.

TO GET A HEAD START: The sauce can be prepared, as in step 3 and 5, up to 3 days ahead. Chill, covered. Gently reheat, without much stirring.

Date-Apricot Muffins with Anise

At least a dozen jars of dried fruits and nuts line the shelves in my kitchen at all times. These muffins rely on a time-tested trio, steeped in the culinary heritage of the Middle East, of dates, dried apricots, and pistachios. Enjoy these chewy muffins on their own, or with orange marmalade and butter. In the mood to splurge? Dish them up for brunch with Brandied Apricot Butter (see sidebar).

Chopped dates will often stick together in one big chunk. Separate the pieces by tossing them with 1 teaspoon of additional sugar before you add them to the batter. MAKES 12 MUFFINS

....

MUFFINS

2 cups white whole wheat flour
  (8 1/2 ounces)

1/4 cup sugar

1 1/2 teaspoons baking powder

1/2 teaspoon baking soda

1/2 teaspoon ground cinnamon

1/2 teaspoon ground anise seeds,
  preferably freshly ground

1/2 teaspoon fine sea salt

1/2 cup chopped dried dates

1/4 cup chopped dried apricots

3 large eggs, at room temperature

1/2 cup honey

1/3 cup extra-virgin olive oil

3/4 cup freshly squeezed orange juice

2 teaspoons finely grated orange zest

1/2 cup chopped unsalted toasted
  pistachios (see page 37)

TOPPING

2 tablespoons sugar

1/2 teaspoon ground anise seeds

3 tablespoons finely chopped
  unsalted toasted pistachios

1 Position a rack in the center of the oven and preheat to 375°F. Lightly butter a standard-size 12-cup muffin pan, preferably nonstick, or coat with cooking spray.

2 To make the muffins, whisk together the white whole wheat flour, sugar, baking powder, baking soda, cinnamon, anise seeds, and salt in a large bowl. Scatter the dates and apricots on top and toss to combine. Make a well in the center. In a medium bowl, lightly whisk the eggs to blend. Whisk in the honey and then the olive oil, orange juice, and zest until smooth, about 1 minute. Add the egg mixture to the center of the flour mixture, and stir with a rubber spatula until just combined. Do not overmix; the batter should look lumpy. Fold in the pistachios. Using a 1/3-cup measure, divide the batter equally among the muffin cups (they will be almost full).

3 To make the topping, combine the sugar and anise seeds in a small bowl. Sprinkle each muffin with 1/2 teaspoon of the sugar mixture, and top with the pistachios.

4 Bake until the muffins are nicely domed and lightly golden and the tops spring back when gently pressed, about 15 minutes. Transfer the pan to a wire rack to cool for 5 minutes, and then gently twist the muffins out of the pan. Eat warm or at room temperature.

TO GET A HEAD START: These muffins freeze well for up to 1 month.

TO VARY IT: Use chopped toasted walnuts or toasted slivered almonds in place of the pistachios.

TO LIGHTEN IT UP: Omit the sugar in the batter for a less-sweet morning muffin—or as an excuse to add your favorite jam. . . .

SEE MEASURING
WHOLE GRAIN FLOUR,
PAGE 28

BRANDIED APRICOT BUTTER

Everyone needs to have at least one delicious breakfast butter in his or her culinary repertoire. Laced with jam or with herbs, these so-called compound butters add a luxurious touch to breakfast with minimal effort. On my brunch table, they are always spiked. But freshly squeezed orange juice can replace the spirits if you have children. No brandy? Use citrus-flavored Grand Marnier or limoncello liqueur. I generously spread this butter on Date-Apricot Muffins with Anise (above) or on Orange-Scented Scones with Dark Chocolate (page 58). **MAKES 3/4 CUP**

1/2 cup (4 ounces, 1 stick) unsalted butter, softened
1/4 cup good-quality apricot preserves
2 tablespoons brandy
1 tablespoon finely grated orange zest
Pinch of fine sea salt

Using the back of a wooden spoon or an electric hand mixer, beat the butter until light and creamy. Add the preserves, brandy, orange zest, and salt and beat until well combined. Chill until firm. Bring to room temperature before serving. The butter will keep in the fridge for up to 1 week.

ALWAYS FRESH CITRUS ZEST ON HAND

When using citrus zest for cooking, I prefer to use unwaxed organic fruit, but they come at a price and are not always available. So whenever I find organic citrus, I keep the peels when I eat the fruit, storing them in a small clear plastic bag in the cheese drawer of the fridge. Leave the bag open to allow for air circulation. The peels will typically last for a couple of weeks. Yes, it is a bit more cumbersome to zest peels without the fruit, but it beats having no good-quality zest at all.

Fig Muffins with Creamy Goat Cheese Filling

The inspiration for these muffins came to me in the wee hours of a sleepless night. I had been mulling for days over a creamy blissful filling when the classic Mediterranean pairing of sweet dried figs and tangy goat cheese came to mind. This is such a winning match that you should try it, even if goat cheese is normally not your thing. Just be sure to look for a mild kind. Of course, you may use cream cheese instead.

The creaminess of goat cheese can vary considerably, as my testers discovered. To get a lush, creamy center, you might have to add up to 2 tablespoons of buttermilk to the filling. But don't worry—even if the filling isn't as creamy as it should be, it will still taste delicious. Just make a note for next time.

MAKES 12 MUFFINS

....

FILLING

3/4 cup crumbled mild soft goat cheese (3 ounces), at room temperature

2 tablespoons honey

1 teaspoon finely grated lemon zest

1/4 teaspoon vanilla extract

MUFFINS

2 cups white whole wheat flour (8 1/2 ounces)

1 1/2 teaspoons baking powder

1/2 teaspoon baking soda

1/2 teaspoon fine sea salt

3 large eggs, at room temperature

3/4 cup packed dark or light brown sugar

1 teaspoon vanilla extract

1/3 cup extra-virgin olive oil

3/4 cup lowfat buttermilk

1 cup chopped dried figs, preferably Turkish or Greek, stemmed (about 10)

3 tablespoons turbinado or granulated sugar, for sprinkling

> **SEE MEASURING WHOLE GRAIN FLOUR, PAGE 28**

1 Position a rack in the center of the oven and preheat to 400°F. Lightly butter a standard-size 12-cup muffin pan, preferably nonstick, or coat with cooking spray.

2 To make the filling, combine the goat cheese, honey, lemon zest, and vanilla extract in a small bowl. Beat with a fork until smooth.

3 To make the muffins, whisk together the white whole wheat flour, baking powder, baking soda, and salt in a large bowl. Make a well in the center. In a medium bowl, lightly whisk the eggs to blend. Gently whisk in the brown sugar and vanilla extract, and then the olive oil and buttermilk until smooth, about 1 minute. Add the egg mixture to the center of the flour mixture, and stir with a rubber spatula until just combined. Do not overmix; the batter should look lumpy. Fold in the dried figs.

4 Using a soup spoon, fill each muffin cup nearly half full. Add a bit more than 1 teaspoon of the goat cheese filling to the center of each muffin, gently pressing in. Top with the remaining batter. (The filling should not be visible.) Generously sprinkle the muffins with the turbinado sugar.

5 Bake until the muffins are nicely domed, the edges start to brown, and the tops spring back when gently pressed, about 13 minutes. Transfer the pan to a wire rack to cool for 5 minutes before gently twisting the muffins out of the pan. Cool them completely on the rack, or eat warm.

TO GET A HEAD START: The muffins can be baked 1 day ahead and stored in an airtight container at room temperature, or frozen for up to 1 month.

TO VARY IT: Use 1 teaspoon orange zest instead of lemon zest in the filling.

Orange-Scented Scones with Dark Chocolate

Fancy pastry shops in Greece have long wooed their customers with rich dark chocolate confections that rival French classics. Aromatic local oranges often play a starring role, a luscious combination that inspired the flavor in these scones. Do I need to add that these are best with a bit of butter? And when I make them for brunch or in the late afternoon, a bowl of lightly sweetened brandied whipped cream always somehow emerges on the table on cue.

A blend of white whole wheat and whole wheat pastry flour is key to the light texture of these small treats. You can increase the amount of chocolate to $1/2$ cup if you are feeling indulgent. Some of my testers also boosted the orange zest to $11/2$ tablespoons—it's your choice. In any case, get the best-quality dark chocolate you can afford. A good-quality semisweet or milk chocolate is fine if a bit more sweetness is what you are after. MAKES 12 MINI-SCONES

....

SCONES

1 cup white whole wheat flour (4 1/4 ounces)

1 cup whole wheat pastry flour (4 ounces)

1/4 cup granulated sugar

2 1/2 teaspoons baking powder

1/2 teaspoon fine sea salt

6 tablespoons chilled unsalted butter, cut into 1/2-inch pieces

1/3 cup chopped toasted walnuts (see page 37)

2 ounces chopped dark chocolate with 70 percent cocoa content (about 1/3 cup)

1 large egg

1 tablespoon finely grated orange zest (from 1 large orange)

3/4 cup chilled heavy whipping cream, plus extra for brushing

Turbinado sugar or additional granulated sugar, for sprinkling

BRANDIED WHIPPED CREAM (OPTIONAL)

1 cup chilled heavy whipping cream

1 tablespoon granulated sugar

1 tablespoon brandy

1 Position a rack in the center of the oven and preheat to 400°F. Lightly butter a baking sheet or line with parchment paper.

2 Whisk together the white whole wheat and whole wheat pastry flours, granulated sugar, baking powder, and salt in a large mixing bowl. Scatter the butter on top. Using a pastry blender or your fingers, quickly rub the butter into the flour mixture until it resembles coarse meal with some uneven pebbles. Stir in the walnuts and chocolate. Make a well in the center.

3 Whisk together the egg, orange zest, and cream in a 2-cup liquid measure. Add about 3/4 cup of this egg-cream mixture to the center of the flour mixture and fold in using a rubber spatula; stir in some or all of the remaining liquid until a shaggy dough just comes together (you might have a bit of the cream mixture left). Gather with your hands and give the dough 4 to 6 gentle turns inside the bowl.

4 Cut the dough in half and transfer to a lightly floured work surface. Pat each half into a 5-inch circle, about 1 inch thick. Using a long, sharp knife dipped in flour, cut each circle into 6 small wedges. Place the wedges 2 inches apart on the baking sheet. Brush the scones with cream and generously sprinkle with turbinado sugar.

SEE MEASURING WHOLE GRAIN FLOUR, PAGE 28

5   Bake until the scones are golden with brown edges and firm to the touch, rotating the baking sheet halfway through, 16 to 18 minutes. Transfer to a wire rack to cool a bit. Eat warm or at room temperature.

6   While the scones cool, prepare the whipped cream: using an electric hand mixer at medium speed, whip the cream, sugar, and brandy until soft peaks form.

TO GET A HEAD START: You like to sleep in on the weekend? Prepare the scones the night before through step 3, cover with plastic wrap, and chill. Bake in a preheated oven straight from the fridge (they will need a few extra minutes to turn golden). Brandied whipped cream can be prepared up to 3 hours ahead. Chill, covered. The scones will freeze well for at least 1 month.

TO LIGHTEN IT UP: You can replace the cream with half-and-half for a less rich but still delicious scone.

ARE YOUR SCONES TOO DENSE?

Real British scones are quite different from many scones sold in the United States. Here scones are often sweeter, denser, and more cakelike, while British scones ideally turn out crumbly and light. To reach this consistency, it is crucial not to overwork the dough. When stirring and folding the liquids into the flour mixture (as in step 3), be sure to gather the dough briskly and to add just enough liquid for the dough to come together (the amount you need depends on the humidity as well as on the flour you use). Knead gently, not more than 10 seconds.

After baking, the most, tender scones will have a shaggy look, with cracks on top and slight bulges on the sides. Pastry chef Frank Tegethoff, of the King Arthur Flour Baker's Hot Line, calls them gentle "curvatures." Knead the dough more and the scones will not bake up with these cracks and bulges, but this neater appearance comes at a price: less tender scones. You choose!

Lemon-Rosemary Scones

If I had to choose between rosemary and lemon, I don't think I could. I can't imagine living without either of them, so I combine them often. These scones are quick to make, and ever so slightly and deliciously tangy because of the addition of sour cream. Serve with orange marmalade and butter, or accompanied by lightly sweetened Greek yogurt. **MAKES 8 SCONES**

1 cup white whole wheat flour (4 1/4 ounces)

1 cup whole wheat pastry flour (4 ounces)

1/4 cup sugar, plus extra for sprinkling

1 1/2 teaspoons baking powder

1/4 teaspoon baking soda

1/2 teaspoon fine sea salt

5 tablespoons chilled unsalted butter, cut into 1/2-inch pieces

3/4 cup sour cream

2 teaspoons finely grated lemon zest

2 teaspoons minced fresh rosemary

1/2 cup lowfat buttermilk, plus extra for brushing

SEE MEASURING WHOLE GRAIN FLOUR, PAGE 28

1 Position a rack in the center of the oven and preheat to 425°F. Lightly butter a baking sheet or line with parchment paper.

2 Whisk together the whole wheat flour, whole wheat pastry flour, sugar, baking powder, baking soda, and salt in a large bowl. Scatter the butter on top. Using a pastry blender or your fingers, quickly rub the butter into the flour mixture until it resembles coarse meal with some uneven pebbles.

3 Using a fork, beat the sour cream, lemon zest, and rosemary in a small bowl to blend. Add to the flour mixture, stirring and folding until pebbly. Add almost all the buttermilk (reserving about 2 tablespoons) and gently bring a rough, patchy dough together with your hands. If a fair bit of flour remains, add just enough reserved buttermilk to gather the dough. Give the dough 4 to 6 gentle turns inside the bowl.

4 Transfer to a lightly floured work surface and pat into a 7-inch circle, about 1 inch thick. Using a long, sharp knife dipped in flour, cut into 8 wedges. Place the wedges 2 inches apart on the prepared baking sheet. Brush with buttermilk and sprinkle generously with sugar.

5 Bake until the scones are golden with brown edges and firm to the touch, rotating the baking sheet halfway through, 20 to 25 minutes. Transfer the scones to a wire rack to cool a bit. Serve warm or at room temperature.

TO GET A HEAD START: See the Orange-Scented Scones with Dark Chocolate (page 58) for make-ahead instructions. Scones freeze well for at least 1 month.

TO VARY IT: Use 2 teaspoons orange zest instead of lemon zest.

TO LIGHTEN IT UP: Use 3/4 cup plain whole-milk Greek yogurt instead of the sour cream for tangier scones with a little less richness. Lowfat sour cream and 2 percent Greek yogurt will work—though personally, I would opt for mini-scones with fuller flavor (for shaping directions, see Orange-Scented Scones with Dark Chocolate). They will need a few minutes less baking time.

Tangerine-Lavender Coffee Cake

I have yet to visit the southeast of France, where purple-hued lavender fields stretch as far as the eye can see. But I have always used the pungent-sweet herb in my cooking. Tangerines with their delicate sweetness, barely acidic, strike a perfect balance in this easy coffee cake. But other citrus varieties are a fine choice as well (see below). Enjoy the cake on its own, or serve it with a bowl of creamy yogurt and freshly cut fruit. Its complex flavors make for a lovely dessert as well—top with sweetened whipped cream, or with a scoop of orange or lemon sorbet. Be sure you make this cake 1 day ahead to allow its flavors to meld—if you can resist taking a bite.

To avoid a sticky mess when measuring honey, spray or spread a thin film of oil in the cup measure—the honey will flow out smoothly. **MAKES 1 (8-INCH SQUARE CAKE) TO SERVE 12**

---

4 or 5 tangerines

1 cup golden or dark raisins

1¹/2 cups white whole wheat flour (6¹/2 ounces)

¹/2 cup fine cornmeal, preferably stone-ground (2 ounces)

¹/4 cup sugar

2 teaspoons baking powder

2 teaspoons dried lavender buds

¹/2 teaspoon baking soda

¹/2 teaspoon fine sea salt

2 large eggs, at room temperature

¹/2 cup honey

¹/4 cup extra-virgin olive oil

¹/2 cup lowfat buttermilk

1 teaspoon vanilla extract

Confectioners' sugar, for dusting

> SEE MEASURING
> WHOLE GRAIN FLOUR,
> PAGE 28

1 Position a rack in the center of the oven and preheat to 325°F. Lightly butter the bottom and sides of an 8-inch square glass baking dish or coat with cooking spray. Line the bottom of the pan with parchment paper, and lightly butter the paper as well. Dust the pan with flour, tapping out excess.

2 Finely grate the zest of the tangerines until you have 1 tablespoon. Squeeze the fruit to get ¹/2 cup juice. Set zest and juice aside. In a small bowl, toss the raisins with 1 tablespoon of the white whole wheat flour.

3 Whisk together the remaining white whole wheat flour, cornmeal, sugar, baking powder, lavender, baking soda, and salt in a large bowl. Make a well in the center. In a medium bowl, lightly whisk the eggs to blend. Gradually whisk in the honey until it is incorporated, beating quite vigorously, followed by the olive oil, about 1 minute. In a small bowl, combine the buttermilk, tangerine juice, zest, and vanilla extract, and stir until smooth; gradually whisk into the egg mixture. Add the wet ingredients to the dry ingredients in 2 additions, stirring well in between with a rubber spatula until just blended. Fold in the raisins. Pour the batter into the pan.

4 Bake until the cake is golden and a cake taster or a toothpick inserted into the center comes out clean with just a crumb or two, 40 to 45 minutes. Transfer to a wire rack to cool for about 10 minutes. To unmold the cake, loosen around the edges with a small sharp knife and invert out of the pan onto a flat plate or a small square tray. Remove the parchment paper and invert again onto a wire rack to cool completely, right side up. Just before serving, dust with confectioners' sugar and cut into 12 squares.

TO VARY IT: Use ¹/2 cup juice and 1 tablespoon zest from 1 grapefruit (preferably Ruby Red) instead of tangerines, or flavor the cake with orange zest and juice.

Walnut Spice Breakfast Cake

While living in Greece as a child, I couldn't get enough of syrup-infused cakes, at once sticky, sweet, and sensual. This cake is inspired by two childhood favorites: a classic Greek *karidhopita* (walnut cake) and an orange-infused semolina cake. This cake features a good dose of cloves, a spice popular in Greece, and barley flour as a nod to my ancestors on Mount Olympus. I did tone down the syrupy part a bit to create a moist breakfast cake for American palates. For a deliciously crumbly cake in the European tradition, be sure someday to try the Greek Walnut-Barley Cake (page 204) in the dessert chapter.

I prefer dark brown sugar to bring the flavors together, but light brown works fine. Freshly grinding the cloves and nutmeg in a spice mill or with a mortar and pestle will reward you with deeper flavor.

MAKES 1 (8-INCH SQUARE CAKE) TO SERVE 12

CAKE

1 1/2 cups white whole wheat flour (6 1/2 ounces)

1/2 cup whole grain barley flour (2 ounces)

2 teaspoons baking powder

1 teaspoon ground cinnamon

3/4 teaspoon ground cloves

1/2 teaspoon baking soda

1/4 teaspoon ground nutmeg

1/2 teaspoon fine sea salt

2 large eggs, at room temperature

3/4 cup packed dark or light brown sugar

2/3 cup plain whole-milk or lowfat Greek yogurt

1/2 cup freshly squeezed orange juice

2 teaspoons finely grated orange zest

1/4 cup extra-virgin olive oil

1 cup coarsely chopped toasted walnuts (see page 37)

SEE MEASURING
WHOLE GRAIN FLOUR,
PAGE 28

SYRUP, AND TO FINISH

1/4 cup freshly squeezed orange juice

1/4 cup packed dark or light brown sugar

1 small strip orange zest (1 inch by 1 inch)

2 whole cloves

1/4 cup coarsely chopped toasted walnuts

1   To make the cake, position a rack in the center of the oven and preheat to 325°F. Lightly butter the bottom and sides of an 8-inch square glass baking dish, or coat with cooking spray. Line the bottom of the pan with parchment paper, and lightly butter the paper as well. Dust the pan with flour, tapping out excess.

2   Whisk together the whole wheat flour, barley flour, baking powder, cinnamon, cloves, baking soda, nutmeg, and salt in a large bowl. Whisk the eggs and brown sugar in a medium bowl until well blended. In a small bowl, combine the yogurt with the orange juice and zest, stirring until smooth; gradually whisk into the egg mixture, followed by the olive oil. Add the wet ingredients to the dry ingredients in 2 additions, stirring well in between with a rubber spatula until just blended. Fold in 1 cup of the walnuts. Spread the batter in the pan, evening out the top with the spatula.

3   Bake the cake until a cake tester or toothpick inserted into the center comes out almost clean, with a few moist crumbs attached, about 35 minutes.

4   While the cake is baking, prepare the syrup. Combine the orange juice, brown sugar, zest, and cloves in a small heavy-bottomed saucepan and bring to a boil over medium-high heat, stirring a few times. Adjust the heat to maintain a simmer and cook, uncovered, for 4 to 5 minutes until thickened (you will have a scant $1/4$ cup). Remove and discard the zest and cloves, and set aside to cool.

5   When the cake is done, transfer the pan to a wire rack. Using a toothpick, pierce the top in about 18 places and, while the cake is still hot, brush the syrup over the cake 3 to 4 times, allowing it to seep in each time. Sprinkle with the remaining walnuts and let cool for 30 minutes. To unmold the cake, loosen around the edges with a small sharp knife, and invert onto a flat plate or a small square tray; remove the parchment paper and invert again onto a wire rack, right side up. Cool completely or enjoy warm. Cut into 12 squares.

TO GET A HEAD START: Don't hesitate to bake this cake 1 day ahead, as its aroma only gets better. Store in an airtight container at room temperature.

Pine Nut Bread with Fennel and Sun-Dried Tomatoes

This easy quick bread, studded with sun-dried tomatoes and fragrant pine nuts, lends opulence to your breakfast table. The two short resting periods are key to a well-risen loaf, slightly dense with an appealing chew—it is whole wheat, after all. Serve with Mediterranean Baked Eggs (see sidebar, page 68) for brunch, or at any other time of day with a bowl of soup. Or slice it, still warm, to complement an assortment of cheeses and olives. While quick breads normally don't last well, this loaf's aromas are still vibrant when you reheat slices in a toaster the next day. Some sun-dried tomatoes are very salty, so take a small bite and reduce the quantity of salt to 1 teaspoon, if necessary. MAKES 1 (1¹/₂-POUND) LOAF

....

3 cups white whole wheat or regular whole wheat flour (12³/₄ ounces)

4 teaspoons baking powder

1¹/₄ teaspoons fine sea salt

1 teaspoon sugar

1¹/₂ teaspoons crumbled dried oregano (not powdered)

2 teaspoons fennel seeds

³/₄ teaspoon crumbled dried sage (not powdered)

¹/₃ cup toasted pine nuts (see page 37)

¹/₂ cup drained and chopped oil-packed sun-dried tomatoes, 1¹/₂ teaspoons oil reserved (see page 138)

1¹/₂ cups chilled whole or lowfat milk (12³/₄ ounces)

> **SEE MEASURING WHOLE GRAIN FLOUR, PAGE 28**

1 Whisk together the whole wheat flour, baking powder, salt, sugar, oregano, fennel, and sage in a large bowl. Stir in the pine nuts, and sprinkle the sun-dried tomatoes across the top. Make a well in the center and add the milk. Using a dough whisk (see page 30) or a fork, and starting from the center, gradually stir in the flour until most of it is incorporated (some flour may remain at the sides). Gather the moist dough inside the bowl with lightly floured hands (if the dough is wet, sprinkle it with flour). Incorporate any remaining flour and bring together, with 5 to 7 gentle turns, into a lumpy ball. Cover the bowl with a dish towel and set aside to rest for 15 minutes.

2 Meanwhile, position a rack in the bottom third of the oven and preheat to 400°F. Lightly grease a 9 by 5 by 3-inch loaf pan with ¹/₂ teaspoon of the tomato oil, or coat with cooking spray.

3 Turn out the shaggy dough onto a lightly floured work surface. Lightly flour your hands and gently knead about 8 turns until smooth, while forming an oblong loaf about 7 inches long. Place the loaf, seam at the bottom, in the prepared pan. Brush with the remaining 1 teaspoon of the tomato oil. Using a very sharp knife, make 3 or 4 diagonal cuts across the top, ¹/₂ inch deep. Cover the loaf with a dish towel and let sit for 10 minutes.

4 Bake until the loaf is well risen, crusty, and nicely browned. A cake tester or a toothpick inserted into center should come out clean (an instant-read thermometer should register 200°F), about 55 minutes. Transfer to a wire rack to cool for 10 minutes. Cut with a sharp serrated knife and serve warm or at room temperature.

TO GET A HEAD START: This bread freezes well for up to 1 month.

TO VARY IT: Use toasted slivered almonds (see page 37) to replace pricier pine nuts.

Sweet Zucchini Bread with Mint

Fresh and dried mint is used across the Mediterranean to flavor countless dishes, from grilled meat kebabs to salads and savory pie fillings. Here the herb, which grows with abandon (you might also say takes over) in so many gardens, is combined with golden raisins and lemon zest, giving the classic zucchini walnut bread a novel twist. Spearmint is my first choice, but any mint will do.

MAKES 1 LOAF, 12 SLICES

....

¹/₄ cup (2 ounces, ¹/₂ stick) unsalted butter, cut into 4 pieces

1 cup white whole wheat flour (4¹/₄ ounces)

¹/₂ cup whole wheat pastry flour (2 ounces)

1¹/₂ teaspoons baking powder

¹/₂ teaspoon fine sea salt

2 cups loosely packed grated zucchini (¹/₂ pound or 2 small)

¹/₂ cup loosely packed chopped fresh mint

¹/₂ cup golden raisins

1 tablespoon finely grated lemon zest

1 tablespoon freshly squeezed lemon juice

3 large eggs, at room temperature

¹/₄ cup extra-virgin olive oil

³/₄ cup packed light brown sugar

1¹/₂ teaspoons vanilla extract

1 cup coarsely chopped toasted walnuts (see page 37), plus 3 walnut halves for garnish

SEE MEASURING WHOLE GRAIN FLOUR, PAGE 28

1 Position a rack in the center of the oven and preheat to 325°F. Butter a 9 by 5 by 3-inch loaf pan, or coat with cooking spray. Dust with flour, tapping out excess. Melt the butter in a small saucepan over low heat. Set aside.

2 In a medium bowl, whisk together the whole wheat flour, whole wheat pastry flour, baking powder, and salt. In a separate medium bowl, combine the zucchini, mint, raisins, lemon zest, and juice.

3 In a large bowl, beat the eggs using a hand mixer at low speed until blended. Increase the speed to medium, gradually adding the olive oil and the brown sugar, and beating until the mixture becomes thick and foamy, 1 to 2 minutes. Beat in the melted butter and vanilla extract until well blended. Decrease the speed to low, add the zucchini mixture, and then slowly add the flour mixture until just blended. Do not overmix. Fold in 1 cup of the walnuts using a rubber spatula. Scrape the batter into the loaf pan, leveling the top with the spatula. Gently press 3 walnut halves across the top.

4 Bake until the bread has risen and is light golden brown, and a cake tester or toothpick inserted into the center comes out clean, 55 to 65 minutes. Transfer the pan to a wire rack to cool for about 10 minutes. Loosen around the edges with a small sharp knife, and unmold the bread; transfer to a wire rack, right side up, to cool completely, or enjoy warm.

TO GET A HEAD START: Zucchini bread can be baked 1 day ahead. Store in an airtight container or wrapped in plastic wrap at room temperature.

TO LIGHTEN IT UP: For a heart-healthy bread, feel free to omit the butter entirely and use a total of ¹/₂ cup olive oil instead.

TO VARY IT: My sister-in-law, Yasmin, an avid baker and cook, made muffins with the batter. She filled the cups of a standard muffin pan about ³/₄ full, and baked them at 325°F until light golden brown, about 40 minutes.

Wild Rice Frittata with Mushrooms and Crisped Prosciutto

This is the frittata I make for Sunday brunch when everyone is famished. Thanks to the addition of deliciously chewy wild rice, this baked omelet is nourishing enough to last you through the day. Three kinds of mushrooms and baked Parmesan cheese infuse the frittata with deep meaty umami flavor. But even one type of mushroom gives it enough aroma. Be sure to cook the rice while you do your *mise en place*—French for lining up your ingredients—for the recipe. **SERVES 6**

WILD RICE

1 cup water

¹/₂ cup wild rice

FRITTATA

6 large eggs

2 tablespoons chopped fresh flat-leaf parsley

¹/₂ teaspoon fine sea salt

¹/₂ teaspoon freshly ground black pepper

¹/₄ teaspoon ground nutmeg

1 tablespoon extra-virgin olive oil

1 cup chopped red onion, cut into ¹/₄-inch dice (about 1 small)

1 tablespoon minced fresh rosemary, or 1 teaspoon dried

1 pound mixed mushrooms, such as cremini, white button, or shiitake, halved if large and sliced ¹/₄ inch thick (about 7 cups)

¹/₂ cup finely grated Parmesan cheese (about 1 ounce)

2 ounces chopped prosciutto (about ¹/₂ cup)

1 To prepare the wild rice, bring the water and rice to a boil in a small heavy-bottomed saucepan. Decrease the heat to maintain a simmer, cover, and cook until the kernels are tender but still slightly chewy, 40 to 50 minutes. Remove from the heat, cover, and steam for 10 to 15 minutes, if you have time. Drain any remaining liquid and set aside to cool.

2 While the wild rice is steaming, make the frittata. Position a rack about 4 inches below the heat source and preheat the broiler. In a large bowl, using a large whisk, beat the eggs, the parsley, ¹/₄ teaspoon of the salt, ¹/₄ teaspoon of the pepper, and the nutmeg. Set aside.

3 Heat the olive oil over medium heat in a 10-inch cast-iron (or other ovenproof) skillet until shimmering. Add the onion, the remaining ¹/₄ teaspoon salt, and the remaining ¹/₄ teaspoon pepper; cook, stirring, until the onion softens, about 3 minutes. Increase the heat to medium-high; stir in the rosemary, followed by the mushrooms. Cook, stirring frequently, until the mushrooms release their liquid, 3 to 5 minutes. Decrease the heat to medium-low and stir in the rice to heat through, about 1 minute.

4 Pour the egg mixture evenly over the rice and vegetables and cook, partially covered, until set around the edges, about 5 minutes. Sprinkle with the cheese and prosciutto. Place the pan under the broiler and broil until the frittata is puffed, the top is nicely browned, and the eggs are set, 2 to 3 minutes. Transfer to the stove top and let sit for 5 minutes.

5 I normally cut the frittata in the pan. But you can loosen the edges by running a metal spatula all around and underneath, and then carefully slide it onto a serving plate. Cut into 6 wedges and serve warm.

TO GET A HEAD START: The wild rice, as in step 1, can be made ahead (see page 23). Also, use presliced mushrooms and look for quick-cooking or instant wild rice varieties, which cook in as little as 10 minutes (for sources, see page 219).

TO MAKE IT VEGETARIAN: Omit the prosciutto, and boost the amount of Parmesan cheese to ³/₄ cup if you like.

MEDITERRANEAN BAKED EGGS

Serving eggs in individual ramekins is an easy way to make a splash at brunch. For a nicely warmed yolk, oozing into the tomato sauce, you'll have to watch carefully to avoid overcooking them. (Please note that the eggs are not fully cooked, in case salmonella is a concern in your area.) Serve with slices of whole wheat baguette, which you can toast on a lower shelf in the oven at the same time, flipping them once halfway through. If you want to pull out all the stops, pair with freshly baked Pine Nut Bread with Fennel and Sun-Dried Tomatoes (page 64). This recipe will make twice as much tomato sauce as you need. You can use the leftover sauce for pasta the next day. Just reheat and sprinkle with crumbled goat cheese and shaved Parmesan—dinner is ready. SERVES 6

TOMATO SAUCE
1 tablespoon extra-virgin olive oil
1 cup finely chopped yellow onion
1 tablespoon minced fresh thyme, or
    1 teaspoon dried
1/2 teaspoon dried oregano
1 clove garlic, minced
1 bay leaf
1/2 teaspoon fine sea salt
1 teaspoon paprika
1/8 teaspoon cayenne pepper (optional)
2 tablespoons tomato paste
1 (28-ounce) can diced tomatoes
1/2 teaspoon red wine vinegar
1/2 teaspoon brown or granulated sugar

EGGS
6 large eggs
Fine sea salt and freshly ground black pepper

1 To make the tomato sauce, heat the olive oil in a large saucepan over medium heat. Add the onion, thyme, oregano, garlic, bay leaf, and 1/4 teaspoon of the salt; cook, stirring frequently, until the onion starts to soften, about 3 minutes. Add the paprika and cayenne and cook, stirring, until fragrant, about 30 seconds. Add the tomato paste and cook until it darkens, another 30 seconds. Add the tomatoes and the remaining 1/4 teaspoon salt and bring to a boil over medium-high heat. Decrease the heat to maintain a light boil and cook, uncovered, until sauce starts to thicken, 10 to 15 minutes. Season with the vinegar and brown sugar. Remove the bay leaf and set aside to cool. You will have about 31/2 cups sauce, about double what you will need.

2 Meanwhile, position a rack in the center of the oven and preheat to 375°F. Butter six 6-ounce ramekins and set in a rimmed baking dish.

3 To finish, place 1/4 cup of the tomato sauce in each ramekin and then break an egg on top. Bake until the whites are solidified and the yolks have just started to set, about 10 minutes. Using tongs, carefully transfer the ramekins to a wire rack. The eggs will continue to cook until the ramekins have cooled enough to be served, about 10 minutes. Sprinkle with salt and pepper, and serve right away.

TO GET A HEAD START: The tomato sauce can be prepared up to 3 days ahead. Chill, covered.

Olive Bread with Bacon and Thyme

Smoked bacon and briny olives are a match made in heaven. And if they are married in a crusty whole wheat loaf with a soft, chewy crumb, that's paradise—for anyone with German and Greek roots. Try this cross-cultural breakfast loaf and judge for yourself. The amount of bacon in this loaf is moderate—I tried it with much more (only a Bavarian would approve) and with less (not worth your time). Serve this bread with an omelet and sausages, or alongside a bowl of soup for supper. I love to drizzle slices with olive oil, warm from the oven.

Do allow for resting time—your loaf will rise stunningly. For a lighter loaf, you can use 2 cups whole wheat flour (8$^1/_2$ ounces) and 1 cup whole wheat pastry flour (4 ounces). Some olives are very salty; take a bite and reduce the amount of salt in the recipe to 1 teaspoon, if necessary. **MAKES 1 (1$^1/_2$-POUND) LOAF**

---

2 ounces smoked bacon, chopped (about $^1/_2$ cup)

3 cups whole wheat flour (12$^3/_4$ ounces)

4 teaspoons baking powder

1$^1/_4$ teaspoons fine sea salt

$^3/_4$ teaspoon sugar

$^1/_2$ teaspoon freshly ground black pepper

$^1/_2$ cup finely chopped pitted black and green olives (about 20)

2 tablespoons chopped fresh thyme, or 2 teaspoons dried

1$^1/_2$ cups chilled lowfat buttermilk (12 ounces)

SEE MEASURING WHOLE GRAIN FLOUR, PAGE 28

1   First, crisp the bacon. Line a plate with paper towels. Cook the bacon in a small skillet over medium heat, stirring occasionally, until it is lightly browned and crisp at the edges, about 5 minutes. Using a slotted spoon, transfer the bacon bits to the paper towel–lined plate to drain and let cool.

2   Whisk together the whole wheat flour, baking powder, salt, sugar, and pepper in a large bowl. Scatter the bacon, olives, and thyme across the flour mixture and stir in. Make a well in the center and add the buttermilk. Using a dough whisk (see page 30) or a fork, and starting from the center, gradually stir in the flour until most of it is incorporated (some flour may remain at the sides). Gather the moist dough inside the bowl with lightly floured hands (if the dough is wet, sprinkle it with flour). Incorporate any remaining flour and bring together, with 5 to 7 gentle turns, into a lumpy ball. Cover the bowl with a dish towel and set aside to rest for 15 minutes.

3   Meanwhile, position a rack in the bottom third of the oven and preheat to 400°F. Lightly grease a 9 by 5 by 3-inch loaf pan with olive oil, or coat with cooking spray.

4   Turn out the shaggy dough onto a lightly floured work surface. Lightly flour your hands and gently knead about 8 turns until smooth, while forming an oblong loaf about 7 inches long. Place the loaf, seam at the bottom, in the pan. Using a very sharp knife, make 2 diagonal cuts that cross in the center, $^1/_2$ inch deep. Dust the loaf with flour, cover the pan with a dish towel, and let sit for 10 minutes.

CONTINUED, PAGE 70

5   Bake until the loaf is well risen, crusty, and nicely browned. A cake tester or a toothpick inserted into center should come out clean (an instant-read thermometer should register 200°F), about 55 minutes. Transfer to a wire rack to cool for 15 minutes. Cut with a sharp serrated knife and serve warm or at room temperature.

TO GET A HEAD START: Buy pitted olives, and if they are marinated, even better for flavor. This bread is best eaten on the same day, or you can reheat it in the toaster the next day. It freezes well for 1 month.

TO MAKE IT VEGETARIAN: Replace the bacon with 1/4 cup sautéed red onions (about 3/4 cup raw, chopped).

DECADENT CHOCOLATE-HAZELNUT BUTTER

Europeans find it hard to resist the chocolate-hazelnut spread Nutella, which they slather on pretty much everything, from breakfast toast to crepes and cookies. Here is a scrumptious adult version with dark chocolate and a shot of rum. A jar of it makes a great holiday gift. Not as smooth as commercially made spread, it is reminiscent of the simple origins of this treat. And don't hesitate to use good-quality milk chocolate for a change. This butter can be stored in the fridge for up to 10 days. It's sinfully good when slathered on a slice of the Floating Sesame Loaf (below), especially the variation with raisins and hazelnuts. MAKES ABOUT 1 CUP

1/2 cup toasted hazelnuts (see page 37)
2 tablespoons sugar
2 ounces good-quality dark chocolate with
    70 percent cocoa content, finely chopped
1/2 cup heavy whipping cream
1 tablespoon dark rum or bourbon (optional)
1/8 teaspoon vanilla extract

1   Place the nuts and the sugar in the bowl of a food processor fitted with the steel blade. Process until very fine, about 30 seconds.

2   Put the chocolate in a small bowl. Heat the cream in a small heavy-bottomed saucepan over medium to medium-high heat until almost boiling (it will steam, and the small bubbles around the rim will become lively). Pour the cream over the chocolate and set aside for 5 minutes. Gently whisk until well blended, and then add the ground nut mixture, rum, and vanilla extract. Transfer to an 8-ounce Mason jar or other airtight container and allow to cool, uncovered, about 1 hour. (There will be a little extra for you to nibble on.) Close the jar, and refrigerate overnight for the chocolate butter to firm up and the flavors to meld—if you can wait that long. Serve at room temperature.

TO LIGHTEN IT UP: Not possible.

Floating Sesame Loaf

If you are you intimidated by yeast dough, try this surprising technique, which turns bread making into a game and puts an impressive loaf of bread on your table—effortlessly. The method takes all the guesswork out of yeast breads: no need to fuss with rising times, rising volumes, and temperatures. Best of all, kneading is minimal. In 1½ hours or less, you will pull a soft and chewy 100 percent whole wheat loaf out of the oven. This dough is amazingly forgiving, and a bit silly to boot: it is left to rise in a stockpot filled with cold water. Yes, you read correctly, water. Your kids will love it—so get them involved! Everyone will be waiting around the pot for the dough ball to float to the surface, a signal that it is ready to be shaped and baked. In Germany, we call this *kinderleicht*, easy enough for a kid to do once you get the hang of it.

For the most appealing crust, use a baking stone if you have one. Preheat the stone right from the start, in step 1. If you own a pizza peel, sprinkle it with cornmeal and set the bread directly on it without using parchment paper, in step 6. MAKES 1 ROUND (1¼-POUND) LOAF

………

2½ cups regular whole wheat or white whole wheat flour (10¾ ounces), plus 3–7 tablespoons as needed

5 tablespoons toasted sesame seeds (see page 37)

2 teaspoons instant or rapid-rise yeast

1 teaspoon sugar

1 teaspoon fine sea salt

1¼ cups lukewarm water (90°F to 100°F)

Medium or coarse cornmeal, for sprinkling

> **SEE MEASURING WHOLE GRAIN FLOUR, PAGE 28**

1 Fill a stockpot or a 4-quart saucepan (about 5 inches high) with cold tap water to 1 inch below the rim.

2 Whisk together the whole wheat flour, 3 tablespoons of the sesame seeds, and the yeast, sugar, and salt in a large bowl. Make a well in the center of the flour mixture and add the water. Using a wooden spoon or a dough whisk (see page 30), and starting from the center, gradually stir in the flour until a pretty moist dough forms and all the flour has been incorporated.

3 Scrape the sticky mass onto a well-floured work surface. Sprinkle with 1 scant tablespoon of flour. Knead the dough with floured hands, incorporating additional flour by the ½ tablespoonful just until the dough is supple and smooth with a slight tackiness, about 2 minutes. Depending on the flour you use and the humidity, you should need only 2 to 5 tablespoons (the dough will continue to absorb more flour at the expense of lightness, but don't add more!). Quickly form a round ball, folding any loose ends into the bottom, and gently deposit the dough into the water in the stockpot.

4 Meanwhile, position a rack in the bottom third of the oven and place a large baking sheet (or a 10-inch cast-iron skillet) on it. Preheat oven to 425°F. While you wait for the dough to rise, which typically takes 7 to 15 minutes (up to 30 minutes), sprinkle a 12 by 16-inch piece of parchment paper with cornmeal. Generously flour your work surface.

5 Once the dough rises to the surface of the water (it will slowly puff like a balloon before popping up), remove it with both hands, letting excess water drain between your fingers. Transfer the dough—it will

CONTINUED, PAGE 72

feel like wet clay—to the work surface. Dry and then flour your hands, and dust the wet surface of the dough with 1 scant tablespoon flour. Working briskly, give the dough not more than a few gentle turns, adding flour by the $^1/_2$ tablespoonful, and then gently stretch the "skin" or surface of the dough from the top to the bottom all around to form a ball with a few loose ends at the bottom. (This stretching is a handy little step—otherwise your loaf might crack around the sides. However, cracks are no more than an optical flaw, which, in my opinion, is also the beauty of handmade.) Kneading and shaping should not take longer than 40 seconds and should not incorporate more than 1 to 2 tablespoons of flour. The dough can be quite slack, even stretchy.

6   Transfer the dough to the parchment paper. It will look somewhat flat. Cover with a dish towel (not terry cloth) and let rest for 15 to 20 minutes. After that, brush with water and gently press the remaining 2 tablespoons sesame seeds all over the surface. Using a sharp knife, make three $^1/_4$-inch-deep cuts across the loaf. Transfer the parchment paper with the dough to the baking sheet (or set in the cast-iron pan).

7   Bake until the loaf is well risen and light golden brown and the bottom sounds hollow when tapped (or when an instant-read thermometer inserted into the center registers 200°F), 25 to 30 minutes. Remove the parchment paper 10 minutes before the end of baking for a better crust. Transfer the bread to a wire rack to cool completely—about 2 hours, for best flavor and texture—before cutting. The loaf might have quite a crust at first, but it will soon soften nicely. Wait if you can!

TO VARY IT: To form a sesame bread ring: At the end of step 5, once you have formed the dough ball, create the ring. Flour your hands. Holding the dough in both hands, gently form a hole in the middle by pulling the center apart—first with both your thumbs from the top, and then molding it with the rest of your fingers from the bottom. The hole should be at least 3 inches wide. Or make a hazelnut-raisin loaf: Use naturally sweeter white whole wheat flour (instead of regular whole wheat) for a more appealing loaf, and add 1 tablespoon sugar (not 1 teaspoon). Instead of the sesame seeds, measure $^1/_4$ cup dark raisins and $^1/_2$ cup toasted chopped hazelnuts. Add the raisins and $^1/_4$ cup of the hazelnuts to the dough in step 2 (instead of sesame seeds). And in step 6, gently press the remaining $^1/_4$ cup hazelnuts (instead of sesame seeds) all over the surface.

THE MAGIC OF WET DOUGH

I am including this bread in this book because its unusual technique made me into the passionate baker I am today. As you work with this dough, you might wonder—what a strange, wet and wobbly mixture—but don't worry, just keep going. When I made it for the first time, I was inexperienced and thoroughly afraid of yeast dough. In front of me was a tiny recipe with twenty lines, and I never really knew what I was doing—but I succeeded nonetheless, pulling an amazing loaf from my old oven. And I have made many more since. The idea of letting a yeast dough rise in water is from a recipe in the German magazine *Natur*, which named it "Happy Bucket Bread." Instead of a bucket, I use a stockpot or a tall saucepan. Curious about the origins of this method, I tracked down one of the recipe developers after more than twenty years. She wasn't able to locate

or to remember the original source for this bread. In my large library, I certainly have never come across anything even resembling this method.

Wet doughs such as this one and the Aroma Bread with Coriander and Fennel (page 74) are great for the novice baker because you can succeed without any kneading or serious baking skills. A so-called wet dough has a high ratio of water to flour by weight. In this floating bread, the water is added twice over: once during initial mixing, and then by dropping the dough into the pot and submerging it. The ample amount of water in the dough helps with gluten formation, which is what kneading normally does. And while you might not know exactly when your dough ball will rise to the surface (I do the dishes in the meantime, with an occasional glance at the pot), you will be smitten when it finally does.

Aroma Bread with Coriander and Fennel

The use of countless aromatics to flavor bread lies at the center of Germany's rich whole grain baking culture. Breads are often prepared with different grains and grinds of flour to achieve distinctively textured loaves. In this 100 percent whole grain loaf, I use spelt for its pleasing mild flavor, but you can use regular whole wheat flour (see below). Yes, this is a thick-crusted loaf, unlike any bread you will find in a U.S. supermarket or pretty much anywhere else, but the inside will be chewy and soft with seeds and spices. Give it a day, and the crust will soften from the humidity in the air. Enjoy this unusual aromatic bread with cheese and cold cuts as a simple supper, or use as a base for a nourishing sandwich. It's also delicious with a bowl of soup.

This is an effortless no-knead bread made using an old technique, most recently revived by New York master baker Jim Lahey. I have taught students to make a slow-fermentation bread with minimal yeast for years, albeit in a plain old loaf pan—initially inspired by a recipe by German cookbook author Luise Brüggemann. I credit Lahey with introducing me to the use of a lidded heavy pot and a simple folding technique to get a truly spectacular artisanal bread—no wonder his method has won him cult status. If the lid of your Dutch oven has a plastic knob, be sure to wrap it in aluminum foil so it doesn't melt in the high heat of the oven. MAKES 1 (2-POUND) LOAF

....

3 cups whole grain spelt flour (12 ounces)

1 cup whole grain rye flour (3³/4 ounces)

¹/2 cup coarse or medium stone-ground whole grain cornmeal (2 ounces)

¹/2 cup sunflower seeds

¹/4 cup flax or sesame seeds

2 tablespoons aroma spice blend (see sidebar)

1¹/2 teaspoons fine sea salt

¹/4 teaspoon rapid-rise or instant yeast

¹/2 cup whole wheat, rye, Kamut, or spelt berries, soaked overnight and drained (optional)

2 cups cold water

Cornmeal, for sprinkling

SEE MEASURING
WHOLE GRAIN FLOUR,
PAGE 28

1   To prepare the dough, start at least 12 hours ahead. Whisk together all the ingredients except the whole grain berries and the water in a large bowl. Scatter the grain berries on top and add almost all the water. Stir with a dough whisk (page 30) or a wooden spoon until the flour is incorporated. The dough should be wet and sticky to the touch, like firm oatmeal; otherwise, add a bit more water. But don't worry too much about the liquid-to-flour ratio, as this is a forgiving dough. Cover loosely with plastic wrap and let sit at room temperature to ferment for at least 12 hours and up to 18 hours.

2   The next day, finish the bread. Sprinkle a linen or cotton kitchen towel (not terry cloth) with cornmeal and generously flour your work surface. Using a bench scraper or a rubber spatula, scrape the stringy, bubbly dough onto the work surface. Using floured hands, fold it exactly 4 times, always toward the center—from the right and from the left, as well as from the top and the bottom. Turn the loaf upside down so the fold is at the bottom, and set it on the kitchen towel. Fold the towel over the loaf to cover, and let sit for about 1 hour.

3   After about 30 minutes, position a rack in the bottom third of the oven and preheat to 475°F. Place a 4¹/2- to 5¹/2-quart cast-iron pot or Dutch oven with its lid in the center of the rack. After about 1 hour, your loaf should have nicely risen. (When you press it with your finger about ¹/4 inch deep, the dimple should remain; if not, wait 15 more minutes.)

But again, don't worry too much—I have sometimes been less than precise and still succeeded.

4 Using thick pot holders, carefully remove the cast-iron pot from the oven and place it on a couple of folded kitchen towels (to avoid cracking); uncover. Unwrap the dough, sprinkle with a bit more cornmeal, and invert directly from the kitchen towel into the pot, seam side up (it might look a bit wiggly; that's normal). If the dough doesn't drop into the center, shake the pot once or twice (use caution, it is hot!).

5 Cover with the lid and bake for 30 minutes. Uncover and bake until the loaf is nicely browned and an instant-read thermometer inserted into the center registers 200°F, 20 to 25 minutes. Using thick pot holders, remove the loaf from the cast-iron pot and transfer to a wire rack. If you can resist, allow to cool completely, about 3 hours, before cutting the loaf with a sharp serrated knife. And a sharp knife it must be— this is a German-style bread, after all.

TO VARY IT: You can use 3 cups regular whole wheat flour (13 ounces) for a slightly denser loaf. If you don't have a cast-iron pot, use a 10-inch cast-iron skillet. Bake until an instant-read thermometer registers 200°F, 40 to 45 minutes. You can also bake the bread in a 9 by 5 by 3-inch loaf pan. Grease the pan well with oil and sprinkle with 1 to 2 tablespoons flax seeds or sesame seeds. After folding the dough as in step 2, drop it seam side up right into the pan. Cover with a dish cloth for about 1 hour (do the finger-poke test as in step 3). After 30 minutes, place a rack in the bottom third of the oven and preheat to 425°F. Bake until an instant-read thermometer registers 200°F, about 60 minutes. Transfer the pan to a wire rack to cool for about 5 minutes. Run a knife around the edges, unmold, and return to the wire rack, right side up, to cool completely before cutting. For a nicer crust when using a skillet or a loaf pan, slide a second rack with a broiler tray into the lowest level of your oven when preheating. After you place the loaf in the oven, carefully add about 1 cup hot tap water to the tray. Stand back so the steam doesn't hit you!

TO TIME IT: Soak the whole grain berries the morning before, no later than lunchtime. Mix the dough (as in step 1) in the late afternoon or evening. Finish and bake the loaf (steps 2 through 5) in the morning, but no later than 18 hours after you start the dough.

HERBED FETA IN OLIVE OIL

Whenever I don't know what to do with leftover fresh herbs, I prepare this marinated feta, a staple in my mom's house in Greece. She doesn't measure anything and uses any fresh herb her Mediterranean garden will provide. Use this recipe as inspiration and do the same. This feta will last up to 1 week in the fridge. Serve herbed feta together with the Aroma Bread with Coriander and Fennel (page 74) or the Pine Nut Bread with Fennel and Sun-Dried Tomatoes (page 64). It's delicious also as part of an appetizer spread, with whole wheat baguette or a crusty sourdough loaf to mop up the fragrant oil. Leftover marinating oil can be used as a salad dressing, or heat it gently and pour over poached white fish or steamed vegetables, combined with a drizzle of lemon juice. MAKES 8 APPETIZER SERVINGS

2 slices feta (preferably sheep's milk),
   about 1/2 inch thick (8 to 10 ounces total)
2 tablespoons chopped fresh mint
2 tablespoons chopped fresh oregano

1 teaspoon minced fresh rosemary
1 teaspoon finely grated lemon zest
1 or 2 cloves garlic, minced
1/4 teaspoon freshly ground black pepper
1/8 teaspoon dried chile pepper (optional)
Extra-virgin olive oil, for marinating
2 teaspoons red wine vinegar, for drizzling

1 Place both slices of feta in a glass or plastic container big enough to fit them side by side.

2 In a small bowl, combine all the other ingredients except the olive oil and vinegar in a small bowl. Press the mixture gently onto the feta slices, creating an herbal layer. Carefully pour enough olive oil into the container to cover the feta and herbs. Chill, covered, for at least 2 hours and up to 1 day. The olive oil will solidify when chilled, so be sure to serve at room temperature. Cut the feta into cubes and drizzle with the vinegar.

Pumpernickel (German Whole Grain Rye Bread)

Real German pumpernickel is a supremely chewy and dense delicacy—unlike what you might find in your local supermarket. It is traditionally baked with two ingredients only: water and rye. An unusual baking process transforms the slightly tangy grain into a naturally sweet bread: the loaves are baked in sealed steam chambers at very low temperatures for up to 24 hours. This no-knead pumpernickel is inspired by traditional recipes. Allow two days for its easy but slow preparation and wait to eat it until the third day, as the bread is too moist to eat immediately (see below). To contrast its natural sweetness, serve pumpernickel thinly sliced with an assortment of cold cuts and aromatic cheeses such as Gouda or blue cheese. It's also delicious with liverwurst or pâté. My personal favorite: slathered with good-quality butter and a sprinkle of coarse sea salt.

Pumpernickel will keep at cool room temperature for 3 to 5 days. Wrap in a dish towel and store in a bread box, or place the wrapped loaf on a wooden board and cover with a turned-over bowl. Pumpernickel flour is a coarse whole grain rye flour (for sources, see page 219). MAKES 1 (2¹/₄-POUND) LOAF

....

*3¹/₂ cups pumpernickel flour
(13 ounces)*

*1 cup whole wheat flour
(4¹/₄ ounces)*

1¹/₂ teaspoons fine sea salt

*¹/₂ cup whole rye berries, soaked
overnight and drained*

*2 cups lukewarm water
(90°F to 100°F)*

2 teaspoons extra-virgin olive oil

*2 teaspoons molasses, preferably
blackstrap*

> SEE MEASURING
> WHOLE GRAIN FLOUR,
> PAGE 28

1 Start 2 days ahead. Grease a 9 by 5 by 3-inch loaf pan with olive oil (or a 13 by 4 by 4-inch *pain de mie* pan). Cut a rectangular piece of parchment paper the size of the bottom of the pan, place inside, and grease that as well.

2 Whisk together the pumpernickel and whole wheat flours and the salt in a large bowl. Sprinkle the rye berries across. Make a well in the center. Thoroughly combine the water, oil, and molasses in a liquid measuring cup or in a medium bowl with a fork. Add the water mixture to the center of flour mixture. Stir, using a wooden spoon or a dough whisk (see page 30), until a dense and heavy, claylike mass forms (you will need a strong arm here!). Scrape the dough into the pan. Moisten your hands with water and press it gently but firmly into the form including the corners, and even out the top. Run your fingers lengthwise along the top of the loaf to create shallow ridges. Cover the pan loosely with waxed paper (or with the lid). Let sit at room temperature for at least 18 to 24 hours and up to 28 hours (see sidebar, page 78). The loaf should feel slightly puffy when gently pressed (it might have a few cracks). If you look closely, it will have risen a bit, at best a scant ¹/₂ inch.

3 The next day, bring a large kettle with about 6 cups of water to a boil. Meanwhile, position 1 rack in the center of the oven and a second rack just below it. Place an empty roasting pan on the lower rack. Preheat the oven to 225°F. Remove the waxed paper and seal the loaf pan with a double layer of aluminum foil (or with the lid). Partially slide out the

CONTINUED, PAGE 78

PUMPERNICKEL (GERMAN WHOLE
GRAIN RYE BREAD), CONTINUED
FROM PAGE 77

NO YEAST—JUST NATURAL LEAVENERS

This pumpernickel dough rises without any help from rising agents such as commercial yeast or baking powder. Instead, it gets a lift through natural leavening, activated by wild yeast spores in the air and the yeast and bacterial spores in the flour. That's why I like to start pumpernickel on a warm summer day—your loaf will rise best. Ideally, the temperature should be in the 80s during the day, and in the 70s at night. It's perfect if you have a warm spot in your kitchen (a gas stove with a pilot light, for example). In cooler climes (in the low 70s), you will just have to wait a bit longer, up to 28 hours. At that point, if you don't have time for the extended baking, just place the loaf, loosely covered, in the fridge and bake it the next day. Allow the loaf about 2 hours to come to room temperature before baking.

lower rack. Carefully fill the roasting pan with about 1/2 inch of boiling water. Place the loaf pan with the dough on the center rack.

4   Bake for 4 hours and then remove the foil and check for doneness. The loaf will have risen nicely, and the top should be darkened and firmed up (it should resist when gently pressed with a finger). If not ready, reseal it, bake for 15 more minutes, and then check again.

5   Return the uncovered loaf to the oven and increase the temperature to 325°F. Add more boiling water to the roasting pan if necessary. Continue baking until an instant-read thermometer inserted into the center of the loaf registers 205°F, about 20 more minutes.

6   Transfer the pan to a wire rack to cool for 5 to 8 minutes, and then loosen the edges with a knife and unmold the pumpernickel (smell the sweetness!). Remove the parchment paper and return the bread to the wire rack to cool completely, at least 2 hours. Wrap in a clean dish towel and allow to sit at cool room temperature for at least 4 more hours and preferably overnight before cutting into thin slices, using a very sharp serrated knife.

TO TIME IT: Two days ahead in the morning, soak the rye berries. Combine the dough (as in steps 1 and 2) in the early evening of the same day. Bake the loaf (as in steps 3, 4, and 5) on the next day by noon, or at the latest by early evening. Allow to cool and rest overnight. Cut and enjoy on the third day.

Oats: Sweet and Sturdy

Most of us have relegated oats, a supremely nourishing grain, to breakfast. We eat sweetened little pouches of oatmeal on the go, cooked up in the microwave. Or we stir up a pot of steel-cut oats on the weekend when we are less pressed for time. Not in my kitchen anymore. I have passionately taken to eating oats, in all their different shapes and styles, for breakfast, lunch, and dinner—as if to catch up on the years of missing out.

In Greece, where I spent much of my early childhood, this hearty staple is not part of the diet. But oats have long been cultivated in northern Europe because they grow well in its cool, wet climate. So when our family moved back to Germany, my father's home country, the grain was suddenly everywhere. My schoolmates ate a breakfast bowl of rolled oats, with cold milk and sprinkled with sugar. I quickly learned to prepare warm oatmeal for breakfast, perfect for the icy winters of Bavaria, where we lived in a suburb of Munich. Friends recommended it as a remedy for mild stomachaches, praising its calming and healing properties. And my dad remembered the plain oatmeal soup of his childhood—a pauper's meal, largely forgotten today. Not as creamy as British porridge, it is cooked with milk, sugar, and a little butter and served warm or cold.

But more than anything, I fell hard for muesli when growing up in Germany. This Swiss national food, a combination of rolled oats, dried fruit, and nuts, was first introduced in the twentieth century by Swiss physician Maximilian Bircher-Benner (see "The Origins of Muesli," page 43). Germans treasure their bowl of muesli—as if they are the better Swiss. Order *Müsli* in a good coffeehouse for a late breakfast on a Sunday, being sure to arrive with an empty stomach. If the establishment is any good, you will find a hefty bowl of oats and other grain flakes in front of you, topped high with freshly cut fruit of the season, nuts, and—my first choice—a mound of softly whipped cream. You may, of course, choose yogurt instead.

But oats, with their natural sweetness and pecanlike tinge, can be so much more than nutritious breakfast fare. They have become my personal über-grain. Oats can be an enticing savory component of any meal. I have long been spellbound by whole oats, the actual grain kernels. Especially when freshly harvested, they are so supple and soft that I sometimes just chew on a few raw grains while cooking them.

Just to give you a few ideas, I have sautéed whole oats as a pilaf with onions, currants, and toasted hazelnuts, topped with a curried cream sauce, and served next to Broccolini or carrots— a match made in heaven. And I once paired them with chicken in a Mediterranean-inspired skillet sauté with bell peppers, tomatoes, and lots of fresh herbs. Or try them as a side in Warm Oat Berries with Walnuts and Gorgonzola (page 96). Admittedly, I have a very personal theory (not substantiated by any facts) why whole oats haven't caught on with a broader public. Their correct name is, hold your breath, groats. Just try saying that out loud! I believe the term does injustice to this extraordinarily pleasing grain. So seek out whole oats more often, and please call them call oat berries.

Last but not least, oats have to be mentioned for the special qualities they lend to baked goods. Their gentle chew and slight density make them memorable in pancakes, muffins, and cookies. Classic honey oatmeal bread for breakfast is a great start to the day. Or think of the satisfying chew of an old-fashioned oatmeal raisin cookie and the nourishing sturdiness of Anzac cookies, once added to care packages for soldiers from Australia and New Zealand. Even classic shortbread, which goes back to the twelfth century, traditionally had oats in its veins. It used to be made from leftover oat bread, sprinkled with sugar and left to harden in the residual heat of the oven. Some bakers have started to add them back into shortbread dough to fashion its characteristic sweet crumble—an afternoon bite I long for.

CHAPTER 2

SALADS & SIDES

With their versatility and no-fuss preparation, many whole grains are perfect for meals on hectic weekdays. When paired with meat or fish, their delicate, subtle flavors spruce up your dinner menu; or enjoy them on their own in a delicious salad for an appealing one-bowl meal, especially in the summer months.

Like any Greek worth her grain, I'm partial to speedy bulgur, the parboiled cracked wheat used widely across the Mediterranean. Italian polenta, also used in parts of Greece, is another favorite. Quick-cooking millet is my go-to comfort food. And infinitely adaptable whole wheat couscous makes for the fastest side of all.

Then there are truly chewy whole grain berries, satisfying and nourishing at once. I prefer to call them berries instead of kernels, which sounds like work instead of fun. Whole oats with their mild pecan-like flavor (who ever named them groats?) pair well with sweet-tasting vegetables like carrots and beets, as well as with nuts and fruits. Rye berries with their slight sour tang provide a clever foil for assertive vegetables and character cheeses such as Greek haloumi or Swiss Emmental. Wheat berries marry with just about any flavor.

Get to know them all, the fast and the slow grains, from a Middle East–inspired cumin-scented quinoa, to bulgur with butter-roasted almonds, to Parmesan polenta made aromatic with a drizzle of rosemary oil. Or try a lush leek salad with grilled haloumi cheese and rye berries, or a juicy Kamut salad with carrots and pomegranate. Yes, whole grain berries take a little extra time to cook, so prepare them ahead, as I often do, or get them going the moment you come home after work. By the time you prep everything else, your grain berries will be ready. It's easy, you'll see.

Everyone Needs a Masala Dabba

Visit any Indian home where a passionate cook resides and inevitably, sooner rather than later, a much-cherished tool will appear on the kitchen counter, right next to the stove. It is so low-tech and simple, I'm surprised it hasn't made its way into the Western kitchen: a round stainless steel container with a tight-fitting lid. It is the invaluable *masala dabba* or spice box, an ingenious invention for organizing the myriad spices that typically flavor an Indian meal. Inside, there are seven small containers, nestled perfectly around an eighth in the center-filled with olfactory heaven. Always shiny, kept perfectly polished by their owners (not covered with fingerprints like mine), a *masala dabba* is ideal for the countless spices that make Indian dishes so addictively aromatic.

Open the lid and you uncover a spice lover's paradise. Depending on the cook, you might find whole green cardamom pods, out of which chocolate-colored seeds tumble when crushed, for infusing the scrumptiously sweet rice pudding called *kheer*. Or crisp, dry coriander seeds, colored with the many nuances of light wood. There are usually pitch-dark, pungent cloves, resembling the dried flower buds they are. Tiny round mustard seeds, ocher or purplish brown, are a must as well; together with cumin seeds they form the base of many an Indian spice mixture, or masala. A *masala dabba* might also carry intensely yellow turmeric powder and earthy cumin-coriander powder, and maybe *amchur*, an astringent powder from green mangoes that adds tang to curries, chutneys, and marinades.

Considering that I married into a large Indian family, it is no surprise that this practical tool entered my kitchen as well. I received my first *masala dabba* as a gift from my mother-in-law. We bought it in one of Toronto's Indian neighborhood stores, where they are sold next to shiny stainless steel containers for flour, sugar, and rice, another must in an Indian home. Of course, I own a set of those as well.

I bought my second *masala dabba* years later while working with my husband in India. I had seen, and envied, this type at the home of Indian friends. My new spice box is state-of-the-art. It is the Mercedes of *masala dabbas*. Unlike my old solid box, this one has the same basic design, but with a glass lid! This clever invention makes finding your spices a snap. No more stressful fumbling, trying to pry open the metal lid while your mustard seeds are popping away on the stove and onto the kitchen floor. No more hunting for the dash of turmeric that colors so many Indian dishes (and stains your tablecloths forever). To this day, I use both of my spice boxes, the modern transparent one and the old-fashioned "mysterious" one. My reasoning goes like this: since I can see the spices in one box, I can make a fairly good guess about what's in the other one (forgetting how many spices I own and how often I change the contents).

My craze for Indian spices goes way back. And, my friends are surprised to learn, this passion is not connected to my husband's Indian roots. Nor is it really part of my own heritage. In German cooking, spices don't take center stage the way they do in many other parts of the world. And my Greek mom, with her purist taste, relies solely on creative combinations of fresh herbs for her dazzling Mediterranean cuisine. I was first intoxicated by spicy food as a young adult, when I visited Sri Lanka on my very first solo trip abroad.

Food on the island has many similarities to the cuisine of southern India. Soon I found myself abandoning the Western dishes local restaurants cooked up for tourists, from pancakes to omelets to pizza. Why eat what I can get at home? During the heat of the day, I indulged on the first fresh tropical fruit of my life, ripe and juicy mangoes, the soft flesh of papayas, and tiny local bananas with their heady aroma. At night, I wandered around sampling spicy local curries in small beach restaurants. But there was more to come.

Joining a group of hungry fellow travelers, I soon found myself at the jungle hut of a local family who cooked dinner for foreigners for a small fee. Tropical nights are dark, so right after sunset we would traipse with a flashlight through a forest of tall palm trees to a tiny straw-covered home. We sat on the ground and waited, and waited, as the cooking began only once we arrived. There was no electricity, just the light of a lantern next to which a woman briskly chopped and worked away over an open fire, together with her daughters.

We could barely see anything as dish after spicy dish was carried to us in the warm night. Using our fingers, we scooped up countless tongue-tingling curries with rice, often made with unknown ingredients and spices. There were aromatic fish and meat dishes we could not identify, vegetables we had never tasted. But dining in the darkness only enhanced our senses and made for the gustatory adventure of a lifetime. To this day, I can still taste a comforting thick-sauced and starchy curry-made from unripe enormous jackfruit, reminiscent of chestnuts.

It didn't take long for the countless spices of the Indian subcontinent to invade my kitchen in Germany. Many were not easy to find at the time. My spice obsession evolved parallel to my almost fanatical interest in whole grains. Soon, the many Indian spices I used in my experimental cooking ended up in my whole grain cooking as well. I started adding whole cinnamon bark and cloves to the cooking water of wheat berries, infusing them with an ever-so-slight hint of sweetness. I added a few black, white, and red peppercorns to spruce up millet for dinner. And to this day, just like in India, my brown rice is simmered with a few whole cumin seeds, cardamom pods, and cloves. All this was long before I owned a *masala dabba* to store them in.

Whole spices soon also made it into my freshly ground flour. I started to add them with whole grains to the funnel of my grain mill. Whole coriander, caraway, and fennel seeds are a must when I bake true German whole grain bread. A few cardamom seeds spice up pie crust dough; a dash of anise adds a spell to the white whole wheat I grind for biscotti. And chiles—so prevalent in Asian cooking, despite their roots in the Americas—have permeated almost every meal I cook, be it German, Indian, or Mediterranean.

My two spice boxes have made this obsession easier to manage. Mostly I use them to organize Indian spices, watching carefully that they are compatible. Once, in my excitement, I added ground ginger and ground cinnamon to my *dabba*. Soon both spices tasted like the ground cumin also stored in the box. Lesson learned. Since then, I have mostly filled my masala box with whole seeds and spices. Grinding them fresh, with a mortar and pestle or in a spice grinder, beats store-bought spice powder anyway. So if you have always dreamed of cleaning up your spice cupboard, think of adding at least one of these magic boxes to your kitchen.

Warm Pasta Salad with Spinach and Fresh Mint

For this simple rustic pasta salad I use whole bunches of spinach, and really fresh ones at that, not prewashed leaves in a bag or frozen spinach. For olive oil, reach for the best quality you have on hand to let the few ingredients shine. SERVES 4 TO 6

....

1 bunch fresh spinach with stems (about 3/4 pound; see sidebar)

1/2 pound short-cut whole wheat or whole grain pasta such as penne

1/2 small red onion, cut into 1/4-inch dice (about 1/2 cup)

1 or 2 cloves garlic, minced

1 1/2 tablespoons freshly squeezed lemon juice

1/4 teaspoon fine sea salt, plus more for the pasta water

1/4 teaspoon freshly ground black pepper

1/2 cup pitted, chopped oil-cured black olives (about 15)

1/4 cup plus 2 tablespoons packed chopped fresh mint

3 tablespoons extra-virgin olive oil

1 Bring a large pot of water to a boil. Add the spinach leaves and cook, in two batches if necessary, until wilted, about 1 minute. Remove the leaves with a slotted spoon and transfer to a sieve to drain. Return the water to a rolling boil, salt to taste, and add the pasta. Return to a boil. Cook, uncovered and stirring a few times, until al dente, according to the package directions. Drain the pasta and briefly rinse under cold water.

2 While the pasta is cooking, combine the onion, garlic, lemon juice, 1/4 teaspoon salt, and pepper for the dressing in a small bowl and set aside (this will take the sting from the onion).

3 When the spinach is cool enough to handle, coarsely chop the leaves and stems (you should have about 2 scant cups). Place the spinach, olives, and 1/4 cup of the mint in a large serving bowl. Add the drained pasta.

4 To finish, slowly pour the olive oil into the center of the bowl with the dressing while beating vigorously with a fork to emulsify (don't let the onion bother you). Drizzle the dressing over the pasta salad and toss to combine. Taste and adjust for salt and pepper. Garnish with the remaining 2 tablespoons mint and serve warm or at room temperature.

TO GET A HEAD START: The salad can be completely prepared 4 to 6 hours ahead. Chill, covered. Bring to room temperature before serving and toss with a bit more olive oil to refresh, or gently reheat in a microwave.

TO MAKE IT A FEAST: Top the pasta salad with 1/2 cup crumbled Gorgonzola cheese, other mild blue cheese, or with shavings of Parmesan cheese.

THE SWEET ROOTS OF SPINACH

My Greek grandfather, an avid lover of greens and fresh fish, taught his children that the entire spinach plant is edible—not just the leaves, but also the stems and even the root crown. In fact, for him the root crown—the pale, fleshy section where the stem and the roots meet—was the most delectable part of the vegetable

Look for bunched spinach with the roots attached. Cut off the pale, fleshy root crowns, leaving 1 to 2 inches of the stems attached to the roots. Scrub them under cold running water with a vegetable brush to remove any grit. Cut off the pinkish dried-out root tip, making sure the root crown doesn't come apart. Briefly steam or blanch them until tender; drain. Drizzle with olive oil and a dash of lemon juice, season with salt and pepper, and enjoy.

Barley Salad with Figs and Tarragon-Lemon Dressing

In my ideal world, a whole grain salad delivers sweet and tangy flavors, crunchy and chewy textures, and is savory and refreshing all at once. Here, I wake up the earthy starchiness of barley with crisp celery, chunks of green apples and lemon-infused dried figs. This makes a good match for chicken or pork, or top it with sautéed shrimp and a splash of lemon. Vegetarians can add toasted chopped walnuts or almonds. SERVES 4

BARLEY

2 cups water

3/4 cup pearl barley

1 (2- by 1-inch) strip lemon zest (optional)

3 peppercorns

Pinch of fine sea salt

SALAD, AND TO FINISH

1 lemon

1/4 cup chopped dried figs, preferably Greek or Turkish (4 to 6)

2 stalks chopped celery, halved lengthwise if large, and cut into 1/4-inch slices (1 cup)

1/2 cup finely chopped green onions, white and light green parts (about 4)

1/2 cup chopped tangy apple, such as Macintosh or Granny Smith (about 1/2 apple)

2 tablespoons extra-virgin olive oil

2 to 3 teaspoons honey

1/4 teaspoon fine sea salt

1/4 teaspoon freshly ground black pepper

2 tablespoons finely chopped fresh tarragon

2 tablespoons finely chopped flat-leaf parsley

1 To prepare the barley, bring the water, barley, lemon zest, peppercorns, and salt to a boil in a 2-quart saucepan. Decrease the heat to maintain a simmer, cover, and cook until the barley is tender but still slightly chewy, 30 to 40 minutes. Remove from the heat and, if you have time, let sit, covered, for 5 to 10 minutes. Drain any remaining liquid and transfer the barley to a large serving bowl to cool. Remove the zest and the peppercorns.

2 To prepare the salad, finely grate the zest of the lemon until you have 2 teaspoons zest. Squeeze the fruit to get 2 tablespoons juice (reserve leftover lemon for another use). Place the dried figs in a small bowl and stir in 1 tablespoon of the lemon juice. Set aside. Add the celery, green onions, and apple to the serving bowl.

3 In a small bowl, whisk together the olive oil, the remaining 1 tablespoon lemon juice, the zest, and 2 teaspoons of the honey. Season with the salt and pepper. Taste and adjust the seasoning, adding more honey if you like, and then stir in 1 tablespoon of the tarragon and 1 tablespoon of the parsley.

4 To finish, add the barley and the plumped figs with any juices to the bowl and stir together. Drizzle on the dressing and toss to combine. Allow to sit at room temperature for 15 minutes for the flavors to mingle. Toss again, sprinkle with the remaining 1 tablespoon of tarragon and 1 tablespoon of parsley, and serve.

TO GET A HEAD START: Make the barley, as in step 1, ahead (see page 23). The entire salad can also be prepared up to 8 hours ahead. Chill, covered. Bring to room temperature and refresh with a bit more olive oil before serving.

TO VARY IT: For a more textured dish, you can use whole grain hulled barley, soaked overnight. Or combine 1/4 cup soaked, hulled barley with 1/2 cup pearl barley for a pleasing mixture.

Kamut Salad with Carrots and Pomegranate

Across the Middle East, cinnamon is used not only to highlight the flavor of sweets but also in savory dishes—as in this Moroccan-inspired carrot salad. I toss it here with slender Kamut berries, which contribute their distinct buttery chew. Vibrantly colorful and deliciously juicy, this salad steals the show on my holiday table. Try it also next to steak, grilled lamb, or a simple roast chicken. **SERVES 4 TO 6**

KAMUT

1 cup water

1/2 cup Kamut berries, soaked overnight and drained

SALAD, AND TO FINISH

2 1/2 cups shredded carrots (about 3 medium)

1/4 cup plus 2 tablespoons golden raisins

3 tablespoons freshly squeezed orange juice

1 tablespoon freshly squeezed lemon juice

1 teaspoon honey

1/4 teaspoon ground cinnamon

1/4 teaspoon fine sea salt

2 tablespoons extra-virgin olive oil

1/4 cup toasted, chopped walnuts (see page 37)

1/4 cup pomegranate seeds, for garnish (optional)

1 To prepare the Kamut, bring the water and the Kamut berries to a boil in a small heavy-bottomed saucepan. Decrease the heat to maintain a simmer, cover, and cook until the Kamut berries are tender but still slightly chewy, 50 to 60 minutes. Remove from the heat and, if you have time, let it sit, covered, for 10 to 15 minutes. Drain any remaining liquid and transfer to a large serving bowl to cool.

2 Once the Kamut has cooled, make the salad. Add the carrots and golden raisins to the serving bowl. In a small bowl, whisk together the orange and lemon juices, honey, cinnamon, and salt until smooth. Gradually whisk in the olive oil in a thin stream.

3 To finish, pour the dressing over the salad and toss to combine. Taste and adjust for salt. Let sit at room temperature for 15 minutes to allow the flavors to come together. Toss again before serving; sprinkle with the walnuts and garnish with the pomegranate seeds.

TO GET A HEAD START: Make the Kamut berries, as in step 1, ahead (see page 23). In a hurry on the day of a party? The salad (without the walnuts and pomegranate seeds) can be prepared 4 to 6 hours ahead. Chill, covered. Bring to room temperature before serving.

TO VARY IT: You can use about 1 1/2 cups cooked farro, spelt, or hard or soft wheat berries if Kamut is hard to find (for cooking instructions, see page 25).

HOW TO SEED A POMEGRANATE

Chefs will use different ways to get to the glistening and juicy-crisp seeds of a pomegranate, a gorgeous fruit with blood-red leathery skin, revered since antiquity. I use a method that has worked well for me over the years. Have a medium-size bowl ready. Rinse the pomegranate and cut it lengthwise into quarters with a sharp serrated knife. Using both hands and working over the bowl, gently pull apart each piece to release the seeds that are nestled between skin "chambers." Remove any little skin pieces that might drop into the bowl. Be sure to wear an apron!

Bulgur with Butter-Roasted Almonds and Cinnamon

I remember digging a spoon into a plate of bulgur studded with roasted nuts and sweet spices in Turkey as a kid. Always someone with a sweet tooth, I thought this sumptuous dish with an everyday grain was as good as dessert. I have re-created this cinnamon-laced childhood dish, which can be done at the last minute—but only with butter (no substitutions possible!) It's delicious with lamb chops, chicken, or spicy Italian sausages. For more on varieties of bulgur, see page 10. SERVES 4

1³/4 cups water

1 cup medium-coarse bulgur

³/4 teaspoon fine sea salt

2 tablespoons unsalted butter

¹/4 cup toasted whole almonds, skin on (see page 37)

¹/4 teaspoon ground cinnamon

Pinch of cayenne pepper

1 Pour the water into a small saucepan and bring to a boil. Stir in the bulgur and salt, and return to a boil. Decrease the heat to maintain a simmer, cover, and cook until the water is absorbed, 12 to 15 minutes. Remove from the heat, cover, and set aside to steam for 5 minutes. Taste and adjust for salt.

2 While the bulgur steams, melt the butter over medium heat in a large skillet or saucepan, preferably stainless steel. Cook, watching attentively, until the aroma of the butter becomes deep nutty-sweet, the color turns golden brown, and the bottom of the pan fills with brown specks, 3 to 5 minutes. Add the almonds, cinnamon, and cayenne and cook, stirring, until fragrant, about 1 minute.

3 Add the bulgur to the skillet (it might splatter!), stir to combine, and serve right away.

TO LIGHTEN IT UP: You can cut the butter to 1 tablespoon if you must, but butter it has to be.

Parmesan Polenta with Rosemary Oil Drizzle

One summer, the rosemary bushes in our Boston garden grew so tall that I started to wonder if their roots reached all the way to Greece. As an endless stream of fragrant, spidery branches moved into our kitchen, the intense bittersweet herb made it into almost every meal. Last but not least, we infused olive oil with its scent. Drizzled over polenta, with freshly grated Parmesan cheese, the rosemary oil takes this peasant dish from everyday staple to festive side. You can use instant polenta when in a hurry, but regular polenta or stone-ground whole grain cornmeal will reward with richer flavor and a nice mouthful of texture. For more on types of polenta, see page 11, and for notes on cooking polenta, see the sidebar on page 106. Spoon the polenta next to pan-fried shrimp or chicken. SERVES 4 TO 6

....

POLENTA

2 cups water

2 cups low-sodium chicken broth or vegetable broth

$1/2$ teaspoon fine sea salt

1 cup polenta, corn grits, or stone-ground coarse cornmeal

ROSEMARY OIL

3 tablespoons extra-virgin olive oil

6 small rosemary sprigs, about 2 inches long, rinsed and patted dry

TO FINISH

1 tablespoon unsalted butter

1 teaspoon minced fresh rosemary

$1/4$ teaspoon freshly ground black pepper

$1/8$ teaspoon red pepper flakes (optional)

2 ounces finely grated Parmesan cheese (about 1 heaped cup), plus extra for serving

1 To make the polenta, pour the water and the broth into a large heavy-bottomed saucepan and bring to a boil over medium-high heat. Add the salt. Using a large whisk, slowly add the polenta in a thin stream, and continue whisking for 1 more minute. Decrease the heat to maintain a gentle bubble. Cover and cook until the polenta grains swell and become tender, about 25 minutes (30 minutes for coarse cornmeal), stirring vigorously every few minutes with a wooden spoon to keep the polenta from sticking to the bottom.

2 While the polenta is cooking, prepare the rosemary oil. Heat the olive oil and the rosemary sprigs in a small skillet over medium-low heat until the oil starts to sizzle. Cook for 1 minute, pressing on the twigs with a wooden spoon to submerge them into the oil. Remove the skillet from the heat and set aside to infuse for 15 minutes. Using tongs, remove and discard the sprigs. Pour the rosemary oil into a small serving bowl.

3 To finish, stir the butter, rosemary, and both peppers into the polenta, followed by the cheese. Taste and adjust for salt and pepper. Serve right away, drizzling a bit of rosemary oil on top of each serving, and passing more cheese around.

TO GET A HEAD START: Rosemary oil can be prepared up to 1 week ahead. Chill, covered. Bring to room temperature before using. Leftover oil can be drizzled over steamed vegetables or mashed potatoes. It's also delicious brushed on grilled meat or strong-flavored fish.

TO LIGHTEN IT UP: Omit the butter entirely or halve the amount, and reduce the amount of Parmesan cheese to $1/2$ cup if you like.

Lemon Quinoa with Currants, Dill, and Zucchini

Delicate quinoa is a more recent addition to my European-inspired grain universe. I often reach for it when I'm pressed for time. This tangy dish, studded with plump currants, is a mixture of a soothing rice pilaf and a refreshing salad. Pair it with grilled or pan-seared salmon or shrimp, or with sautéed chicken breast. For a light summer dish, simply top with crumbled feta, or ricotta salata for the Italian variation below, or just spoon some creamy yogurt over it. **SERVES 4 TO 6**

....

QUINOA

1 tablespoon extra-virgin olive oil

1 cup chopped green onions (about 6)

3/4 teaspoon fine sea salt

1 cup quinoa, well rinsed and drained

2 cups water

1/2 cup dried currants

1 lemon

TO FINISH

2 cups shredded zucchini (about 2 small)

4 tablespoons toasted sesame seeds (see page 37)

4 tablespoons chopped fresh dill

1/4 teaspoon freshly ground pepper

1 To make the quinoa, heat the olive oil in a medium saucepan over medium heat. Add the green onions (the oil might splatter!) and 1/4 teaspoon of the salt and cook, stirring frequently, until the dark green parts wilt but do not turn brown, about 2 minutes. Add the quinoa and cook, stirring occasionally, until the grains start to crackle and turn dry, about 3 minutes. Add the water, the currants, and the remaining 1/2 teaspoon salt; bring to a boil. Decrease the heat to maintain a simmer, cover, and cook until the water is absorbed, 15 to 20 minutes.

2 Meanwhile, finely grate the zest of the lemon until you have 1 teaspoonful, and then squeeze the lemon until you have 2 tablespoons juice.

3 To finish, remove the pan from the heat. Stir the zucchini, lemon juice and zest, 2 tablespoons of the sesame seeds, 2 tablespoons of the dill, and the pepper into the quinoa. Taste and adjust for salt and pepper. Cover and let sit for 3 minutes.

4 Transfer the quinoa to a serving bowl, sprinkle with the remaining 2 tablespoons each of sesame seeds and dill, and serve.

TO VARY IT: For an Italian-inspired side, replace the sesame seeds with toasted pine nuts (see page 37), use chopped fresh basil instead of dill, and omit the lemon juice.

Saffron Couscous

The fewer ingredients you use in cooking, the higher their quality has to be. Saffron is a case in point. For many years, I found the flavor of saffron in my cooking rather underwhelming—until my Iranian friend Golnaz brought me a tiny package of the crimson-red threads from her home country. The first time I used it, the delicate aroma of saffron permeated a bowl of simple risotto, enveloping every kernel with its ethereal scent and painting our meal a subtle orange hue. This memorable dinner subsequently inspired the Saffron Risotto with White-Wine Clams and Peas (page 182). Here I infuse whole wheat couscous with saffron, creating a luxurious side to pair with soupy mussels or salmon. Don't even ponder omitting the fat, as it allows the elusive fragrance of the spice to bloom. **SERVES 4 TO 6**

1/2 teaspoon loosely packed saffron threads

3 tablespoons hot water

1 3/4 cups low-sodium chicken broth or vegetable broth

1 tablespoon extra-virgin olive oil or unsalted butter

1/4 teaspoon fine sea salt

1 1/4 cups whole wheat couscous

1   Heat a small heavy-bottomed skillet over medium heat for 2 to 3 minutes. Add the saffron and toast until the threads darken ever so slightly, 30 seconds to 1 minute, stirring with a wooden spoon and watching closely. Immediately scrape the threads into a small bowl and crush them with your fingers. Cover with the hot water and let sit for at least 5 minutes.

2   Meanwhile, pour the broth, olive oil, and salt into a 2-quart saucepan and bring to a boil. Remove the saucepan from the heat. Stir in the couscous and the saffron, together with any of its colorful liquid. Cover and let sit until the liquid is absorbed, about 10 minutes.

3   Taste and adjust for salt. Fluff with two forks and serve right away.

PRECIOUS SAFFRON

Saffron, the world's most expensive spice, is the dried stigma of the *Crocus sativus* flower. It is harvested by hand, and it takes about thirteen thousand threads to get one ounce of the precious spice. And it has been highly valued since antiquity: Pliny describes the smuggling of saffron in the first century AD. Saffron flavor varies, depending on its region of origin. High-quality saffron comes from Italy, Spain, Iran, and the Kashmir region of India. So if you are not impressed the first time, try a different source for your spice. Saffron should be stored in a cool, dry place in a jar or tin with a tight-fitting lid.

Leek Salad with Grilled Haloumi Cheese and Rye Berries

Haloumi, a textured goat and sheep's milk cheese, popular across the Middle East, is irresistibly chewy and will not melt when grilled or roasted. Take this salad to a barbecue and char the cheese right there for a smoky touch, or use a broiler anytime. *Pecorino Romano* can stand in for the haloumi but it lacks the same lip-smacking chewiness. Both cheeses can be quite salty, so you may want to go easy when adding the salt. **SERVES 4 TO 6**

....

RYE

1¹/2 cups water

3/4 cup rye berries, soaked overnight and drained

SALAD

2 medium leeks, cleaned and cut into 3/4-inch segments (about 4 cups)

1/2 cup low-sodium chicken broth or vegetable broth

1 (2- by 1-inch) strip orange zest, white pith removed (optional)

1/4 cup chopped oil-packed sun-dried tomatoes, drained, 2 teaspoons oil reserved (see page 138)

1/4 cup chopped fresh mint, plus 2 tablespoons for garnish

2 tablespoons nonpareil capers

3/4 teaspoon fennel seeds

1/4 teaspoon fine sea salt

1/4 teaspoon freshly ground black pepper

TO FINISH

1/4 pound haloumi cheese

1¹/2 teaspoons dried crumbled oregano or thyme

1/4 teaspoon freshly ground black pepper

1/8 teaspoon dried red pepper flakes (optional)

1 To prepare the rye, bring the water and the rye berries to a boil in a small heavy-bottomed saucepan. Decrease the heat to maintain a simmer, cover, and cook until the berries are tender but still slightly chewy, 50 to 60 minutes. Remove from the heat, cover, and steam for 10 to 15 minutes if you have time. Drain any remaining liquid and transfer to a large serving bowl to cool.

2 While the rye cools, prepare the salad. Bring the leeks, chicken broth, and orange zest to a boil in a large saucepan. Decrease the heat to maintain a simmer, cover, and cook until the leeks are soft, 5 to 7 minutes. Drain the leeks, and add them to the serving bowl with the rye berries. Add the sun-dried tomatoes, 1/4 cup of the mint, and the capers, fennel seeds, salt, and pepper. Taste and adjust the seasoning, keeping in mind that capers and haloumi are quite salty.

3 To finish, position a rack about 6 inches below the heat source and preheat the broiler. Cut the haloumi cheese into thin slices, about 1/4 inch thick, and put them on a plate. Sprinkle with the oregano, pepper, pepper flakes, and reserved 2 teaspoons of tomato oil; rub the oil and spices all over to coat the slices on both sides (work gently, as haloumi breaks easily). Transfer the cheese to a medium cast-iron skillet or a broiler pan.

4 Broil the haloumi until the slices just start to brown at the edges, about 5 minutes, turning once with a spatula. (Watch closely as you don't want the cheese to dry out.)

5 Top the salad with the haloumi. Sprinkle with the remaining 2 tablespoons mint, and serve right away.

TO GET A HEAD START: Make the rye berries, as in step 1, ahead (see page 23). The salad (without the haloumi) can be prepared 4 to 6 hours ahead. Chill, covered. Bring to room temperature before serving.

TO VARY IT: A great stand-in for the rye in this dish would be about 2 cups cooked whole oat berries (for cooking instructions, see page 25).

Summer Tabouli with Farro

Mild-tasting farro, an ancient wheat variety, stands in for bulgur in this refreshing tabouli, a riff on the classic Middle Eastern salad (for more on varieties of farro, see page 16).

Be sure to choose sweet vine-ripened tomatoes from a farmers' market or your garden. Like my Greek mom, I chop the parsley quite coarsely—it adds a nice rustic touch. Bring this to a summer barbecue, where you can pair it with grilled fish drizzled with lemon juice, or with beef kebabs. For a simple vegetarian meal, top the tabouli with a handful of good-quality feta or Greek *manouri* cheese.

SERVES 4 TO 6

....

FARRO

2 cups water

1 cup farro

2-inch sprig rosemary, or
  1/2 teaspoon dried (optional)

TABOULI, AND TO FINISH

2 cups coarsely chopped tomatoes
  (3/4 pound)

1 cup loosely packed chopped
  flat-leaf parsley leaves

1/2 cup finely chopped red onion

3/4 teaspoon minced hot green chile
  (optional)

3 tablespoons extra-virgin olive oil

2 tablespoons freshly squeezed
  lemon juice

1 tablespoon red wine vinegar

3/4 teaspoon fine sea salt

1/4 teaspoon freshly ground black
  pepper

1 To prepare the farro, bring the water, farro, and rosemary to a boil in a small heavy-bottomed saucepan. Decrease the heat to maintain a simmer, cover, and cook until the farro is tender but still slightly chewy, 20 to 25 minutes. Remove the rosemary sprig, drain any remaining liquid, and transfer the farro to a large serving bowl to cool.

2 Once the farro has cooled, make the tabouli by adding the tomatoes, parsley, onion, and chile to the serving bowl. In a small bowl, whisk together the olive oil, lemon juice, vinegar, salt, and pepper. Taste and adjust the seasoning.

3 To finish, pour the dressing over the tabouli and toss to combine. Set aside for 10 minutes for the flavors to mingle, and serve.

TO GET A HEAD START: Make the farro, as in step 1, ahead (see page 23).

Cumin-Scented Quinoa with Red Beets

The sweet crunchiness and superb simplicity of raw shredded beets are overlooked and underrated. I think they are a delicacy. Combine this humble root vegetable with ancient quinoa and wait for these two earthy flavors to merge into a divine union. I like to blend red beets into burgundy-colored quinoa for a stunning crimson-colored side. On hot days, add a dollop of sumac-spiced yogurt and serve with chicken, lamb, or pork, or with an oil-rich fish such as pan-fried or grilled bluefish. To save time on dish duty, I use the large holes of a box grater and my muscles to shred raw beets (beware of splatters!), but feel free to use a food processor fitted with a shredding disk. And no, I never wear gloves. The red beet stains wash off easily, plus they show that I love to cook.

If you don't have whole cumin seeds at home, in step 1 add 1 teaspoon ground cumin together with the quinoa to the saucepan and cook, stirring, until the quinoa is hot to the touch, about 1 minute. Then proceed as directed. SERVES 4

QUINOA

1 tablespoon extra-virgin olive oil

1 teaspoon whole cumin seeds

1 cup red quinoa, well rinsed and drained

1 3/4 cups water

3/4 teaspoon fine sea salt

1/2 teaspoon sumac (optional; see sidebar)

SUMAC YOGURT TOPPING, AND TO FINISH

1 cup plain whole-milk yogurt

1 clove garlic, minced

1/2 teaspoon sumac, for sprinkling, or 1 teaspoon freshly squeezed lemon juice

1 1/4 cups shredded raw red beet (about 1 medium-sized beet, rinsed and peeled)

1 to 2 tablespoons freshly squeezed lemon juice

1 or 2 pinches of cayenne pepper (optional)

1 Heat the olive oil in a medium saucepan over medium heat until shimmering. Add the cumin seeds (they will sizzle) and cook, stirring, until the seeds darken and become fragrant, 30 seconds. Stir in the quinoa (it may splatter!) and cook, stirring frequently, until hot to the touch, about 1 minute. Add the water, salt, and sumac and bring to a boil. Decrease the temperature to maintain a simmer, cover, and cook until the liquid is absorbed, 15 to 20 minutes.

2 Meanwhile, make the sumac yogurt topping. Beat the yogurt and the garlic in a small bowl with a fork until smooth. Sprinkle with sumac and set aside.

3 To finish, remove the saucepan from the heat. Stir in the shredded beet, cover, and steam for 3 to 5 minutes. Stir in 1 tablespoon lemon juice and a pinch or two of cayenne. Taste, adjusting for salt and lemon juice, and serve with the yogurt topping.

TO VARY IT: White quinoa and golden beets combine for an equally attractive preparation.

SUMAC

Sumac is a dark red powder made from the crushed dried berries of a small Mediterranean tree. Widely used across the Middle East for centuries, it gives a sharp acidic kick to salads and roasted meats or fish. You can sprinkle sumac on top of hummus, or flavor rice with it. Its amazing, complex flavor contributes not only tanginess, but also sweet and bitter notes.

Warm Oat Berries with Walnuts and Gorgonzola

Most of us think of oats as a breakfast food. Try this side and think again—it will steal the limelight from trendy farro in an instant. Whole oat berries have a pleasing chew and an ever-so-slight toasty sweetness, inviting this pairing with pan-roasted walnuts and just-melted Gorgonzola cheese. Serve next to grilled or pan-fried steak and tuna, or offer it with simple sautéed greens such as spinach or chard. **SERVES 4 TO 6 SERVINGS**

....

OATS

1¼ cups water

1 cup whole oat berries (oat groats)

⅛ teaspoon fine sea salt

TO FINISH

1 tablespoon extra-virgin olive oil

½ cup coarsely chopped walnuts

3 teaspoons chopped fresh thyme

½ cup coarsely chopped pitted green olives

¼ teaspoon fine sea salt

¼ teaspoon freshly ground black pepper

2 teaspoons red wine vinegar

¾ cup crumbled Gorgonzola or other mild blue cheese (3 ounces)

1 To prepare the oats, bring the water, oat berries, and salt to a boil in a small saucepan. Decrease the heat to maintain a simmer, cover, and cook until the oats are tender but still slightly chewy, 30 to 40 minutes. Remove from the heat, cover, and set aside to steam for 10 to 15 minutes if you have time. Drain any remaining liquid.

2 To finish, heat the olive oil in a 10-inch skillet over medium heat until shimmering. Add the walnuts and 2 teaspoons of the thyme and toast, stirring frequently, until fragrant, about 3 minutes. Decrease the temperature if the walnuts darken too fast. Add the oats, olives, salt, and pepper. Cook, stirring, until heated through, about 2 minutes. Taste and adjust for salt and pepper (keeping in mind that olives can be salty). Sprinkle with the vinegar and remove from the heat. Briskly stir in ½ cup of the cheese until it just starts to melt. Top with the remaining ¼ cup cheese, sprinkle with the remaining 1 teaspoon thyme, and serve right away.

TO GET A HEAD START: Make the oats, as in step 1, ahead (see page 23).

TO VARY IT: Use 2½ cups cooked Kamut or soft wheat berries if you can't find whole oat berries (for cooking instructions, see page 25).

Tomato-Infused Bulgur Pilaf with Fresh Basil

When an abundance of fresh vine-ripened tomatoes piles high on my mother's kitchen counter in Thessaloniki, she cooks up a simple pot of juicy bulgur with the fruit. This classic pairing is born out of necessity in the heat of summer in many parts of the Mediterranean. It nicely accompanies lamb chops, flank steak, chicken breast, or grilled shrimp.

I like to add the fruity heat of Aleppo pepper (for more, see sidebar page 117), but you may replace it here with 1 teaspoon paprika and a good dose of black pepper. If you like a more textured side, use coarse bulgur. You may need up to an additional 3/4 cup broth (for a total of 2 1/4 cups liquid) and a total cooking time of 20 to 25 minutes (for more on varieties of bulgur, see page 10). I often prepare double the amount, as this side reheats well and freezes nicely for up to 1 month (add a bit of water when reheating). I don't mind that the basil darkens a bit, as it also intensifies the flavor. SERVES 4

1 tablespoon extra-virgin olive oil

1 cup red onion, cut into 1/4-inch dice (about 1 small)

1 clove garlic, peeled and crushed

1/2 teaspoon fine sea salt

2 tablespoons tomato paste

1/2 to 1 teaspoon Aleppo pepper

1 1/2 cups low-sodium chicken broth or vegetable broth

1 cup coarsely chopped fresh tomatoes or diced canned tomatoes

1 cup medium-coarse bulgur

1/4 cup chopped fresh basil, plus 2 tablespoons for garnish

1   Heat the olive oil in a 3- or 4-quart saucepan over medium heat until shimmering. Add the onion, garlic, and 1/4 teaspoon of the salt. Cook, stirring frequently, until the onion softens and starts to brown at the edges, about 5 minutes. Add the tomato paste and Aleppo pepper and cook, stirring, until the mixture darkens, about 1 minute. Add the broth, the tomatoes with their juices, and the bulgur and bring to a boil, stirring and scraping the bottom of the pan.

2   Decrease the heat to maintain a simmer, cover, and cook until the liquid is absorbed and the bulgur is tender but still slightly chewy, about 15 minutes. Add a tad more water if necessary. Remove the saucepan from the heat and season with the remaining 1/4 teaspoon salt. Taste for salt and adjust, and then stir in 1/4 cup of the basil. Cover and set aside for 3 minutes. Garnish with the remaining 2 tablespoons basil and serve.

TO VARY IT: Make this a light meal by adding 1 cup coarsely crumbled feta cheese. Stir in 1/2 cup of the feta together with the 1/4 cup basil to soften the cheese while the bulgur sits. Top with the remaining 1/2 cup feta when adding the basil garnish and serve.

Spicy Millet with Yogurt and Fresh Herbs

Never ever say you are serving millet for dinner, unless the trend gods declare it the next super grain. I'm working on this. For now, I continue to hide it whenever possible, as too many of us still consider millet to be bird food. Here, lots of garden-fresh herbs and a good-quality yogurt will do the trick, creating a refreshing and creamy summer side. Adding the seeds of a chile gives a nice kick. If you have a few fresh sage leaves, chop them finely and toss them in as well. Serve with sautéed shrimp, which you can drizzle with a bit of lemon. Any leftovers will harden in the fridge, but a quick warming in the microwave will restore this side's softness. **SERVES 4**

MILLET

1 tablespoon extra-virgin olive oil

1/2 cup chopped green onions (about 3), dark green parts reserved and finely chopped

1 bay leaf

1 cup millet

2 cups water

3/4 teaspoon fine sea salt

TO FINISH

1 cup plain whole-milk yogurt

1/4 cup packed finely chopped basil

1/4 cup packed finely chopped mint

1/2 serrano chile with seeds, minced

1/4 teaspoon freshly ground black pepper

Finely grated Parmesan cheese, for garnish

1 To make the millet, heat the olive oil in a medium saucepan over medium heat. Add the green onions (the oil might splatter!) and the bay leaf and cook, stirring frequently, until the green onions wilt but do not turn brown, about 2 minutes. Add the millet and cook, stirring, until hot to the touch, 2 to 3 minutes.

2 Add the water and salt and bring to a boil, stirring once. Decrease the heat to maintain a simmer, cover, and cook until the water is absorbed, 15 to 20 minutes. Remove the bay leaf.

3 To finish, stir in the yogurt, herbs, chile, and pepper. Taste and adjust for salt and pepper. Garnish with all or some of dark green onion tops and serve right away, passing the grated cheese.

TO VARY IT: Feel free to combine any fresh herbs you have at home, such as dill and parsley, dill and mint, or basil and parsley.

Spring Pilaf with Artichokes and Green Peas

This quick dinner side is perfect for the days when you are tired, overworked, and simply done with the day. Most of the ingredients come from the freezer or the pantry—and they combine quickly for an invigorating meal. Sweet green peas, artichoke hearts, and any fresh herbs on hand will remind you why cooking beats takeout. No green onions? Yellow onions will do. And artichoke hearts marinated in olive oil work just as well. I use instant brown rice here for a quick dinner. Adjust the amount of broth according to the package directions. Of course, this pilaf is most delicious with your own parboiled brown rice (see "to vary it" below). Pair with grilled chicken or sautéed shrimp. SERVES 4

....

1 tablespoon extra-virgin olive oil

1 cup chopped green onions (about 6)

1/2 teaspoon fine sea salt

2 teaspoons minced fresh rosemary, or 1 teaspoon dried

1 clove garlic, minced

2 cups instant brown rice

1 3/4 cups low-sodium chicken broth or vegetable broth

1 cup green peas (do not thaw if using frozen)

2 tablespoons chopped fresh dill or flat-leaf parsley, plus 2 tablespoons for garnish

1/4 teaspoon freshly ground black pepper

8 quarters artichoke hearts, jarred or frozen (do not thaw)

Finely grated Pecorino Romano or Parmesan cheese, for serving

1 Heat the olive oil in a large saucepan over medium heat. Add the green onions and 1/4 teaspoon of the salt and cook, stirring frequently, until the dark green parts wilt but do not brown, about 2 minutes. Add the rosemary and garlic and cook, stirring, until fragrant, about 1 minute. Add the rice and stir until the kernels are coated with oil. Add the broth, and stir in the green peas and 2 tablespoons dill. Season with the remaining 1/4 teaspoon salt and the pepper; nestle the artichoke pieces into the rice and bring to a boil.

2 Decrease the heat to maintain a simmer, cover, and cook until the liquid is absorbed, about 5 minutes. Remove from the heat, cover, and let sit for 5 minutes.

3 Taste and adjust for salt and pepper. Serve, sprinkled with the remaining 2 tablespoons dill and passing the cheese.

TO VARY IT: Use 1 recipe long-grain parboiled rice (see page 26). In step 1, you will add about 3 cups parboiled rice (instead of 2) and reduce the amount of broth to 3/4 cup (instead of 1 3/4 cups). Cook for 10 (instead of 5) minutes in step 2.

Orange and Lemon Couscous

This side is tangy, but deliciously so. Ample fresh juice from two kinds of citrus transforms whole wheat couscous into a succulent dish that even the busiest cook can easily make. Serve with pork roast or alongside the Roast Chicken with Orange, Lavender, and Thyme (page 179). SERVES 4

2 large oranges

1 lemon

3/4 cup low-sodium chicken broth
    or vegetable broth

1 tablespoon extra-virgin olive oil

1/2 teaspoon fine sea salt

1/4 teaspoon freshly ground black
    pepper

1 cup whole wheat couscous

2 tablespoons finely chopped
    flat-leaf parsley

1   Finely grate the zest of 1 orange, and squeeze the oranges until you have about 3/4 cup juice. Finely grate the zest of the lemon, and squeeze 1 lemon half to get 2 tablespoons juice. (Reserve the remaining lemon for another use). Whisk together the orange juice, lemon juice, and zest in a liquid
    measuring cup or small bowl.

2   Bring the chicken broth, olive oil, salt, and pepper to a boil in a 2-quart saucepan. Remove the pan from the heat. Stir in the juice mixture and the couscous. Cover and let sit until the liquid is absorbed, about 10 minutes.

3   Taste and adjust for salt and pepper. Fluff the grain with two forks, sprinkle with the parsley, and serve right away.

Speedy Chickpea Couscous with Pesto

A double boost of basil, from the pesto and the fresh leaves, gives this whole wheat couscous a flavor lift. It's perfect for busy weeknights when you are starving for quick and easy carbs. Home-cooked chickpeas taste best, but canned chickpeas work fine when you're in a rush. And pesto from a jar is a perfectly good replacement for homemade. Serve next to sautéed fish or chicken. SERVES 4

1 1/2 cups low-sodium chicken broth
    or vegetable broth

1 cup whole wheat couscous

3/4 cup canned chickpeas, rinsed
    and drained (about half of a
    14-ounce can)

3 tablespoons pesto

4 tablespoons chopped fresh basil

1 clove garlic, minced

1/2 teaspoon fine sea salt

1/4 teaspoon freshly ground pepper

1   Pour the broth into a medium saucepan and bring to a boil. Remove the saucepan from the heat. Stir in the couscous, chickpeas, pesto, 2 tablespoons of the basil, garlic, salt, and pepper. Cover and let sit until the liquid is absorbed, about 10 minutes.

2   Taste and adjust for salt and pepper. Fluff with two forks, sprinkle with the remaining 2 tablespoons basil, and serve right away.

TO VARY IT: Garnish with 1/4 cup chopped toasted pistachios (see page 37); or make it a light meal with crumbled ricotta salata, goat cheese, or feta cheese and a few olives.

Greek-Style Cornbread with Feta and Thyme

When my mother and her literature-loving friends meet to discuss poetry, it's her old-fashioned Greek cornbread that steals the show. Listening to her talk about these gatherings, I have come to believe that the group cherishes cornbread, traditionally rich in eggs and cheese, more than the lofty lines of verse. Here is a lighter version for contemporary tastes—yet with a generous amount of feta cheese to enrich your every bite. Be sure not to crumble the feta too finely, and for information on measuring flour see page 28. I like to use a cast-iron skillet, which endows the cornbread with a golden brown crust. In Greece, we eat it as a light lunch with a simple salad. Of course, this cornbread also works nicely with soup, or it can be served as part of a lazy, delectable brunch table.

In the unlikely event that you anticipate leftovers, transfer any remaining cornbread from the skillet to a wire rack to cool—to avoid a soggy bottom. Reheat leftover cornbread wedges in the microwave or in a moderate oven, or freeze for up to 1 month. And if you don't have a cast-iron skillet, you can use a 9-inch glass pie dish. Preheat the dish at 400°F and bake the cornbread at the same temperature, about 20 minutes. **SERVES 6 TO 8**

....

2 cups stone-ground, medium-coarse, whole grain cornmeal (8 ounces)

1 cup whole wheat pastry flour (4¹/₄ ounces)

1 teaspoon baking powder

³/₄ teaspoon baking soda

¹/₂ teaspoon fine sea salt

¹/₂ teaspoon dried crumbled oregano

¹/₄ teaspoon freshly ground black pepper

¹/₈ teaspoon red pepper flakes (optional)

2 large eggs

¹/₄ cup extra-virgin olive oil

1 ¹/₂ cups lowfat buttermilk

1 tablespoon minced fresh thyme, or 1 teaspoon dried

6 ounces feta cheese, coarsely crumbled into ¹/₄-inch pieces (about 1¹/₂ cups)

1 tablespoon unsalted butter

1 Position a rack in the center of the oven and place a 10-inch cast-iron skillet on it; preheat the oven to 450°F.

2 Whisk together the cornmeal, pastry flour, baking powder, baking soda, salt, oregano, pepper, and pepper flakes in a large bowl. Make a well in the center. In a medium bowl, lightly whisk the eggs to blend. Gently whisk in the oil, buttermilk, and thyme until smooth. Add the egg mixture to the center of the flour mixture, and stir with a rubber spatula until just combined. Do not overmix; the batter should look lumpy. Fold in the feta cheese.

3 Using a thick oven mitt, carefully remove the hot skillet from the oven. Add the butter and tilt carefully to coat the bottom and the sides. It will sizzle and brown fast for great flavor. Scrape the batter into the hot skillet, leveling the top with a spatula. Reduce the oven temperature to 400°F.

4 Bake until the edges of the cornbread turn golden brown and a toothpick inserted into the center comes out clean, 20 to 25 minutes. Let sit for 5 minutes before cutting into wedges. Serve warm.

TO VARY IT: For a deliciously textured, more rustic cornbread, replace 1 cup of the medium-coarse cornmeal with coarse stone-ground cornmeal.

Barley with Crisped Prosciutto and Truffle Oil

Aromatic prosciutto, rosemary, and a drizzle of truffle oil transform humble, earthy barley into a side dish fit for royalty. I like a mixture of pearl and hulled barley, blending the comforting creaminess of pearl barley with just enough chewy whole grain. Feel free to use one or the other. Pair with the lemon variation of the Roast Chicken with Orange, Lavender, and Thyme (page 179). Drizzle with truffle oil only at the table to make most of the aroma of this pricey ingredient; you can use a good-quality olive oil in its place, if you must, or if you're serving it as an everyday side. SERVES 4

BARLEY

2 cups water

1/2 cup hulled barley, soaked overnight and drained

1/2 cup pearl barley

1 small bay leaf

1/4 teaspoon fine sea salt

TO FINISH

1 teaspoon extra-virgin olive oil

2 ounces chopped prosciutto (about 1/2 cup)

1 teaspoon finely chopped fresh rosemary

Truffle oil, for drizzling

1 To prepare the barley, bring the water, both kinds of barley, bay leaf, and salt to a boil in a medium saucepan. Decrease the heat to maintain a simmer, cover, and cook until the grain is tender but still slightly chewy, about 40 minutes. Remove the bay leaf. Remove from the heat and, if you have time, let sit, covered, for 5 to 10 minutes. Taste and adjust for salt. Drain any remaining liquid and return to the saucepan. Cover.

2 To finish, heat the olive oil in a medium skillet over medium heat until shimmering. Add the prosciutto and cook, stirring frequently, until lightly browned and starting to crisp, about 3 minutes. Transfer to a small bowl. Stir the rosemary and two-thirds of the crisped prosciutto into the barley. Sprinkle with the remaining prosciutto and serve right away. Pass the truffle oil around the table so everyone can add a drizzle on top.

TO GET A HEAD START: Make the barley, as in step 1, ahead (see page 23). Rewarm over medium heat, adding 1/4 cup water or a bit more and breaking up any lumps with a wooden spoon. The prosciutto can be crisped 1 hour ahead. Set aside at room temperature.

Rustic Fall Polenta with Fontina and Sun-Dried Tomatoes

The beauty of polenta is the ease with which a home cook can take it from everyday to special in an instant. One evening, on a whim, I added a handful of sun-dried tomatoes—to discover a few minutes later that my polenta took on a spectacular auburn hue. The color depends on the tomatoes you use, and sometimes the grain will just turn a light orange. Beautiful? Always! This colorful side brings just enough opulence to an elegant fall dinner, next to chicken, turkey, or braised beef. Or add it to give a Mediterranean twist to your Thanksgiving table.

Some sun-dried tomatoes are very salty—try a small piece—reduce the salt to 1/4 teaspoon, and then adjust to taste after cooking. Kitchen shears come in handy to snip tough sun-dried tomatoes into pieces. For notes on cooking polenta, see the sidebar on page 106. SERVES 4 TO 6

....

POLENTA

4 cups water

1/2 cup coarsely chopped dry-packed sun-dried tomatoes

1/2 teaspoon fine sea salt

1 cup polenta, corn grits, or stone-ground coarse cornmeal

TO FINISH

1 teaspoon dried thyme or oregano

1/2 teaspoon dried sage

1/4 teaspoon freshly ground black pepper

1/2 cup cubed fontina (2 ounces)

2 ounces shaved Parmesan cheese (about 1/2 cup)

1 To make the polenta, bring the water and sun-dried tomatoes to a boil in a large heavy-bottomed saucepan over medium-high heat. Add the salt. Using a large whisk, slowly add the polenta in a thin stream, and continue whisking for 1 more minute. Decrease the heat to maintain a gentle bubble. Cover and cook until the polenta granules swell and become tender, about 25 minutes (30 minutes for coarse cornmeal), stirring vigorously every few minutes with a wooden spoon to keep the polenta from sticking to the bottom. Taste and adjust for salt.

2 To finish, stir in the thyme, sage, and pepper, followed by the fontina cheese. Cover and let sit for 2 minutes to allow the cheese to melt. Top with the shaved Parmesan cheese and serve right away.

TO GET A HEAD START: In a hurry, instant or quick-cooking polenta or grits will do, but they don't bring the same flavor and texture to the dish.

TO VARY IT: In the United States, I have learned to appreciate the stunning varieties of chiles. On occasion, I will drop a whole dried or fresh habanero chile into my polenta for its intense fruitiness. Be sure to remove the chile before serving—habaneros are some of the hottest chiles on the planet. Don't even contemplate adding one if serving the polenta to children.

ON COOKING POLENTA

Italian polenta has the reputation of being hard to cook. Nothing could be further from the truth. All it needs is a good stir once in a while. Admittedly, sometimes this can be a long while, depending on which kind you are cooking. With most polenta or corn grits, the granules are nice and plump when cooked for about 25 minutes (see above), but frankly, when I'm hungry I dig in after 15 minutes. On the other hand, certain kinds of coarse stone-ground polenta from specialty mills take longer to develop their alluring texture and mouthfeel. But once you try them, you might never go back to everyday polenta (see also page 11).

The more water, broth, or milk you add, the more billowy-soft your polenta will become. Some people like their polenta softer; I like mine a bit firmer. This means you can adapt the recipes to your liking, and you should.

What I like best about polenta is that leftovers can be deliciously resurrected. Just spread any remaining polenta into an oiled casserole dish or onto a rimmed baking sheet, about $1/2$ to $3/4$ inch thick (or thicker if you like). Allow to firm up at room temperature and then chill, covered with plastic wrap. For your next meal, cut the firm polenta into triangles or rectangular pieces and pan-fry them in olive oil or butter until golden on both sides. Or oven-bake the polenta pieces, topped just with a bit of butter, or sprinkled with herbs and cheese for a new mouthwatering side.

Corn: Comforting and Uplifting

No grain stirs as much passion in the American soul as corn. Native to the Americas, corn was sacred to the Aztecs and the Maya. The plant reached Europe, and eventually the rest of the globe, only in the early sixteenth century. Its mythical stature inspires Americans to this day—be it as a craving for comforting golden cornbread, a hunger for the light-colored soft clouds of grits, or a love for the crunch of popcorn.

Corn, or maize (derived from the word *mahiz* of the pre-Columbian indigenous *Taíno* people), is the one grain Americans often aspire to eat whole. Magazines, cookbooks, and blogs praise the use of stone-ground corn, its superior flavor and texture, and its better nutritional profile.

Corn, like all grains, is most flavorful when freshly milled as a whole. Its coarse yet supple texture and sweetness are unsurpassed. If you have yet to try freshly milled stone-ground cornmeal from a traditional American mill (for sources, see page 219), compare it someday to its shelf-stable, degerminated cousins whose aromatic germ and bran have been removed. The difference will be as striking as the contrast between a supermarket tomato bought in the dead of winter and one from the farmers' market in mid-August.

When I moved to the United States, the American passion for corn surprised me because in Greece, cornmeal has long been considered the food of the poor. People ate corn when they had not much else to eat. But poverty and lack of resources inspire creativity at the stove. This is why Germans long for the delectable simplicity of *Arme Leute Küche* (poor people's cuisine) and Italy's austere and flavorful *cucina povera* (the cooking of the poor) has become hip and trendy all over.

If you think cornbread is an all-American treat, just visit a family in northwestern Greece. To this day, mothers and grandmothers will whisk cornmeal into delicious rustic pies bursting with leafy greens, feta cheese, and fresh herbs. And while corn conjures up the poverty of the war years for many Greeks, some are rediscovering the simple tastes and virtues of long-forgotten grains such as wheat berries, bulgur, and corn. Crusty farmer's breads are reappearing in trendy city bakeries, their interior crumbly with a light yellow hue from cornmeal, as has the *bobota*, a sweet cornbread studded with raisins or currants, and sometimes soaked in orange-honey syrup.

Cornmeal has always been a staple in my pantry. A bowl of warm polenta has been a comfort food in winter ever since I owned my first set of German-made, heavy-bottomed stainless steel pots. I'm smitten by stone-ground American corn, yet I typically don't bother cooking it for a whole hour. Thirty minutes will have to do for dinner, although patience does reward you with a delectably sweeter mouthful of the grain. Be sure to try it once, or on occasion. Cornmeal in all its variations, polenta being one of them, is infinitely adaptable. You can serve it sweet or savory, finely ground for comfort, or chewy for a more textured side. Cook it in water, stock, or milk; add sugar, honey, and fruit for a warming breakfast; or stir in cheese, sun-dried tomatoes, herbs, and vegetables and dab it with butter for savory meals. To me, cornmeal is a magic hat for kitchen leftovers: throw in what you have on hand, and out comes dinner. This is reason enough to love cornmeal.

Last but not least, there is the awesome sensation of corn *au naturel*, freshly picked, ideally by yourself—standing small in a field between sky-high stalks of corn, searching for the perfectly ripe ear. When I was a kid in Greece, we would sometimes light a fire right there, in the dusk of the evening—the farmer joining us next to the crackling fire to cherish this one grain as is, plain, no salt, not even butter, just the memorable moment when the chewy kernels burst their sweet juice into your mouth. I have since had corn on the cob as a teenager in Germany, when living and working in India, and prepared by my Iranian sister-in-law's parents on a porch in Toronto—proof that the love for these kernels is universal.

CHAPTER 3

SOUPS & STEWS

Don't know what to dish up for dinner tonight? Soups and stews offer an easy way out of this everyday dilemma. Nourishing and warming in the dark months of the year, light and refreshing in the summer—for me, they always fit the bill. They are especially rewarding when your crisper drawer just yields two carrots, a leek, and half a fennel bulb, or any other forgotten vegetables from more ambitious meals. A soup will take it all in, no questions asked. The same goes for leftover whole grains. What to do with the half-cup of brown rice from a couple of days ago? The bit of cooked barley, or quinoa? Just drop them in and spoon up a mesmerizing medley a little while later.

Few things are as calming as lifting the lid of a Dutch oven and inhaling its exhilarating aromas. As your nose travels across the many ingredients simmering inside—sweet and acidic, herbaceous and spicy, meaty or deliciously fishy—cooking does for me what doctors say we all need more often: it functions as an instant relaxation pill. To quote British domestic goddess Nigella Lawson, "Cooking . . . is totally underestimated as a stress killer." How true, and most of all, how convenient. No need for special attire, for running shoes, yoga clothes, or a swimsuit. Just your apron will do, and a wooden spoon. Time-consuming? Take a shower and pour yourself a glass of wine—soup is low-maintenance and allows for such luxury.

Most important, soups and stews get better as they age, which means you can make them ahead for a busy work week, and you will reap the rewards a couple of days later when you spoon up their layered flavors and textures. In this chapter, try a Greek-inspired fish stew with fennel, tomatoes, and a splash of ouzo served over light whole wheat couscous to mop up the fine sauce. Or surprise guests with a lush, slowly simmered lamb stew with red wine, to which I have added wheat berries for a twist. Or how about a barley-lentil stew, flavored with crisped prosciutto and dill? Some of these recipes can be on the table in 30 minutes; others require a bit more time. Your rewards will be manifold: delicious new flavors and textures, wrapped in the comforting warmth of a soup or a stew.

Many Small Bites and One Shot of Ouzo

Going out for dinner with my family in Greece is an all-night affair—so much so that my now much-Americanized self struggles to adjust each time I visit. My extended family—aunts and uncles, cousins, their husbands and kids—rarely pile into their cars to drive to a restaurant before 9:00 P.M. By the time we all get there and settle into our chairs at the table, it can be as late as 10:00 P.M. To say that I am usually famished at this point would be an understatement. One of our family's favorite restaurants lies on the gulf of Thessaloniki, the second-largest city in Greece. It is one of a string of popular bars and outdoor tavernas serving food and a spectacular view. Sitting at the waterfront, we never stop admiring the dazzling lights of the city spread across the dark mirror of the still ocean.

Of course, what we really come for is the evening meal—and foremost its mouthwatering *mezedes*, the countless small plates that to me symbolize the slow start to a Greek dinner. While *meze* traditionally are tiny bites, served midday with wine or spirits as part of a lively debating culture, a ritualistic socializing around food, they have also become cherished appetizer plates served before dinner. Across the Mediterranean, petite plates are served to entice your appetite, help you sit down and relax. In Spain people feast on tapas; Italians enjoy their antipasti. *Meze* or *mezze* is also served in Turkey, Lebanon, and Cyprus. The term *meze* has its roots in the Persian *maze*, "taste" or "snack."

These miniature dishes, usually divided into cold and warm plates, are so varied that they can cover forty items on a restaurant menu. You can choose among tiny oregano- or mint-flavored meatballs, marinated octopus, deep-fried calamari, crisp cheese croquettes, giant white beans with roasted red peppers, bite-size tomato fritters, batter-fried zucchini flowers, and spicy cheese spread, plus familiar *tzatziki*, the thick cucumber-laced garlic yogurt, or fire-roasted eggplant salad, stuffed grape leaves (dolmades), and succulent pan-fried olives.

The moment the first heaping plate is set down, we all compete for slices of delicate zucchini with a crisp flour coating, deep-fried to perfection, with no residue of fat—bite-size delicious. A large platter of traditional Greek salad comes next, with the proverbial vine-ripened tomatoes, red onions, crisp cucumbers, olives, and thick slices of feta cheese roofed across the top—in a pool of aromatic, peppery olive oil to sop up with bread. Next come tiny deep-fried anchovies, a savory-sweet tidbit from the ocean, which we eat bones and all. They're followed by glistening black-skinned halves of charcoal-grilled eggplants, their cross-hatched interior spiced with more than enough minced garlic, parsley, and an ample dose of olive oil.

A rich assortment of finger food like this is, naturally, served with a signature drink: a shot of the Greek spirit ouzo for everyone at the table. To me, this highly aromatic distilled spirit equals home. This Greek national drink simply doesn't taste as good much of the year in Boston—it waits to be savored at the end of a sweltering-hot day, ideally with a slight breeze from the ocean whispering across your filled glass.

Ouzo's dominant note is that of anise. Together with other spices such as coriander, star anise, cloves, and cinnamon, it blends into a superbly aromatic yet delicate sweetness that is just right with any *meze*. In 2006, ouzo won the status of protected designation of origin from the European Union. Today there are many producers, each distilling its own herbal concoction. The French enjoy a similar anise-scented pastis, the Italians sip on sambuca, and in Turkey raki accompanies *meze*.

In the heat of the summer, be sure someday to try ouzo "on the rocks." Pour it with a few ice cubes into a clear, tall slim glass, and watch as the aquatic spirit turns stunningly white, resembling a glass of milk. This so-called louching is the result of an emulsion, created when the essential oils of anise react to the addition of water—a feast for the eyes to accompany the feast on the table.

Acorn Squash Soup with Spicy Yogurt Topping

Made with acorn squash, this savory soup is inspired by the winter pumpkins Greeks use for cooking. During my years in Germany, I fell for the comfort of soups thickened with naturally sweet rolled oats. Here I grind them into coarse meal, which adds an addictive voluptuousness to every spoonful. Serve with the Floating Sesame Loaf (page 71), or, for heartier fare, with the Aroma Bread with Coriander and Fennel (page 74). **SERVES 4 TO 6**

....

SOUP

1/4 cup old-fashioned rolled oats (not instant)

1 tablespoon extra-virgin olive oil

1 cup finely chopped yellow onion (about 1 small)

1 tablespoon minced fresh garlic (about 3 cloves)

3/4 teaspoon fine sea salt

2 pounds acorn squash, peeled, seeded, and cut into 3/4-inch cubes (about 6 cups)

1/2 teaspoon freshly ground nutmeg

1/4 teaspoon freshly ground black pepper

1/8 teaspoon red pepper flakes

1 quart low-sodium chicken broth or vegetable broth

SPICY YOGURT TOPPING, AND TO FINISH

1/2 lemon

1 cup plain whole-milk Greek yogurt

1/4 teaspoon fine sea salt

1/8 teaspoon cayenne pepper, or just a pinch

1/2 to 1 teaspoon sugar

1/4 cup chopped fresh flat-leaf parsley

1 To prepare the soup, grind the oats in a food processor until you have coarse meal, about 20 seconds. If you don't own a handheld blender, do not clean the processor bowl yet.

2 Heat the olive oil in a large saucepan over medium-low heat. Add the onion, garlic, and 1/4 teaspoon of the salt and cook, stirring occasionally, until the onion is glassy and soft, 6 to 8 minutes. Increase the heat to medium, add the squash, and cook until the pieces shine with a coating of oil, stirring, about 1 minute. Sprinkle the oatmeal, nutmeg, pepper, and pepper flakes across the top. Stir and cook until fragrant, about 1 minute. Add the broth and the remaining 1/2 teaspoon salt and bring to a boil, scraping the bottom to release any toasted oatmeal bits. Decrease the heat to maintain a simmer, cover, and cook until the squash is tender, about 8 minutes (a paring knife should glide out easily).

3 While the soup simmers, make the spicy yogurt topping. Finely grate the lemon half until you have 1/2 teaspoon zest. Squeeze the fruit to get 1 tablespoon lemon juice. Add the yogurt, lemon juice, zest, salt, and cayenne to a small serving bowl and beat with a fork until smooth.

4 To finish, puree the soup with a handheld blender in the saucepan, or in batches in the food processor (use caution with hot liquids!). If using a food processor, return the mixture to the saucepan and gently rewarm over medium heat until bubbles appear just below the surface, stirring a few times. Add 1/2 teaspoon of the sugar. Taste for salt, pepper, and sugar and adjust. Ladle the soup into deep plates, spoon a generous tablespoon of topping into each, and garnish with parsley. Be sure to swirl the topping into the soup before you dig in.

TO GET A HEAD START: The soup and the topping can be prepared, separately, up to 3 days ahead. Chill, covered. Gently reheat the soup, stirring occasionally. You can also freeze the soup, but not the topping, for up to 1 month.

TO VARY IT: Use blue hubbard squash, or easily available (and ready-cut if you like) chopped butternut squash.

TO LIGHTEN IT UP: In my perfect culinary universe, whole-milk Greek yogurt is a must to bring these simple flavors together. So give it a try before you go lowfat (which, of course, you can).

Mediterranean Mussels with Farro and White Wine

Pleasingly chewy farro and tender-sweet mussels are culinary siblings of sorts. Both share a rewarding lip-smacking plumpness, which makes them a perfect match in this easy one-pot stew. Don't let the length of the ingredients list keep you from giving it a try—this straightforward preparation is on the table fast. Serve with a crusty baguette to mop up the intensely flavorful, wine-infused mussel juices and extra olive oil to drizzle on top.

 The wine you use does not have to be expensive. Even a downright basic bottle can result in a fruity and aromatic sauce. I prefer smaller, wild-caught mussels, which typically cook in just under 3 minutes. Cultivated mussels might take 5 to 8 minutes. For more on varieties of farro, see page 16.

SERVES 3 OR 4 AS A LIGHT MAIN COURSE, OR 4 TO 6 AS A STARTER

....

FARRO

1¹/₂ cups water

³/₄ cup farro

1 small bay leaf

2 whole peppercorns

Pinch of fine sea salt

STEW

2 pounds fresh mussels in their shells

2 tablespoons extra-virgin olive oil

*1 cup finely chopped yellow onion
    (about 1 small)*

*1 cup thinly sliced carrots
    (about 2 small)*

*1 cup thinly sliced celery stalks
    (1 to 2 pieces)*

2 to 3 cloves garlic, lightly crushed

2 teaspoons minced fresh rosemary

2 bay leaves

1 dried red chile

¹/₂ teaspoon fine sea salt

1¹/₂ cups dry white wine

*1¹/₂ cups chopped fresh or diced
    canned tomatoes with their
    juices, (one 14-ounce can)*

1¹/₂ cups water

¹/₄ teaspoon freshly ground black pepper

1 teaspoon sugar

TO FINISH

*2 tablespoons freshly squeezed lemon juice,
    plus lemon wedges to serve*

2 tablespoons extra-virgin olive oil

¹/₄ cup chopped fresh flat-leaf parsley

1 To prepare the farro, bring the water, farro, bay leaf, peppercorns, and salt to a boil in a 2-quart saucepan. Decrease the heat to maintain a simmer, cover, and cook until the grain is tender but still slightly chewy, 20 to 25 minutes. Remove the bay leaf, drain any remaining liquid, and set aside.

2 While the farro simmers, rinse the mussels under cold running water, brushing to remove sand and residue on the shells. Remove the beards (hairy clumps around the shell) with tweezers or a sharp knife. Discard chipped mussels. Tap any open mussels and discard if they don't close. Set the cleaned mussels aside.

3 To make the stew, heat the olive oil in a large Dutch oven or heavy-bottomed pot over medium heat until shimmering. Add the onion, carrots, celery, garlic, 1 teaspoon of the rosemary, the bay leaves, chile, and ¹/₄ teaspoon of the salt. Cook, stirring frequently, until the vegetables soften, 3 to 5 minutes. Increase the heat to medium-high, add ¹/₄ cup of the white wine, and cook until syrupy and the liquid is almost gone, about 2 minutes. Add the tomatoes, the water, the remaining 1¹/₄ cups white wine, the pepper, and the remaining ¹/₄ teaspoon salt; bring to a

CONTINUED, PAGE 114

boil. Cook, uncovered, at a lively simmer until the carrots are crisp-tender, about 5 minutes. Stir in the sugar.

4 Add the mussels and the farro together with the remaining 1 teaspoon rosemary to the pot and bring to a boil. Cover and steam over medium to medium-high heat, shaking the pot once or twice in between, until the mussels open, 2 to 3 minutes. Remove from the heat, and discard any unopened mussels.

5 To finish, add the lemon juice. Taste for salt and pepper and adjust. Drizzle the mussels with the olive oil and serve right away in deep plates, garnished with parsley and with lemon wedges on the side.

TO GET A HEAD START: Make the farro, as in step 1, ahead (see page 23). The stew, as in step 3, can be prepared up to 3 days ahead. Reheat before adding the mussels and farro, as in step 4. The mussels should be bought the day they are cooked. For a speedy, light dish, omit the farro altogether, and do not add the water to the stew.

TO VARY IT: Easily available and affordable pearl barley plumps up nicely to compete with farro in this dish, or simply use leftover brown rice. You will need about 2 cups cooked grain (for cooking instructions, see page 25).

Fish and Fennel Stew with Ouzo over Couscous

Every passionate cook knows that a swig of alcohol in the saucepan mightily rewards the eater later on. In Greece, this kick inevitably comes from the popular anise-flavored spirit ouzo (see page 110), which adds a blissful licorice touch to this fish stew. I like to serve this dish in the summer or fall when fennel, with its delicate feathery fronds, is at its peak. Be sure to keep a handful of the aromatic sprigs for garnish (and save the rest to flavor soups and salads). **SERVES 6**

....

STEW

2 tablespoons extra-virgin olive oil

1 1/2 cups chopped yellow onion (about 1 medium)

2 cloves garlic, minced

1 large bay leaf

2 medium fennel bulbs (about 1 1/2 pounds), cored, quartered, and thinly sliced crosswise (about 4 cups)

1/4 cup ouzo or other anise-flavored liqueur

2 cups vegetable broth

1 (28-ounce) can diced tomatoes

1 1/2 pounds skinned halibut, mahi mahi, tilapia, or other white-fleshed fish, patted dry and cut into 1-inch pieces

2 tablespoons freshly squeezed lemon juice

Fine sea salt and freshly ground black pepper

COUSCOUS

1 1/2 cups water

1 tablespoon extra-virgin olive oil or unsalted butter

3/4 teaspoon fine sea salt

1 1/4 cups whole wheat couscous

TO FINISH

1/2 to 1 teaspoon sugar

1/4 teaspoon freshly ground black pepper

1 tablespoon extra-virgin olive oil

1/4 cup finely chopped fennel fronds

1   To make the stew, heat the olive oil in a Dutch oven or large heavy-bottomed pot over medium heat until shimmering. Add the onion, garlic, bay leaf, and fennel and cook, stirring frequently, until the vegetables soften, about 5 minutes. Add the ouzo and cook until syrupy and almost no liquid remains, about 2 minutes. Add the broth and tomatoes and bring to a boil. Decrease the heat to maintain a simmer, cover, and cook until the vegetables are crisp-tender, 15 to 17 minutes.

2   While the stew simmers, place the fish in a large glass or other non-reactive bowl. Allow to sit at room temperature for 15 minutes, and then drizzle with the lemon juice and season with salt and pepper. Set aside for a few minutes.

3   Meanwhile, make the couscous. Pour the water, olive oil, and salt into a heavy medium saucepan and bring to a boil. Remove the saucepan from the heat. Stir in the couscous, cover, and let sit until the liquid is absorbed, about 10 minutes.

4   To finish, add the fish to the stew, stir—gently to keep the pieces intact—and return to a simmer. Cook, leaving the lid slightly askew, until the fish is fork-tender and opaque throughout, 3 to 4 minutes. Add 1/2 teaspoon of the sugar and the pepper. Taste and adjust for sugar, salt, and pepper. Remove from the heat, drizzle the stew with the olive oil, and let sit, with the lid slightly askew, for 3 minutes.

5   Fluff the couscous with a fork and divide among deep plates. Scoop the fish stew over the couscous and garnish each serving with some fennel fronds.

TO GET A HEAD START: The stew without the fish, as in step 1, can be prepared 1 day ahead. Just before serving, proceed with step 2 and gently reheat the stew before adding the fish, as in step 4.

Bulgur-Lentil Soup with Minted Olive Oil Butter

The rustic simplicity of this classic Turkish soup has mesmerized me since childhood. Variations are served in Greece as well. As the red lentils disintegrate, they form the backbone of a thick, nourishing one-pot meal with the pleasing chewiness of bulgur. Passionate Mediterranean cooks will simmer the soup for 40 minutes, and if you have time, do it—you will be rewarded with chunky, supple spoonfuls as the starch in the lentils continues to congeal. If you prefer a smoother soup, you can puree part or all of it in batches in a blender or food processor fitted with the metal blade (use caution with hot liquids!). Return the soup to the same pot, cover, and gently rewarm over medium heat, stirring. Serve as a light meal in the summer or as a warming first course in the colder months, together with toasted whole wheat pita wedges.

I often double or triple the amount of minted olive oil butter, as it tastes delicious drizzled on whole grain bread or over brown rice (chill, covered, and briefly reheat in the microwave). Or use it to brush on burgers such as the Lamb Burgers with Bulgur and Mint (page 136). For more on varieties of bulgur, see page 10. SERVES 6

....

SOUP

1 tablespoon extra-virgin olive oil

1 tablespoon unsalted butter, or more olive oil

1 medium-size yellow onion, cut into 1/4-inch dice (about 1 1/2 cups)

1/2 teaspoon fine sea salt

1 tablespoon minced garlic (about 3 cloves)

1 1/2 teaspoons paprika, or 1/2 teaspoon Aleppo pepper (see sidebar)

1/8 teaspoon cayenne pepper (optional)

2 tablespoons tomato paste

1 1/2 cups coarsely chopped fresh or diced canned tomatoes, preferably fire-roasted (one 14-ounce can)

1/2 cup coarse bulgur

1/2 cup split red lentils, picked over, rinsed, and drained

2 cups low-sodium chicken broth or vegetable broth

3 cups water

1 to 2 tablespoons freshly squeezed lemon juice

1/2 to 1 teaspoon sugar

1/4 teaspoon freshly ground black pepper

MINTED OLIVE OIL BUTTER

1 tablespoon extra-virgin olive oil

1 tablespoon unsalted butter

2 teaspoons dried spearmint

Pinch of cayenne pepper, or 1/4 teaspoon Aleppo pepper

1 To prepare the soup, heat the olive oil in a large pot over medium heat until shimmering. Add the butter and wait until the foam almost subsides. Add the onion and 1/4 teaspoon of the salt and cook, stirring occasionally, until the onion softens and turns light golden, about 5 minutes. Add the garlic, paprika, and cayenne and cook, stirring, for 1 minute. Add the tomato paste and cook until it darkens, 1 minute. Add the tomatoes (there might be splatter!) and adjust the heat to maintain a lively simmer. Cook, uncovered, stirring once or twice and scraping the bottom to release any browned bits, until the mixture thickens slightly, about 3 minutes.

2 Stir in the bulgur, lentils, broth, water, and remaining $1/4$ teaspoon salt; bring to a boil. Decrease the temperature to maintain a simmer, cover, and cook until the soup thickens, with the bulgur retaining a slight bite, at least 25 minutes but ideally 40 minutes. Season with 1 tablespoon of the lemon juice, $1/2$ teaspoon of the sugar, and the pepper. Taste and adjust the seasoning. Cover and let sit for a few minutes.

3 While the soup sits, make the minted olive oil butter. Heat the olive oil and butter in a small skillet over medium heat. Once the butter has melted, add the mint and cayenne (it will sizzle!) and stir until fragrant, 15 seconds. Immediately remove the skillet from the heat and pour the minted olive oil butter into a small serving bowl.

4 Divide the soup among 6 bowls, drizzling on a bit of the minted olive oil butter.

TO GET A HEAD START: The soup can be prepared up to 3 days ahead. Chill, covered, or freeze for up to 1 month. It will thicken in the fridge, so just add a bit more water or broth when reheating.

Chicken Stew with Artichokes and Dried Apricots over Brown Rice

Sweet dried apricots, bittersweet artichokes, and fragrant orange zest lend sublime fruitiness to this colorful stew, transporting you straight to the Mediterranean. Despite its lengthy ingredients list, this is a no-fuss dish. I like to brown tender pieces of chicken breast on one side only, and not all around, to keep the meat juicy while still providing enough browned bits to add flavor to the sauce. Tangy-sweet dried Blenheim apricots are my first choice, as they beautifully complement the layers of flavors.
SERVES 6

....

BROWN RICE

2¹/2 cups water

1¹/2 cups long-grain brown rice

¹/2 teaspoon fine sea salt

CHICKEN STEW

1¹/2 pounds skinless boneless
  chicken breasts (3 to 4 pieces),
  trimmed, patted dry, and cut into
  1-inch pieces

2 tablespoons extra-virgin olive oil

1¹/2 tablespoons unsalted butter, or
  more olive oil

1 medium-size yellow onion,
  cut into ¹/4-inch dice (about
  1¹/2 cups)

2 stalks celery, halved lengthwise if
  large, and sliced ¹/4 inch thick
  (about 1 cup)

²/3 pound carrots, sliced ¹/4 inch
  thick (about 1¹/2 cups)

1 tablespoon minced garlic (about
  3 cloves)

2 tablespoons white whole wheat or
  regular whole wheat flour

3 cups low-sodium chicken broth

1 cup dry white wine such as Pinot Grigio

¹/2 pound frozen quartered artichoke hearts
  (about 2 cups; do not thaw)

4 (1¹/2 by ¹/2-inch) strips orange zest,
  white pith removed

³/4 teaspoon fine sea salt

¹/4 teaspoon freshly ground black pepper

1 cup dried apricots, cut or snipped in half

TO FINISH

1 to 2 tablespoons freshly squeezed lemon juice

¹/4 cup chopped fresh flat-leaf parsley

1   Start making the brown rice about 15 minutes before you cook the stew. Bring the water to a boil in a 2-quart saucepan with a tight-fitting lid. Add the rice and salt and return to a boil, stirring once. Decrease the heat to maintain a simmer, cover, and cook until the rice is tender and the water is absorbed, 35 to 45 minutes. Remove from the heat, cover, and let sit for 5 to 10 minutes. Fluff with two forks before serving.

2   To make the stew, season the chicken pieces with salt and pepper. Heat 1 tablespoon of the olive oil in a large Dutch oven or heavy-bottomed pot over medium-high heat until shimmering. Add half the chicken pieces and cook on 1 side only until golden brown, 2 to 3 minutes. Using a heatproof spatula, transfer the chicken pieces to a large plate. Add the remaining tablespoon of the olive oil and repeat with the remaining chicken.

3   Decrease the heat to medium, add 1 tablespoon of the butter, and wait until it melts. Add the onion, celery, carrots, and garlic; cook until the onion softens, stirring frequently and scraping the bottom of the pan to loosen browned bits, about 3 minutes. Sprinkle with the flour and cook, stirring, 1 to 2 minutes.

4   Add the broth, wine, artichoke hearts, orange zest, the salt and pepper, stirring and scraping the bottom of the pot to loosen the browned bits. Cover, leaving the lid slightly askew, and bring to a gentle boil. Decrease the heat to maintain a simmer and cook for 3 minutes. Add the apricots and the chicken, with any accumulated juices; return to a simmer and cook until the carrots are tender and the chicken is done, 5 to 7 minutes.

5   To finish, remove the stew from the heat. Add 1 tablespoon of the lemon juice. Taste for salt, pepper, and lemon juice and adjust. Stir in the remaining 1/2 tablespoon butter, cover, and let sit for 3 minutes. Sprinkle with parsley and serve in deep soup plates over brown rice.

TO GET A HEAD START: Use parboiled brown rice (see page 26) and finish cooking it when you start the stew. The stew, up through step 4, can be made 1 day ahead. Chill, covered. Gently warm just to a simmer over medium heat, adding a bit more water or broth to thin if needed. Finish as in step 5.

Lamb Stew with Wheat Berries in Red Wine Sauce

One of the first meals I learned to cook when I moved away from home was lamb stew. I couldn't imagine living without the enticing pungent sweetness of lamb, the meat I most closely associate with lavish feasts and festive meals in Greece. I always add a pinch of cinnamon, common in Greece and Turkey for tomato-based meat dishes. This one-pot meal can be completely prepared ahead—perfect for an evening with friends. Serve the stew with garlic-infused yogurt spooned on top, and with a crusty bread or baguette to mop up the flavorful raisin-spiked sauce. For maximum flavor, prepare the garlic yogurt a day ahead. SERVES 4 TO 6

....

WHEAT BERRIES

2 cups water

1 cup soft whole wheat berries, soaked overnight and drained

GARLIC YOGURT

1 cup plain whole-milk Greek yogurt

2 cloves garlic, minced

Fine sea salt

STEW, AND TO FINISH

1 (28-ounce) can whole tomatoes

1 cup dry red wine, such as Cabernet Sauvignon

2 tablespoons good-quality balsamic vinegar, plus extra for seasoning

1/2 teaspoon paprika

1 1/4 pounds lamb shoulder, trimmed of fat and cut into 1-inch cubes

2 tablespoons (or more) extra-virgin olive oil

1 1/2 cups chopped onion (about 1 medium)

2 cloves garlic, thinly sliced lengthwise

1 (3-inch) cinnamon stick

1 bay leaf

1 teaspoon fine sea salt

2 tablespoons tomato paste

1 pound carrots, cut 1/4 inch thick (about 3 cups)

3/4 cup dark raisins

1 teaspoon brown sugar

1/4 teaspoon freshly ground black pepper

1   To prepare the wheat berries, bring the water and the wheat berries to a boil in a heavy-bottomed medium saucepan. Decrease the heat to maintain a simmer, cover, and cook until the wheat berries are tender with a slight chew, about 45 minutes. Remove from the heat, cover, and set aside to steam for 10 to 15 minutes, if you have time. Drain, reserving the cooking liquid (about 1/2 cup).

2   Meanwhile, prepare the garlic yogurt. Beat the yogurt in a small bowl with a fork until smooth. Stir in the garlic and season with salt. Chill, covered, until ready to serve.

3   To make the stew, place the tomatoes with their juices, wine, vinegar, and paprika in a large bowl. Using a wooden spoon or your hands, gently crush the tomatoes and combine the mixture.

4   Pat the lamb dry with paper towels and season with salt and pepper. Heat the oil in a large Dutch oven or large heavy-bottomed saucepan over medium-high heat until shimmering. Working in 2 or 3 batches, cook the lamb until browned on all sides, adding a bit more oil if the pan goes dry, about 5 minutes per batch. Using a slotted spoon, transfer the lamb to a plate. Decrease the heat to medium; add the onion, garlic, cinnamon, bay leaf, and 1/4 teaspoon of the salt. Cook, stirring constantly, until the onion softens, 2 to 3 minutes. Add the tomato paste and cook for 30 seconds, stirring. Add the tomato mixture (it may splatter!), the meat with its accumulated juices, the carrots, and the remaining 3/4 teaspoon salt, scraping the bottom of the pot. Bring

CONTINUED, PAGE 122

to a boil. Decrease the heat to maintain a simmer, cover, and cook for 30 minutes.

5   Add the raisins, the wheat berries, and, if needed, enough of the reserved cooking liquid to just cover the vegetables (the tips of the carrots will show). Return to a boil. Decrease the heat to maintain a simmer, cover, and cook until the lamb is fork-tender, about 40 minutes. Add more cooking liquid or water to thin, if you like.

6   To finish, season with the brown sugar and pepper, as well as a dash more balsamic vinegar. Taste and adjust the seasoning, and serve with the garlic yogurt spooned on top or alongside.

TO GET A HEAD START: Make wheat berries, as in step 1, ahead (see page 23). Or cook the soaked wheat berries while you assemble the ingredients. The stew can be prepared 1 to 2 days ahead—it will only get tastier.

TO VARY IT: It is worth tracking down soft wheat berries here, as hard wheat berries are more chewy and typically need longer to cook. This dish is also delicious when using about 2 1/2 cups cooked spelt or Kamut berries (for cooking instructions, see page 25).

Greek Egg and Lemon Soup with Chicken and Brown Rice

Classic avgolemono—a delicious, velvety swirl of lemon and eggs—is used in myriad ways in Greece: as a tangy finish for soups, braised vegetables, and stuffed grape leaves, or to lighten rich, meaty stews made with lamb or pork. According to Aglaia Kremezi, an authority on Mediterranean food, this characteristic sauce was probably introduced to fifteenth-century Greece by Sephardic Jews fleeing persecution in Spain. Mine is a light silky soup. Like my purist mom, I don't use cornstarch to give the soup more body—only eggs and a good whisking. SERVES 4

....

SOUP

1 bone-in, skin-on chicken breast half (about 1 pound)

Fine sea salt and freshly ground black pepper

6 cups low-sodium chicken broth

1/2 cup thinly sliced green onions (about 3)

1 clove garlic, lightly crushed

1/2 recipe parboiled short-grain brown rice (see page 26; about 1 1/4 cups cooked)

AVGOLEMONO, AND TO FINISH

2 or 3 lemons

2 large eggs, separated, at room temperature

1/2 cup finely chopped fresh dill or flat-leaf parsley

1 Season the chicken breast with salt and pepper. Bring the chicken, broth, green onions, and garlic to a boil in a large saucepan, covered. Decrease the heat to maintain a simmer and cook until the chicken breast is no longer pink in the center, 20 to 25 minutes.

2 Using tongs, transfer the chicken breast to a cutting board and set aside to cool a bit. Add the rice, return to a simmer, cover, and cook until the rice is tender, about 10 minutes.

3 Meanwhile, juice the lemons. Measure 1/4 cup juice and set it aside in a small bowl. Set 2 more tablespoons aside in a separate little bowl. Reserve the remaining lemon juice for serving at the table. Once the chicken is cool enough to handle, remove the skin of the breast and discard. Pull the meat off the bones and shred it.

4 When the rice is ready, make the avgolemono. In a medium nonreactive heatproof bowl, beat the egg whites vigorously with a large balloon whisk until frothy and multiplied in volume several times, about 2 minutes. Continuing to whisk vigorously, add the yolks, then slowly pour in the 1/4 cup lemon juice. Now the egg mixture should have lots of body and a light yellow color. Gradually pour 1 ladleful of the hot chicken broth into the egg mixture, whisking all the while, to temper it. Add a second ladleful of broth in the same way.

5 To finish, slowly pour the egg-broth mixture back into the soup, whisking continuously. Return the chicken to the pot and add 1/4 cup of the dill. Switch to a wooden spoon and very gently heat for 2 minutes over medium heat, stirring all along—do not bring the soup to a boil or the eggs will curdle. There will now be a thick, foamy layer on top of the soup. It will subside as you serve, while adding a sublime silky texture. Taste for salt and pepper and adjust. Add 1 or 2 more tablespoons of the remaining lemon juice to taste.

6 Ladle the soup into deep plates or bowls. Garnish each serving with some of the remaining fresh dill and freshly ground pepper, and serve with more lemon juice on the side.

Barley-Lentil Stew with Mushrooms, Crisped Prosciutto, and Dill

In the waning days of summer—when the nights come early and you can smell the fall moving in—this is the stew I cobble together in my kitchen. It is light, yet substantial enough to carry me comfortably through those first crisp evenings. A jumble of grains, legumes, and vegetables, this stew also connects me to my roots in the Mediterranean, where barley has been served since antiquity. Hulled whole grain barley adds texture, pearl barley comforting starchiness.

Instead of the two kinds of barley, you may use $^1/_2$ cup of a single type, whatever you have on hand. Widely available brown lentils can be used, however, they turn mushy more easily. Green lentils, also called French or Puy, have a firmer texture, as do black Beluga lentils. A surprise ingredient—soy sauce, with its deep umami flavor—lends an earthy finish. Serve on its own or with crusty sourdough bread, with a dab of butter. SERVES 4

....

GRAIN-LENTIL MIXTURE

2 cups water

$^1/_4$ cup hulled barley, soaked overnight and drained

$^1/_4$ cup pearl barley

$^1/_4$ cup green or black lentils, picked over and rinsed

1 large bay leaf

1 dried red chile

STEW, AND TO FINISH

2 tablespoons extra-virgin olive oil

4 ounces prosciutto, chopped (about 1 cup)

2 medium leeks, white and light green parts, sliced $^1/_4$ inch thick (about 3 cups)

$^1/_2$ pound cremini mushrooms, halved if large, and sliced $^1/_4$ inch thick (3 cups)

$^1/_2$ bunch chard or spinach, leaves chopped (about 2 cups) and stems sliced $^1/_4$ inch thick

2 cloves garlic, lightly crushed

2 teaspoons dried marjoram

1 teaspoon dried crumbled oregano

$^1/_2$ cup chopped fresh dill

2 cups vegetable broth

1 cup water

1 corner Parmesan cheese rind (optional)

2 tablespoons reduced-sodium soy sauce, plus extra for seasoning

$^1/_4$ teaspoon freshly ground black pepper

$^1/_2$ cup sour cream or plain whole-milk Greek yogurt, beaten until smooth

1   To parboil the grain-lentil mixture, bring the water, both kinds of barley, lentils, bay leaf, and chile to a boil in a heavy-bottomed medium saucepan. Decrease the heat to maintain a simmer, cover, and cook for 20 minutes.

2   Meanwhile, start the stew. Line a small plate with paper towels. Heat 1 tablespoon of the olive oil in a heavy-bottomed large saucepan over medium heat until shimmering. Add the prosciutto and cook, stirring frequently, until lightly browned and crisp, about 3 minutes. Using a slotted spoon, transfer $^1/_4$ cup of the prosciutto to the paper-lined plate and set aside.

3   Add the leeks, mushrooms, chard stems, and garlic and cook, stirring frequently, until the vegetables soften and mushrooms release much of their liquid, about 3 minutes. Add the dried herbs and cook for 1 minute, then stir in $^1/_4$ cup of the dill. Add the broth, water, Parmesan rind, 1 tablespoon of the soy sauce, and the pepper.

SAVORY STEMS

Many recipes call for only the leaves of chard, spinach, or kale and discard a sweet and delicious part of the vegetable, the stems. I always chop them finely and add them right at the start, together with the onions for example, for a richer base in stews, stir-fries, or frittatas.

4   Transfer the parboiled grains and lentils, including any remaining cooking liquid, to the vegetables and bring everything to a boil. Decrease the heat to maintain a simmer, cover, and cook until the barley is tender but still slightly chewy, about 20 minutes.

5   To finish the stew, remove the Parmesan rind, bay leaf, and chile, and season with the remaining 1 tablespoon soy sauce. Taste and adjust for pepper (I like to spice it up a bit), salt, or soy sauce (don't add both, as soy sauce is very salty). Stir in the chard leaves, drizzle with the remaining 1 tablespoon olive oil, and remove the saucepan from the heat. Let sit, covered, for 3 to 5 minutes to allow the leaves to soften.

6   Ladle the stew into bowls. Garnish each serving with a dollop of sour cream, a bit of the reserved crisped prosciutto, and some of the remaining ¼ cup dill. Serve right away.

TO GET A HEAD START: Barley and lentils, as in step 1, can be parboiled 3 days ahead. Do not drain. Cover and chill. The stew, up through step 5, can be prepared 1 day ahead. Chill, covered.

TO MAKE IT VEGETARIAN: Simply omit the prosciutto.

Fire-Roasted Tomato Stew with Eggplant and Farro

A trio of tomatoes—oil-packed sun-dried tomatoes, tomato paste, and fire-roasted tomatoes—coupled with a hearty beef broth gives this stew an opulent intensity. Soft, pliable eggplant, plump, sweet raisins, and a hint of cinnamon are combined with nutty, sweet farro, alluring even in the dead of winter when tomatoes come from a can (for more on varieties of farro, see page 16). A few parsnips, once forgotten in my vegetable drawer during a bone-chilling February, are a surprisingly delicious addition, their sweet, floral fragrance complementing the rich aromas of the stew. Kick-starting the cooking of eggplants in a microwave removes some of their moisture for a more supple outcome. This is the place where you want to use soaking liquid left from making your own oil-packed sun-dried tomatoes to replace some of the broth (for a recipe, see page 138). Leftovers taste ever so good the next day. SERVES 6

FARRO

1 cup water

1/2 cup farro

Pinch of salt

STEW

1 eggplant (about 1 pound)

2 tablespoons extra-virgin olive oil

1 medium-size red onion, cut into 1/4-inch dice (about 1 1/2 cups)

1 clove garlic, lightly crushed

1/2 teaspoon fine sea salt

1/2 pound parsnips or carrots, halved or quartered lengthwise depending on size, and sliced 1/2 inch thick (about 2 cups)

3/4 teaspoon ground cinnamon

2 tablespoons tomato paste

1 (28-ounce) can whole fire-roasted tomatoes, crushed

2 1/2 cups low-sodium beef broth

1/2 cup dark raisins

1/4 cup drained, chopped oil-packed sun-dried tomatoes (see page 138)

1/4 teaspoon freshly ground black pepper

TO FINISH

1 teaspoon sugar

1 tablespoon extra-virgin olive oil

1/4 cup chopped fresh flat-leaf parsley

Plain whole-milk yogurt, for serving

1 To prepare the farro, bring the water, farro, and salt to a boil in a small heavy-bottomed saucepan. Decrease the heat to maintain a simmer, cover, and cook until the grain is tender but still slightly chewy, 20 to 25 minutes. Drain any remaining liquid.

2 Meanwhile, prepare the eggplant for the stew. Cut the eggplant lengthwise into eight pieces (cut into quarters, then each quarter in half again), and then cut each piece into 1/4-inch slices. You will have about 6 cups of eggplant. Place half on a large microwave-safe plate and drizzle with 1 tablespoon water. Microwave on high for 2 minutes, or until the pieces start to soften. Transfer the slices to a medium bowl, and repeat with the remaining eggplant.

3 To make the stew, heat the olive oil in a large heavy-bottomed saucepan over medium heat until shimmering. Add the onion, garlic, and 1/4 teaspoon of the salt. Cook, stirring occasionally, until the onion is light golden with a few brown edges, about 8 minutes. Stir in the parsnips, eggplant, and cinnamon and cook, stirring, until fragrant, about 1 minute. Stir in the tomato paste and cook for 1 minute.

4 Add the canned tomatoes with their juices, scraping the bottom of the saucepan to release any browned bits. Add the broth, raisins, sun-dried tomatoes, pepper, and the remaining 1/4 teaspoon salt and bring to a boil. Decrease the heat to maintain a simmer, cover, and cook until the eggplant is soft and the parsnips are tender, 20 to 25 minutes, stirring once or twice.

5   To finish, stir in the farro and season with the sugar. Add a bit more water to thin, if you like. Taste and adjust for salt and pepper. Remove from the heat, drizzle with the olive oil, and let sit for 3 minutes. Garnish with the parsley and serve in deep plates, spooning some yogurt on top or on the side.

TO GET A HEAD START: Make the farro, as in step 1, ahead (see page 23). The stew can be prepared up to 3 days ahead. Chill, covered.

TO VARY IT: Add $1^1/_2$ cups cooked bulgur or wheat berries instead of farro (for cooking instructions, see pages 24–25). Or, for a speedy, light dish, omit the farro and serve with a baguette or sourdough bread. In addition, you can stir in $1^1/_2$ cups cooked chickpeas (one 15-ounce can) in step 4 together with the tomatoes, and thin with a bit more water if needed.

TO MAKE IT VEGETARIAN: Just use vegetable broth instead of beef broth.

ROASTED PROSCIUTTO ROLLS WITH FIGS AND ROSEMARY

These packages deliver all you could ask for in one mouthwatering bite: sweet and salty, crisp and crunchy. They will disappear the moment you set them on the table. Best of all, they are a cinch to assemble. On a chilly day, pair them for brunch with the hearty Aroma Bread with Coriander and Fennel (page 74). Or serve the rolls as an appetizer, for example with the Fire-Roasted Tomato Stew with Eggplant and Farro (page 126). Don't skimp on the oil here, as prosciutto can dry out fast under the broiler. If your figs are very large, use only half a fig per roll. MAKES 8 ROLLS, TO SERVE 4

8 dried figs, preferably Greek or Turkish, stemmed
8 thin slices prosciutto (4 ounces)
1 teaspoon minced fresh rosemary
Freshly ground black pepper
8 toasted walnut halves (see page 37)
Extra-virgin olive oil, for brushing

1   Position a rack on the lowest shelf of the oven, about 4 inches from the bottom, and preheat to 375°F. Thoroughly brush a small rimmed baking sheet with olive oil, or coat with cooking spray.

2   Place the figs in a small bowl and cover with hot water for 10 to 15 minutes. Drain and pat dry.

3   Arrange the prosciutto slices side by side on a work surface. Sprinkle with the rosemary and season well with pepper. Slice the figs in half, but not all the way through, so they can be opened up like a book. Put a walnut half in the center of each and close. Place 1 fig on the bottom third of each prosciutto slice and roll up, using a toothpick to fasten the package. Transfer to the baking sheet.

4   Brush the prosciutto rolls generously with olive oil, or coat with cooking spray. Roast for a total of 5 to 7 minutes, until the prosciutto is crisp and browned, turning once, using tongs, and brushing or spraying halfway through. Serve at once.

TO GET A HEAD START: The prosciutto rolls, up through step 3, can be prepared 2 hours ahead. Set aside at room temperature.

TO VARY IT: Use large pitted dried prunes instead of figs.

Barley: Mild and Adventurous

Barley is central to the cultural fabric of Bavaria, the southern German state in which I spent my teenage years, yet many Bavarians have not tasted the grain in a meal since World War II. Locals are devoted to the grain. They like to recite a hymn to barley: "*Hopfen und Malz, Gott erhalt's,*" translated as "hops and malt, may God preserve it." But the malt they rave about is the sprouted and dry-roasted barley used in making beer.

Bavarians *love* beer. Locals have it at all times of the day, for breakfast, lunch, and dinner—and as a snack in between. They drink it in huge beer halls during the cold season, and in lush beer gardens under the wide canopy of trees in the summer. Munich is the self-declared "beer capital of the world." But despite the fact that I was raised in its suburbs, after my father's job posting in Greece ended and we moved back to Germany, I remained pretty aloof from the all-encompassing beer culture around me.

Then one day my neighbor and friend Hildegard served the grain barley to me for the first time. I was in my mid-twenties, and she had come over with a home-cooked meal. I didn't even know you could eat the grain. Barley is for beer production, isn't it? Why would anyone consider cooking with the crop? Then I was drawn in by the faint earthy aroma, unfamiliar to me, wafting from my plate. Earlier in the day, she had bought crisp summer zucchini at the farmers' market. She had cut them in half lengthwise, hollowed them out, and prepared a filling from coarsely milled barley. The grits were first cooked and combined with sautéed onions, a medley of herbs, and a mild farmer's cheese. Hildegard then baked the zucchini until the cheese in their grain-filled centers melted and its ingredients melded into a light, mouthwatering summer dish. This left me longing for more.

I have since discovered the dual faces of barley. Many people are familiar with pearl or pearled barley in a hearty stew, simmered with spicy sausages, richly flavored beef, or smoked ham hock. Barley is a sucker, so to speak—it will absorb any flavors and sauce from its surroundings and flourish. The result is a supremely comforting soup or stew with character, perfect for the cold winter months.

On Greek islands, whole barley is coarsely milled for rustic loaves that are double-baked into thick farm-style rusks. It has the color of café au lait, so fittingly described by Greek-food expert and author Diane Kochilas. Until a generation ago, locals would eat this tough bread for breakfast, mellowed by dipping in wine. Today these crude rusks are often served as a bread salad, first briefly soaked in water and then combined with tomatoes, olives, and feta cheese, drizzled with olive oil. I remember carrying the dark rusks with me while hiking across islands in Greece—as part of a rustic picnic, eaten on top of a mountain overlooking the sun-drenched Aegean Sea. We also packed feta cheese, olives, and boiled eggs, as well as juicy tomatoes and fresh grapes. On lucky days, we were able to marry the rusks with fresh goat cheese, bought by the side of the road. A farmer would hang his cheese baskets on a clothesline in the yard, swinging in the wind to ripen and for wandering tourists to see.

To me, there is also a sweet, ambrosial character to this ancient grain. With its unobtrusive mildness, it pairs exquisitely with soft, tender vegetables like zucchini, eggplant, and squash of all kinds. Barley's inviting, delicate flavor also makes it splendid for desserts. A sweetened porridge, often made from barley and called *belila* by Sephardic Jews, is one luscious example. In Britain, people cherish barley pudding, dotted with currants and served with cream. It's a gratifying treat, divine in its simplicity. I also like to use the flour in ethereal holiday cookies, spruced up with candied orange peel and almonds.

One of my favorite barley dishes is a bread enhanced with walnuts, finely chopped rings of leek caramelized in butter and beer. The result is a memorable loaf, with a balmy sweetness that defies its heartiness. Maybe the beer culture of Bavaria did, after all, have an impact on a school kid imported from Greece.

CHAPTER 4

BURGERS, SAVORY CAKES, & MORE

Everyone loves finger food. At its most appealing, the classic Greek appetizer platter *meze* comes with tiny beef kebabs, melting cheese fritters, hot zucchini cakes, and more—whatever the chef dreams up that day. Whole grains, with their distinct flavors and textures, expand this sensory universe. Think juicy lamb burgers with bulgur, or bright oatcakes with crunchy pine nuts, Brie, and aromatic sun-dried tomatoes. By making grain cakes you are reviving a succulent "leftover" tradition. After all, they were a natural innovation by frugal homemakers who wanted to serve their families something delicious instead of the same old grain from the night before.

Here's all you need to create a myriad of new burgers, fritters, and grain cakes: combine leftover grains with minced meat, fish, or cheese. Add herbs, spices, eggs, and a binder, if needed. Mash, shape, and pan-fry: your super-fast dinner is ready. Don't forget the ketchup and the mustard. This is fast food first-class. Any way you roll or shape them, these moist bites are also great party food. But don't ever call them whole grain patties, that's so twentieth-century.

Smelling Cows and Cutlets

Of all the senses we use to navigate through life, the sense of smell is most central to my being. My nose leads the way, whether I like it or not. As a five-year-old in Greece, I remember being hypnotized by the heavenly smell of a dark blue ball of heavy-duty rubber. I have never been able to understand why I was so mesmerized by this unusual scent, which I can recall to this day. But transfixed I was. As a teenager, the capability of my nose became the envy, and joke, of my friends. I was able to distinguish the perfumes my girlfriends were wearing. I fell head over heels for someone just because he smelled divine. And I could blindly tell cheeses, spices, and flowers apart—later to be followed by wine and any other food. To this day, I always know what my neighbors are having for dinner—even through brick walls.

Most of my life, this heightened sense of smell has served me well. Only on occasion has my hypersensitive olfactory organ been a cause for sorrow, especially when traveling in some of my favorite countries in Asia and the Middle East. Imagine crossing a road in New Delhi, for example: Sacred cows relieve themselves anywhere and everywhere. Auto rickshaws spew acidic clouds of black fumes. And dark corners at night become, well, I don't need to get into details. It is in those moments that I believe I suffer more than anyone on the planet. The only consolation: nasal rewards are never far from those plain stinky moments. There are street vendors hawking their freshly fried samosas. Others offering hot, spicy potato "cutlets," aka savory cakes—not to forget my favorite pastry wallahs, who boil down gallons of sweet milk in huge iron vats for the preparation of traditional Indian sweets. I can detect them miles, okay, yards away.

I understood early on that my sensitive nose served me best in my favorite pastime, cooking and baking. Otherwise I never paid much attention to it; after all, I was used to my "super-nose." That all changed a few years ago, when I read an enchanting story by Monica Bhide in the *Washington Post*. In it she describes never being allowed to taste food while cooking for her Hindu family. In fact, she learned to add the correct amount of spices just by sight and smell. The reason: her grandmother insisted that the first serving of food be reserved for the gods—in this case via the revered street cows, for whom a plate of freshly cooked food was left outside the house each night. While I was raised not as a Hindu but by a Greek Orthodox mother and a Catholic German dad, I realized that I don't taste the food I cook either! I almost never take a spoonful of this, or a bite of that. Instead, I navigate through all my cooking with my nose on top of the stove. And until that instant, I had been completely unaware of this curious habit.

The effect of cooking by scent is twofold: by inhaling the potent aromas a dish releases, I am almost always able to tell what's missing—except salt, that is. I know when dinner needs a dash more cayenne or a hint of cumin. I smell when the mussels could benefit from a tad more wine, or a handful of fresh tomatoes to balance their rich sauce. Most of all, though, I relish the unintended effect of cooking with my nose: instant relaxation. As meat or fish, herbs and spices, vegetables and grains meld their many aromas, they build a castle of steam so rich and powerful that it bolts me in place when I open the lid of my pot. Breathing in the perfect blend of spices, the addictive fragrance of caramelized onions, the enticing marriage of carrots and tomatoes in a wine-braised lamb stew is rewarding, before I taste a single spoonful. It is then that I can feel the weight of my workday falling off, my body's tense muscles unwinding, and the stress of the day waning.

And when baking, it is my nose, not the timer, that reports the exact moment when biscotti turn golden, that informs me of the instant to check on the Tangerine-Lavender Coffee Cake (page 61), that tells me the almonds are toasted just right. No need to wait for the timer to go off. No need to gauge by eyesight. My nose is almost always right. The only lesson I had to learn: when the sublime aroma of butter cookies reaches my nostrils, *run*. Stay put just a few more moments, and the long-awaited sweets will be beyond repair.

GRAIN BURGER BASICS

Nothing beats grain cakes and burgers when you have leftover grain from last night's dinner. Instead of reheating the grain, which can be oh-so-boring, use it to create a flavorful new centerpiece of a meal, or make it into an innovative side—this is how grain cakes were invented in the first place. The recipes in this chapter are meant to inspire you and generally work best when you use leftover grain, or cook the grain the night before. Before long, you will come up with your own creations.

If you are not familiar with making whole grain cakes and burgers, give yourself a break if they don't turn out perfect the first time around. As with all cooking, it does take a bit of practice to form a grain burger so that it retains its shape and doesn't fall apart when cooked or flipped. Here are some tricks to help you along:

- If you have time, make your grains the night before (when not using leftover grains). Chilling hardens the starch in grains—it's called retrogradation—which makes it easier to shape them into burgers or cakes. The starches will soften again when heated.

- Don't shape grain burgers into roundish mounds. They will hold up better if they are formed instead into flat cakes shaped like a car tire, an even thickness all around.

- Most grain cakes hold up better when chilled for 30 minutes, which also means you can make them ahead, often up to 6 hours. So don't skip this step, especially when you are still practicing the shaping. Plus, start with a smaller size, by making, for example, twelve smaller 2-inch burgers instead of eight larger ones.

- Chopping add-ins such as onions and sun-dried tomatoes finely (about 1/8 inch dice) also helps the mixture to come and stay together.

- And last but not least, always use a gentle hand when turning the burgers in the pan or on the baking sheet.

Over the years, I have tried many different cooking methods to coax the most flavor out of whole grain cakes and fritters. I believe nothing beats pan-frying in a bit of olive oil in a cast-iron skillet. This browning in a little fat unlocks their flavors beautifully, and it's also what my Greek grandmother always did, albeit using olive oil by the truckload. One more plus for the diet-conscious: I have noticed that I actually eat less of pan-fried cakes compared to baked ones—I find them more satisfying.

However, if you wish, by all means bake your grain patties in a preheated 425°F oven. Place them on a well-oiled baking sheet, brush the tops with olive oil or spray with cooking spray, and bake for 10 to 14 minutes on each side or until they are nicely browned, turning them carefully once and brushing or spraying with oil again.

All grain cakes, including the buckwheat-feta burgers and the quinoa cakes, are perfect for a party buffet, as they can be prepared ahead and served at room temperature. When serving them this way, I like to shrink them for bite-size appeal.

Instead of 8 large burgers or cakes, you can prepare 16 smaller cakes about 2 inches in diameter, or 32 for the zucchini-dill bites (page 141). Once you have divided the grain mixture inside the bowl into eight equal portions, form 2 cakes (instead of 1) out of each portion. Pan-fry, as directed, about 3 minutes on each side. Or bake as described above, 7 to 10 minutes on each side, or until golden brown.

Brie Cakes with Sun-Dried Tomatoes

These richly flavorful cakes reveal pockets of oozing Brie, and burst with the aroma of Mediterranean herbs and sun-dried tomatoes. The cakes, naturally sweet with two kinds of oats, are also perfect finger food, served as part of a buffet. Look for firm (not soft and oozing) Brie when shopping for this recipe; it will be easier to cut. And leave the rind on. Add a bit of the richly flavored oil from the sun-dried tomatoes to the olive oil in the pan for extra aroma. **MAKES 8 TO 12 CAKES, TO SERVE 4**

....

OATS

1 1/2 cups water

3/4 cup steel-cut oats

CAKES

2 ounces firm Brie, cut into
  1/4-inch cubes (about 1/2 cup)

1 1/2 cups quick-cooking oats
  (not old-fashioned rolled oats)

1/2 cup finely chopped red onion
  (about 1/2 onion)

1/3 cup well-drained and chopped
  oil-packed sun-dried tomatoes
  (see page 138)

1/3 cup toasted pine nuts
  (see page 37)

2 large eggs, lightly beaten

1 tablespoon minced fresh rosemary,
  or 1 teaspoon dried

1 tablespoon minced fresh sage,
  or 1 teaspoon dried

1 to 2 teaspoons minced fresh red
  Thai chile (optional)

1/2 teaspoon fine sea salt

1/4 teaspoon freshly ground black
  pepper

YOGURT-KETCHUP SAUCE, AND TO FINISH

1 cup plain whole-milk yogurt

2 tablespoons ketchup

1/2 hot red chile, cut into small rings, or
  1 teaspoon Asian chile sauce such as sriracha

Fine sea salt

2 tablespoons extra-virgin olive oil

1 To prepare the oats, bring the water and oats to a boil in a 2-quart saucepan. Cook, uncovered, for 2 minutes over medium to medium-low heat, stirring a few times. Remove from the heat, cover, and let sit at room temperature until the liquid is absorbed, about 1 hour. Transfer the oats to a large bowl and spread to cool for about 10 minutes.

2 To make the cakes, add the Brie and all the remaining ingredients to the bowl with the oats. Using your hands, thoroughly combine the mixture until the ingredients come together.

3 Level the mixture inside the bowl and divide it into 8 equal portions using a butter knife (cut in half like a cake, and then each half into quarters). Moisten your hands with water and form cakes about 3 inches in diameter. Place the cakes on a small baking sheet or large plate.

4 To make the sauce, combine the yogurt, ketchup, and red chile in a small bowl. Season with salt to taste.

5 To finish, heat 1 tablespoon of the olive oil in a large skillet over medium heat until it shimmers. Add 4 cakes and cook 4 to 5 minutes on each side or until golden brown, carefully turning once with a metal spatula. Add the remaining 1 tablespoon olive oil and repeat with the second batch. Serve warm or at room temperature, together with the yogurt-ketchup sauce.

TO GET A HEAD START: Make the oats, as in step 1, ahead (see page 23). The cakes, up through step 3, can be prepared 6 hours ahead. Chill, covered.

TO LIGHTEN IT UP: Bake the burgers instead of pan-frying (see page 133).

Lamb Burgers with Bulgur and Mint

These are the richly spiced juicy meatballs of the Middle East, often prepared with lamb, known as *kofta*. Bulgur gives them texture; cumin and a hint of cinnamon are classic seasonings. I serve them with a garlic-spiked yogurt (the Greek in me adds four cloves per cup of yogurt), but ketchup or mustard can top them off as well. Or vary with any of the other yogurt toppings, such as the Spicy Yogurt Topping (page 111), the Yogurt-Ketchup Sauce (page 134), or the lemony yogurt dip (page 141) replacing the fresh dill with mint to fit the bill. **MAKES 6 BURGERS, TO SERVE 6**

BULGUR

3/4 cup medium-coarse or coarse bulgur

1 1/2 cups hot water

BURGERS

1 pound ground lamb

1 cup grated yellow onion (about 1 medium)

1/2 cup finely chopped fresh mint

1/4 cup finely chopped fresh flat-leaf parsley

2 cloves garlic, minced

1 tablespoon ground cumin

1 teaspoon freshly ground black pepper

1 teaspoon fine sea salt

1/2 teaspoon ground cinnamon

1/2 teaspoon Aleppo pepper (see page 117), or 2 pinches cayenne pepper

1 Place the bulgur in a large bowl and cover with the hot water. Let sit at room temperature until much of the water is absorbed and the kernels are tender with a bit of chew, 20 to 30 minutes. Drain the bulgur in a fine-mesh sieve, pressing on the kernels with your hands to squeeze out as much water as you can.

2 Position a rack about 6 inches from the heat and preheat the broiler. Oil a 12-inch cast-iron skillet or the bottom of a broiler pan.

3 Return the bulgur to the bowl; add the lamb and all remaining ingredients. Combine the mixture thoroughly but gently with your hands, trying to handle as little as possible. Shape into 6 voluptuous burgers, each about 3 inches in diameter, and place them in a single layer in the prepared skillet or broiler pan.

4 To finish, brush the burgers with olive oil and broil until they start browning on the top, about 10 minutes. Flip using a metal spatula, brush with oil again, and broil until nicely browned, about 5 more minutes. Allow to sit for a few minutes—as the meat cools you will be better able to taste the herbs and spices.

TO GET A HEAD START: You can soak and drain the bulgur, as in step 1, a day ahead. Chill, covered. The burgers can be shaped up to 6 hours ahead. Place on a small baking sheet or a large plate, cover with plastic wrap, and chill.

TO LIGHTEN IT: Have your butcher grind leg of lamb for leaner burgers. Brush the burgers generously with oil and broil a little less, about 12 minutes total.

TO VARY IT: For a flavor boost, brush minted olive oil butter (page 116) or rosemary oil (page 89) on the burgers instead of olive oil.

Buckwheat-Feta Burgers with Tangy Parsley Sauce

Buckwheat, a mild, quick-cooking staple much loved in eastern Europe, gets a Mediterranean twist in these succulent meatless burgers, seasoned with briny feta cheese and thyme. Drizzled with Tangy Parsley Sauce, these fragrant burgers can stand on their own. Or serve on slim whole wheat rolls with lettuce, onion, and tomato. Be sure to choose a mild feta to allow the sweet, grassy flavor of buckwheat to shine. **MAKES 8 BURGERS, TO SERVE 4**

....

BUCKWHEAT

1³/4 cups water

1 cup raw buckwheat groats
   (not kasha)

¹/4 teaspoon fine sea salt

TANGY PARSLEY SAUCE

1 cup lightly packed fresh flat-leaf
   parsley, rinsed and patted dry

1 tablespoon freshly squeezed
   lemon juice

1 teaspoon red wine vinegar

4 cloves garlic, peeled

1 teaspoon dried crumbled oregano

¹/2 teaspoon fine sea salt

¹/4 teaspoon red pepper flakes
   (optional)

A few drops of Tabasco sauce

3 tablespoons extra-virgin olive oil

BURGERS

4 ounces mild feta cheese, crumbled
   (about 1 cup)

¹/2 cup finely chopped yellow onion
   (about ¹/2 medium onion)

6 tablespoons quick-cooking oats
   (not old-fashioned rolled oats)

1 large egg, lightly beaten

2 tablespoons chopped fresh thyme,
   or 2 teaspoons dried

¹/2 teaspoon Aleppo pepper (see page 117),
   or 1 teaspoon paprika

¹/4 teaspoon freshly ground black pepper

¹/8 teaspoon dried red pepper flakes

2 tablespoons extra-virgin olive oil

1   To prepare the buckwheat, bring the water, buckwheat, and salt to a boil in a 2-quart saucepan. Decrease the heat to maintain a simmer, cover, and cook until the water is absorbed, about 15 minutes. Remove from the heat, cover, and let sit for 5 to 10 minutes. Transfer the buckwheat to a large bowl and spread to cool for about 20 minutes.

2   Meanwhile, prepare the parsley sauce. Process all the ingredients except the olive oil in a mini-food processor until minced. Slowly add the olive oil and blend to combine.

3   To make the burgers, add all the ingredients except the olive oil to the bowl with the buckwheat. Using your hands, thoroughly combine, and squish the mixture to bring it together.

4   Level the mixture inside the bowl and divide it into 8 equal portions using a butter knife (cut in half like a cake, and then each half into quarters). Moisten your hands with water and form burgers about 3 inches in diameter, pressing firmly to ensure they hold together. Place the burgers on a small baking sheet or large plate.

5   To finish, heat 1 tablespoon of the olive oil in a large skillet over medium heat until it shimmers. Cook 4 burgers at a time, carefully turning once with a metal spatula, about 4 minutes on each side, until golden brown. Add the remaining 1 tablespoon olive oil and repeat with the second batch. Serve warm or at room temperature, accompanied by the parsley sauce.

TO GET A HEAD START: Make the buckwheat, as in step 1, ahead (see page 23). Or use about 3 cups cooked leftover buckwheat (for cooking instructions, see page 24). The burgers, up through step 4, can be prepared up to 6 hours ahead. Chill, covered.

OIL-PACKED SUN-DRIED TOMATOES WITH HERBS

During the many rounds of recipe testing for this book, more than one of my testers remarked warily that oil-packed sun-dried tomatoes taste somewhat underwhelming, or that they simply didn't like them very much. This surprised me. Of course, not everyone has been raised in Greece or Italy, where these flavorful treats are popped in the mouth like nature's candy. But then it hit me: I never buy ready-made oil-packed sun-dried tomatoes in jars. I always reconstitute dry-packed sun-dried tomatoes and marinate them myself to have a steady supply on hand, especially during the dark winter months when I crave a bite of summer.

Oil-packed sun-dried tomatoes are rich in savory umami flavor. Easy to make, they are terrific on sandwiches. I use them also as colorful enrichment for many salads, such as the Leek Salad with Grilled Haloumi Cheese and Rye Berries (page 92). Or serve them as a party nibble, drizzled with a bit of balsamic vinegar, next to an assortment of cheeses, olives, and dried apricots with slices of rustic whole grain bread such as the German-style Aroma Bread with Coriander and Fennel (page 74).

Oil-packing your own sun-dried tomatoes adds two prized ingredients to your cooking: aromatic tomato soaking liquid and richly flavorful tomato-infused olive oil. Use the oil and the soaking liquid, for example, in the Fire-Roasted Tomato Stew with Eggplant and Farro (page 126). The oil will also give a twist to homemade salad dressing, or add it to tomato-based pasta sauce to boost flavor, or simply drizzle it over fresh bread. For an appetizer, slice vine-ripened tomatoes, top with slices of feta or a mild goat cheese, garnish with fresh oregano or thyme, and drizzle with tomato oil. The soaking liquid can be frozen, or stored in the fridge for up to 5 days. I replace some of the broth in soups, stews, and sauces with it. Sometimes, when it's not too salty, I just drink it. My mom does that, of course—where else would I get such an idea? MAKES 1 CUP

TOMATOES

1 cup dry-packed sun-dried tomatoes
(about 1½ ounces)

1 cup boiling water

1 tablespoon balsamic vinegar

TO FINISH

2½ teaspoons herbes de Provence
(for sources, see page 219), or use
Mediterranean Herb Mixture below

3 to 4 cloves garlic, thinly sliced

¼ teaspoon freshly ground black pepper

⅛ teaspoon red pepper flakes (optional)

Fine sea salt

½ cup or more extra-virgin olive oil,
depending on the size of the jar or
container used

1   Place the tomatoes in a small bowl and top
with the boiling water. Stir in the balsamic
vinegar and set aside to steep until the tomatoes are soft and plump, about 15 minutes. Try
one—a bite will also tell you how salty your
tomatoes are. Drain the tomatoes, reserving the
soaking liquid for another use.

2   To finish, leave the tomatoes whole (if you like
to serve them as an appetizer), or chop and
return them to the bowl. Add the herbes de
Provence, garlic, pepper, and red pepper, and

stir to combine. Taste for salt and pepper,
and adjust. Spoon the tomatoes into a half-
pint Mason jar or other small glass container.
Carefully pour in enough olive oil to cover the
tomatoes completely. Using a clean spoon,
gently push any protruding tomatoes into the
oil. Chill, covered, for at least 2 hours and up
to 1 day, to allow the flavors to come together.
Bring to room temperature before serving. Use
the tomatoes within 1 week. The olive oil will
solidify, but will become liquid again at room
temperature. Always use clean utensils when
removing the tomatoes, and cover the remaining ones with more olive oil to create a seal.

MEDITERRANEAN HERB MIXTURE

1 teaspoon fennel seeds

1 teaspoon dried thyme

½ teaspoon dried marjoram

¼ teaspoon dried lavender buds

1   Combine all ingredients in a small bowl and use
for the recipe above (instead of 2½ teaspoons
herbes de Provence). Multiply the ingredients as
needed, and store the herb mixture in a small
jar in a cool dark place for up to 6 months.

Quinoa Cakes with Smoked Trout and Lime Mayonnaise

Moist chunks of smoked trout brightened with lime, serrano chile, and cilantro are a natural foil for the delicate flavor of quinoa. True, this recipe is inspired more by the lush flavors of the Americas than by those of the Mediterranean. Yet these whole grain cakes are so irresistible, I *had* to introduce them to you. Serve these quinoa cakes with lime mayonnaise over salad greens as a light main course. They are also terrific as small party bites. **MAKES 8 CAKES, TO SERVE 4**

....

QUINOA

1¹/4 cups water

³/4 cup quinoa, well rinsed and drained

LIME MAYONNAISE

¹/2 cup mayonnaise

2 teaspoons freshly squeezed lime juice

1 teaspoon finely grated lime zest

¹/4 teaspoon minced serrano chile (remove veins and seeds for less heat)

CAKES

¹/2 pound smoked trout, skinned and torn into ¹/2-inch pieces (about 1¹/2 cups)

¹/2 cup finely chopped green onions (about 3)

¹/2 cup finely chopped cilantro leaves

6 tablespoons plain dry whole wheat or regular bread crumbs

2 large eggs, lightly beaten

1 to 2 teaspoons minced serrano chile (remove veins and seeds for less heat)

1 teaspoon finely grated lime zest

¹/2 teaspoon ancho chile powder

¹/4 teaspoon freshly ground black pepper

¹/4 teaspoon fine sea salt

2 tablespoons extra-virgin olive oil

1 To prepare the quinoa, bring the water and the quinoa to a boil in a 2-quart saucepan. Decrease the heat to maintain a simmer, cover, and cook until the water is absorbed, 10 to 15 minutes. Remove from the heat and let sit, covered, for 5 to 10 minutes. Transfer the quinoa to a large bowl and spread to cool for about 20 minutes.

2 Meanwhile, prepare the mayonnaise. In a small bowl, combine the mayonnaise, lime juice and zest, and the serrano chile. Chill, covered, until ready to serve.

3 To make the cakes, add all the ingredients except the olive oil to the bowl with the quinoa. Using your hands, thoroughly combine, and squeeze the mixture to bring it together.

4 Level the mixture inside the bowl and divide into 8 equal portions using a butter knife (cut in half like a cake, and then each half into quarters). Moisten your hands with water and form cakes about 3 inches in diameter, pressing firmly to ensure they hold together. Place the cakes on a small baking sheet or large plate. If you have time, chill, covered with plastic wrap, for 30 minutes.

5 To finish, heat 1 tablespoon of the olive oil in a large skillet over medium heat until it shimmers. Cook 4 cakes at a time until golden brown, carefully turning once with a metal spatula, about 4 minutes on each side. Add the remaining 1 tablespoon olive oil and repeat with the second batch. Serve warm or at room temperature, together with the mayonnaise.

TO GET A HEAD START: Make the quinoa, as in step 1, ahead (see page 23).

TO LIGHTEN IT UP: Use lowfat mayonnaise or lowfat Greek yogurt instead of regular mayonnaise to make the lime mayonnaise. Bake the burgers instead of pan-frying them (see page 133).

Zucchini-Dill Bites with Pine Nuts

From my Greek mom I inherited a passion for dill, an herb I consider much underappreciated in the United States. This spidery kitchen green livens up many dishes—as in these small oven-baked zucchini cakes. I like serving them with smoked salmon and a lemony yogurt dip, or, for vegetarians, with cubed feta cheese and olives. **MAKES 8 CAKES, TO SERVE 4**

ZUCCHINI BITES

1 pound zucchini (3 small zucchini or 2 medium)

1/2 teaspoon fine sea salt

1/2 medium-size yellow onion, cut into chunks

3/4 cup loosely packed fresh dill

1/4 cup loosely packed fresh basil

3/4 teaspoon dried thyme

1/4 cup pine nuts

1 clove garlic, peeled

1 large egg, lightly beaten

1/2 cup plain dry whole wheat bread crumbs

1/4 teaspoon freshly ground black pepper

LEMONY YOGURT DIP

1 cup plain whole-milk Greek yogurt

2 tablespoons chopped fresh dill

2 teaspoons freshly squeezed lemon juice

Fine sea salt and freshly ground black pepper

1 to 2 teaspoons extra-virgin olive oil

1. To prepare the zucchini bites, shred the zucchini in a food processor using the shredding disk. You should have about 4 cups. Place the shredded zucchini in a sieve, toss with the salt, and set aside to drain for 20 to 30 minutes. Do not clean the processor bowl yet.

2. Position a rack in the center of the oven and preheat to 425°F. Brush a large rimmed baking sheet with olive oil or coat with cooking spray.

3. Fit the food processor with the steel blade and add the onion, dill, basil, thyme, pine nuts, and garlic to the bowl of the processor. Process until finely chopped, about 8 seconds, scraping down the bowl once halfway through. Transfer the ingredients to a large bowl.

4. Wrap the zucchini in a clean dish towel and twist to wring out as much liquid as possible. You should have about 2 cups. Add the zucchini to the bowl as well. Stir in the egg, 1/4 cup of the bread crumbs, and the pepper; mix gently, using your hands or a fork, until combined. Level the mixture inside the bowl and divide it into 8 equal portions using a knife (cut in half like a cake, and then each half into quarters) and form into 21/2 by 1/2-inch cakes.

5. Spread the remaining 1/4 cup bread crumbs on a shallow plate. Press each cake into the bread crumbs to coat on both sides.

6. Transfer the cakes to the prepared baking sheet and gently brush on top with olive oil or coat with cooking spray. Bake until the zucchini cakes are golden brown, about 25 minutes, turning once and brushing or spraying in between.

7. While the cakes are baking, prepare the yogurt dip. Beat the yogurt in a small bowl with a fork until smooth. Add the dill and lemon juice. Season with salt and pepper. Just before serving, drizzle with the olive oil.

8. Serve the zucchini cakes warm, accompanied by the dip.

TO VARY IT: For parties, you can shrink these dill bites further to make fantastic one-bite appetizers. My trusted recipe tester, Karen, served her guests 32 tiny cakes using 1 slightly heaped tablespoon of the mixture per piece; bake these mini-bites for 20 minutes, turning once.

Crispy Brown Rice Cakes with Green Olives, Pecorino, and Sage

The beauty of brown rice is its mild nutty character, a godsend for creative home cooks. Use this recipe as inspiration for a myriad of finger-licking rice cakes—perfect for leftovers. I typically choose short-grain brown rice, but a medium-grain brown rice works equally well. Delicious with ketchup and a dash of Asian hot chile sauce, or with a bit of Indian *chile achar*, a spicy condiment I haven't been able to live without ever since I spent a year working in India (for sources, see page 219).

Serve the rice cakes with oven-baked chicken drumsticks or as a light main, next to a salad of Boston bibb lettuce with lemon-olive oil dressing. Vegetarians may pair them with warm tomato sauce (page 68). **MAKES 8 CAKES, TO SERVE 4**

....

BROWN RICE

1 1/2 cups water

3/4 cups medium- or short-grain brown rice

CAKES, AND TO FINISH

3/4 cup plain dry whole wheat or regular bread crumbs

2 ounces shredded Pecorino Romano *cheese or Greek* kefalotiri, *using the large holes of a box grater (about 3/4 cup)*

1/2 cup finely chopped green onions (about 3)

1/4 cup finely chopped pitted green olives

2 large eggs, lightly beaten

1 tablespoon minced fresh sage, or 1 teaspoon dried

1 teaspoon minced hot green chile, such as serrano (optional)

1/2 teaspoon fine sea salt

1/4 teaspoon freshly ground black pepper

2 tablespoons extra-virgin olive oil

1 To prepare the rice, bring the water and rice to a boil in a 2-quart saucepan with a tight-fitting lid. Decrease the heat to maintain a simmer, cover, and cook until the rice is tender and the water is absorbed, 40 to 45 minutes. Remove from the heat, cover, and let sit for 5 to 10 minutes. Transfer the rice to a large bowl and spread to cool for about 10 minutes.

2 Meanwhile, spread 1/2 cup of the bread crumbs on a shallow plate. Have a small baking sheet on hand.

3 To make the cakes, add the remaining 1/4 cup bread crumbs and all the remaining ingredients except the olive oil to the bowl with the rice. Using your hands, thoroughly combine the mixture until the ingredients come together. No need to be gentle.

4 Level the mixture inside the bowl and divide using a butter knife into 8 equal portions (cut in half like a cake, and then each half into quarters). Moisten your hands with water and form cakes about 3 inches in diameter. Gently press both sides of each cake into the bread crumbs to coat and place on the baking sheet.

5 To finish, heat 1 tablespoon of the olive oil in a large skillet over medium heat until it shimmers. Cook 4 cakes at a time, carefully turning once with a metal spatula, about 4 minutes on each side, until golden brown. Add the remaining 1 tablespoon olive oil and repeat with the second batch. Serve warm or at room temperature.

TO GET A HEAD START: Make the brown rice, as in step 1, ahead (see page 23). Or use 2 1/4 cups cooked leftover rice (for cooking instructions, see page 25). The cakes can be prepared, up through step 4, as much as 6 hours ahead. Chill, covered.

TO LIGHTEN IT UP: Bake the burgers instead of pan-frying them (see page 133).

Sesame-Crusted Fish Sticks with Yogurt Rémoulade

In Greece sesame seeds adorn cookies, bread sticks, and many a savory pie—inspiring this riff on fish sticks. Grinding the seeds adds a flavor boost and helps them adhere to the crunchy coating of panko bread crumbs. I use thick Greek yogurt for a tangy rémoulade, a fresh take on the classic mayonnaise version. Serve with sautéed spinach or a simple green salad. **MAKES 8 FISH STICKS, TO SERVE 4**

FISH STICKS

1/2 cup sesame seeds, preferably unhulled

3/4 cup whole wheat flour

1 large egg

1/4 cup whole or lowfat milk

1 1/2 cups whole wheat panko bread crumbs

1 pound (3 or 4 pieces) skinless firm white fish fillets such as tilapia, mahi mahi, cod, or halibut

Fine sea salt and freshly ground black pepper

RÉMOULADE, AND TO FINISH

1 cup plain whole-milk Greek yogurt

1/4 cup finely chopped dill, plus 1 tablespoon for garnish

3 tablespoons finely chopped cornichons (about 4)

2 tablespoons nonpareil capers, drained

2 teaspoons Dijon mustard

1 teaspoon honey

Lemon wedges, for serving

1 To make the fish sticks, position 1 rack 6 inches from the heat of the broiler. Position a second rack in the center of the oven and preheat to 375°F. Grease a large baking sheet with olive oil, or spray with cooking spray.

2 Place the sesame seeds in the bowl of a food processor fitted with the steel blade and process until they have the texture of coarse nut meal, about a minute and a half for unhulled seeds (a bit less for hulled). You will have about 2/3 cup ground sesame meal.

3 Have 3 shallow bowls or pie plates ready, one of them large. Spread the whole wheat flour over 1 plate. Put the egg and milk in the second one and lightly beat with a fork to blend. On the large plate, spread the panko bread crumbs and the sesame meal, tossing with your hands to combine.

4 Pat the fish fillets dry with paper towels. Cut each fillet lengthwise into 2 pieces, and season with salt and pepper. Dredge each piece in the flour mixture, shaking off any excess. Dip into the egg mixture, allowing the excess to drip off, and coat with the panko-sesame mixture, pressing gently to adhere all around. Transfer the coated fillets to the prepared baking sheet.

5 Spray the fillets with cooking spray and place the baking sheet on the center rack of the oven. Bake until the fish sticks are opaque throughout, 9 to 13 minutes depending on the thickness (test by piercing the thickest part with a paring knife).

6 Meanwhile, make the rémoulade. Beat the yogurt in a small bowl with a fork until smooth. Add the 1/4 cup dill, cornichons, capers, mustard, and honey, and stir to combine. Garnish with the remaining 1 tablespoon dill.

7 Transfer the baking sheet to a wire rack and spray the fish sticks with cooking spray. Heat the broiler. Place the baking sheet on the top rack and broil the fish sticks until golden brown, 2 to 3 minutes. Watch closely so as not to burn them. Serve right away, with the rémoulade and lemon wedges.

Buckwheat: Bold and Almost Instant

Serve a stack of rustic buckwheat pancakes, dripping with maple syrup, to your guests for brunch—and ask if anyone knows what buckwheat looks like. Chances are, the conversation around the table will go quiet, fast. Or pose the question in a trendy soup spot when you are slurping a rich, meaty broth laced with elegant grayish Japanese soba noodles. Quiet, again. Most of us know little about the tiny seeds that give the earthy flavor and color to the flour in both of these signature dishes. Whenever I take the heart-shaped triangular seed grains to a cooking class, participants examine them with the curiosity reserved for mysterious artifacts unearthed from a prehistoric cave.

Most of all, though, I'm surprised that buckwheat hasn't made any inroads into our time-pressed lives. In this day and age, when we grab instant polenta and quick-cooking parboiled rice, why not buy something that actually cooks fast from scratch? A delicious and hassle-free side, on the table in minutes.

Even I have to admit that buckwheat made its entry into my grain universe rather quietly, unlike some whole grains, which forcefully stamped their distinctive characters into my culinary memory for life. My first chew of wheat berries, for example, hit me like the French *coup de foudre*, love at first sight (or bite). Same with barley. Or teff. Not so with buckwheat. Buckwheat simply snuck up on me—and stayed.

It stayed because buckwheat can be prepared at the speed of light: as fast as you can sear and dish up a steak, this side will be ready. It stayed because it is amazingly versatile. And it stayed because I have learned to appreciate its superb but humble flavor and texture. There is nothing sophisticated about buckwheat, which makes it even more appealing to me. For some, buckwheat is an acquired taste. But then so much of what we have not grown up with is, and just needs another try.

Buckwheat comes to your table in two distinct variations. One is the raw grayish-green seed with a white center, a bit hard to find yet worth seeking out for its mild, earthy flavor with grassy undertones. The other is the aromatic toasted kernel, generally referred to as kasha, which adds a marked roasted sweetness; some even detect hints of cocoa. The seeds of buckwheat have delicate skin and a soft crunch, they are not chewy at all, and they cook up into a comforting side dish cherished in eastern Europe. This makes them appealing when you are just exploring the many faces of whole grains.

My own slow passion for buckwheat started with the raw seed grains. Their subdued mildness allows them to be paired with bold flavors, suited to rich meat and vegetable dishes. German recipes pair buckwheat with robust sauerkraut, white wine, and apples, adding sage, marjoram, and lovage. Eastern Europeans have traditionally eaten it as a staple like rice, as well as baked it into sweet puddings. Russian blini, the famous small pancakes, showcase the darkish flour. So do the Italian *pizzoccheri* pasta, the Japanese soba, and the galettes and crepes of Brittany in northern France.

My first experience with toasted buckwheat or kasha, on the other hand, was a disaster. I had simmered the reddish brown seeds in stock, assuming they would turn out similar to their raw cousins—only to find them disintegrating faster then I could turn my back on the pan. I love mush, but this was mush of a different order. It tasted plain awful, akin to wet flour. And so kasha, regrettably, fell off my radar screen for years, until I found a simple yet intriguing recipe. In it the kernels were coated in egg before being added to the pan. This made mecurious. An egg coating? Years had passed since my first-class mush. Why not give it another try? You probably know where this is going: the kasha turned out delectably good. The egg-coated kernels stayed nice and firm, the roasted aroma was addictive, and the meal left a mark on my culinary memory. My husband and I devoured the whole skillet (4 servings!) and cooked up another batch a few days later.

CHAPTER 5

PASTA

Mention whole wheat pasta to your friends, and in all likelihood they will look uninterested at best. "Gritty," "overly chewy," and "wheaty" they might moan. I was lucky: my first experience with whole wheat pasta was homemade, prepared from freshly ground wheat berries, made with farmers' market eggs, kneaded and rolled out by hand and left to dry on a wooden noodle board. Yes, those fettuccine were chewier than their refined white counterparts, and no doubt unusual, but mesmerizing. They were hearty, fresh, and full of flavor, like no pasta I had ever eaten.

I don't remember how this fettuccine was served. But the friend who made it was an exquisite home cook. I'm sure she knew the most important secret when preparing assertive whole wheat pasta: serve it with an equally assertive sauce. Rustic? Yes, and superb. Think walnuts, radicchio, and bacon (page 151), or caramelized onions and spicy tuna (page 154). Still a skeptic? Try whole wheat pasta during the holidays with a fragrant blend of roasted chestnuts, hazelnuts, and fried sage leaves (page 156).

For all practical purposes, the recipes in this chapter are written for store-bought pasta. All of my pasta servings are less than the standard amount of one pound of pasta for four people. But rest assured, these recipes will not leave you hungry. For one, whole grain pasta is more nourishing than refined pasta, and will keep you nicely satisfied as a result. In addition, as with all good pasta, some sauces or toppings will make you swoon with deliciously rich ingredients, which satisfy hunger in other ways. I believe in such cases that less is more, so you can eat your cake and still feel good. I'm also including a recipe for homemade fettuccine made from spelt flour (page 159), in case the fancy strikes you on a quiet weekend. It's so worth a try, at least once.

Today's whole wheat pasta has little in common with its harsh-tasting predecessors from the 1970s and 1980s. Be sure to eat your way through different whole grain pasta brands, be they made of whole wheat, Kamut, farro, spelt, or brown rice. Texture and flavor vary greatly from brand to brand, and there are many new varieties on the market. So take your cue from the Italians, who for centuries have enjoyed pasta made from whole grains such as farro and buckwheat. Perhaps you might even detect a hint of cinnamon in farro pasta. Sometimes I swear I do.

My Life with Two Grain Mills

All my life I have prided myself on having a fairly low-tech, European-inspired kitchen—without much clutter, that is. No fancy stand mixers, tabletop grills, or pressure cookers; they only compete for valuable counter space. I love working with my hands in the kitchen. I blend eggplant and cheeses using a fork for Greek appetizers. I chop onions and carrots for salad, and I freshly grind Indian spices in a mortar with a pestle. Most of all, I love kneading dough. I even treasure working by hand the unforgivably dense whole rye sourdough we crave in Germany. What if it tires me out? I don't need to go to the gym, for one, and I get to eat my own oven-fresh bread. In my stubbornness, I resemble my East African–Indian mother-in-law. To this day, she routinely cooks for thirty, slaving in her kitchen for hours, chopping vegetables, meats, and fish with small beaten-up knives and a ridiculously tiny onion chopper. My husband and I offered to buy her a "proper" food processor, but she refused. And we know better than to go over her head.

I admit I have lied a little about my kitchen—because there is one very fancy kitchen tool I do possess. And it is neither low-tech nor small: I own an attractive and sizable German grain mill. In fact, I own two such decadent objects, one on each side of the Atlantic, as I divide my time between the United States and Germany.

And I admit to more: a secret milling obsession. Almost since the time I started using whole grains in my kitchen more than twenty years ago, I have owned a mill. Why such a lavish expense, not to mention the shrunken work space? Because home-ground flour is sublime. It adds a new dimension to the characteristic aromas of whole grains. As a food writer and cooking instructor, I often use store-bought flour to make sure recipes are replicable with perfect results. But sometimes on a weekend, when I power up my mill and bake for pure pleasure, my husband and I will inhale a bite of a scone and wonder, "Wow, why do these taste so different today?" So sweet, so intensely flavorful?

Similar to fruits and vegetables, whole grain flours are most rewarding at their freshest. They are ravishing when used right after grinding. Their rich spell can be lost within hours. And there is more: a grain mill allows you to create layers of texture and flavor in breads, muffins, cookies, pancakes, and more. I use fine pastry flour for delicate cupcakes and coarse rye meal for an intensely satisfying bread. Sometimes, I grind a third of the flour for a bread loaf into coarse rye for its texture and hearty aroma, and churn out the rest as more finely milled whole wheat to help it rise to perfection. At dinner, freshly ground corn makes for polenta heaven, and delicate dumplings from millet spruce up my winter soup. I use mild and earthy barley for ancient flat breads, toasty oatmeal for naturally sweet cookies, nutty whole wheat and slightly sour rye for breads, and balmy rice flour for comforting sweet puddings.

Milling—albeit not by hand but at the push of a button—makes me pause for a moment. Selecting and holding the colorful kernels in my hand before adding them to the hopper, I appreciate their distinct quality and character and the work that goes into growing them. Stone-milling, in countless variations, has been at the center of meals across cultures since our earliest days. And while we rush through our sometimes insanely paced lives today, I find this thought quite comforting. If you are a passionate baker, especially if you love a fresh homemade loaf, this should be your most important appliance.

To this day, I don't own a stand mixer, but I have a mill on each continent. When working in Europe, I still use the first mill I ever bought. It has a powerful engine, assembled in the former East Germany, and an old-fashioned drawer to collect the flour. The more powerful German mill I use in the United States is truly state-of-the-art. It has a beautiful octagonal beechwood casing and traditional millstones for grinding. I can just place a bowl under its spout and start milling with the touch of a finger. All of this makes my heart race and my pulse quicken. I ponder what kind of sweet bread to whip up next.

Farmers' Market Pasta with Heirloom Tomatoes, Rosemary, and Basil

I admit, I cook even when the thermometer hits 90 degrees on a sweltering day in Boston. But I do appreciate the ease of seasonal meals invented by ingenious cooks in hot climates long ago. Raw pasta sauce is one of them. This is a treat with fresh tomatoes from your own garden, or with juicy-ripe heirlooms from a farmers' market. I smell every tomato I buy (Greeks do that!), and only if I get a whiff of their vibrantly sweet, grassy aroma will I add them to my shopping basket. Don't omit the anchovies here, even if the thought of adding them makes you a bit queasy. If you mince the tiny fish they will blend into the sauce, adding a rich undertone that works especially well with heartier whole grain pasta. Start, if you must, by using just half the amount. SERVES 4

RAW TOMATO SAUCE

1¹/₂ pounds vine-ripened heirloom beefsteak or other juicy tomatoes, coarsely chopped

¹/₂ cup Kalamata or other good-quality black olives, pitted and coarsely chopped

¹/₂ cup loosely packed chopped fresh basil leaves

4 oil-packed anchovy fillets, drained and finely minced (about 2 teaspoons)

2 tablespoons nonpareil capers

2 to 3 cloves garlic, minced

1 teaspoon minced fresh rosemary

1 teaspoon minced fresh hot green chile such as serrano (optional)

¹/₂ teaspoon freshly ground black pepper

¹/₄ teaspoon fine sea salt

¹/₄ cup extra-virgin olive oil

PASTA

Fine sea salt

³/₄ pound whole wheat or spelt linguine

2 tablespoons chopped fresh basil leaves, for garnish

Extra-virgin olive oil, for drizzling (optional)

1 First, make the tomato sauce. Place the chopped tomatoes with their juices in a medium bowl. Add all the other ingredients and stir well to combine. Set aside at room temperature for the flavors to meld, at least 30 minutes and up to 2 hours. Taste for salt and pepper and adjust.

2 While the tomatoes are releasing their sweet juices, bring a large pot of water to a rolling boil. Add salt as you see fit and then the pasta, stirring a few times. Return to a boil with the lid on; uncover and cook at a gentle boil until the pasta is al dente, according to the package directions.

3 To finish, drain the pasta and return it to the pot or to a large serving bowl. Pour the tomato sauce over the pasta and toss to combine. Garnish with the remaining 2 tablespoons basil and drizzle with more olive oil, if you like. Serve at once.

TO VARY IT: Homemade Spelt Fettuccine (page 159) are also delicious here if the fancy strikes you.

Fettuccine with Salmon, Tomatoes, and Golden Raisins

Cumin, coriander, and cinnamon play a starring role in this creamy pasta. This trio of spices is as popular in the eastern Mediterranean as it is in India, where my husband's family has its roots—and when you taste it, you will know why. This is a straightforward preparation despite the lengthy ingredients list—perfect for a relaxing Friday night, and festive enough for serving to dinner guests. SERVES 4

PASTA

Fine sea salt

1/2 pound store-bought whole wheat fettuccine, or other flat wide whole grain pasta or Homemade Spelt Fettuccine (page 159)

SALMON TOMATO SAUCE

3/4 pound skinless salmon fillet

2 tablespoons extra-virgin olive oil

1 cup finely chopped red onion (about 1 small)

1/2 teaspoon fine sea salt

1 teaspoon ground coriander

1/2 teaspoon ground cumin

1/4 teaspoon ground cinnamon

1/8 teaspoon cayenne pepper (optional)

1 tablespoon tomato paste

2 cups finely chopped tomatoes (about 2 medium)

1/2 cup dry white wine

1/2 cup heavy whipping cream

1/2 cup water

1/3 cup golden raisins

1 teaspoon sugar

2 tablespoons finely chopped fresh flat-leaf parsley

1   Bring a large pot of water to a rolling boil. Add salt as you see fit and then the pasta, stirring a few times. Return to a boil with the lid on; uncover and cook at a gentle boil until the pasta is al dente, according to the package directions.

2   While the water is coming to a boil, pan-fry the salmon. Pat the salmon fillet dry and season with salt and pepper. Cut in half crosswise to make it easier to handle, if needed. Heat 1 tablespoon of the olive oil in a 12-inch skillet over medium-high until shimmering. Add the salmon and cook for 2 minutes; flip with a metal spatula and cook for 1 to 2 more minutes, depending on the thickness of the fillet (the fish will not be fully cooked). Transfer the salmon to a cutting board. Once it cools off a little, cut the fillet into 1-inch pieces.

3   To make the tomato sauce, reduce the heat to medium and add the remaining 1 tablespoon olive oil to the same skillet. Add the onion and 1/4 teaspoon of the salt, and cook until the onion softens and just starts to turn golden-brown at the edges, about 3 minutes, stirring and scraping the bottom to release any browned bits. Add the coriander, cumin, cinnamon, and cayenne and cook, stirring, until fragrant, about 30 seconds. Stir in the tomato paste and cook until it darkens, about 1 minute. Add the tomatoes and the white wine, bring to a boil, and cook, uncovered, at a lively simmer for 5 minutes. Add the cream, water, golden raisins, and the remaining 1/4 teaspoon salt and return to a boil. Cook, uncovered, with a gentle simmer until slightly thickened, about 5 more minutes. Stir in the sugar. Taste for salt and adjust.

4   When the pasta is almost ready, return the salmon to the skillet to reheat in the sauce, about 2 minutes.

5   To finish, drain the pasta, reserving 1/3 cup of the cooking liquid. Transfer the pasta to a large serving bowl and pour the salmon tomato sauce on top, adding about half of the reserved cooking liquid and gently tossing for about 1 minute to moisten. Add more cooking liquid by the tablespoon, if needed. Garnish with the parsley and serve at once.

TO MAKE IT VEGETARIAN: Replace the salmon with red lentils. Bring 1 cup water and a scant 1/2 cup dried red lentils to a boil in a small saucepan. Decrease the heat to maintain a simmer, cover, and cook until the lentils are tender but still have a slight bite, 7 to 10 minutes. Drain any remaining liquid and stir the lentils into the sauce in step 4.

Spaghetti with Radicchio, Caramelized Shallots, and Bacon

Crimson radicchio, one of my favorite bitter greens, is completely transformed when roasted in the oven or sautéed in a skillet—from a crunchy salad with a hint of bitterness to a wilted beauty, mellow-sweet with haunting toasted flavors, almost worthy of dessert. Here, it works its magic in a whole wheat pasta dish, enveloped by caramelized shallots and earthy mushrooms. For this recipe you should avoid white button mushrooms, as they can release a lot of liquid, preventing caramelization of the shallots. While Italians might choose pancetta, which is not smoked, I prefer smoky bacon to bring these simple flavors together. SERVES 4

....

PASTA

Fine sea salt

1/2 pound whole wheat spaghetti

RADICCHIO MUSHROOM MIXTURE

3/4 pound cremini mushrooms, or a mixture of cremini and shiitake mushrooms

2 ounces smoked bacon, chopped into 1/4-inch pieces (about 1/2 cup)

1 tablespoon extra-virgin olive oil, plus extra as needed

1 shallot, thinly sliced (about 1/4 cup)

1/2 teaspoon fine sea salt

1 small head radicchio, quartered and sliced 1/4 inch wide (about 1/2 pound)

1 clove garlic, minced

1/4 teaspoon freshly ground black pepper

1/2 cup finely grated Parmesan cheese (1 ounce), plus extra for serving

1 Bring a large pot of water to a rolling boil. Add salt as you see fit and then the pasta, stirring a few times. Return to a boil with the lid on; uncover and cook at a gentle boil until the pasta is just short of al dente, according to the package directions.

2 While the water is coming to a boil, cut the cremini mushrooms in half if large, and slice 1/4 inch thick. Remove and discard the shiitake mushroom stems. Cut the caps in half if large, and slice 1/4 inch thick.

3 Cook the bacon in a heavy-bottomed 12-inch skillet over medium heat, stirring occasionally, until lightly browned and crisp, about 5 minutes. Remove the pan from the heat, but leave the bacon in the pan. Add a bit more olive oil to the rendered fat if needed so that you have about 2 tablespoons fat (or drain the bacon fat and use olive oil only).

4 While the pasta is cooking, prepare the radicchio mushroom mixture. Return the same skillet to the burner and heat over medium-high heat. Add the mushrooms, shallots, and 1/4 teaspoon of the salt. Cook, stirring frequently, until the liquid of the mushrooms evaporates and the shallots start to caramelize, about 5 minutes. Add the radicchio and garlic and cook, stirring, until the radicchio shrivels and turns dark auburn, 2 to 3 minutes. Decrease the heat to medium if the radicchio or the garlic starts to burn. Season with the pepper and the remaining 1/4 teaspoon salt. Remove the pan from the heat if the pasta is not ready. Taste for salt and pepper and adjust (I like this quite peppery), but keep in mind that you will still add salty Parmesan cheese.

5 To finish, drain the pasta (but do not shake off the water), reserving 3/4 cup of the cooking liquid. Return the skillet to the burner, add the pasta and a scant 1/2 cup of the reserved cooking liquid, and return to a boil over medium heat. Add the cheese and cook, tossing vigorously and adding a bit more of the cooking liquid if needed, until the pasta is nicely moistened, 1 to 2 minutes. Toss with 1 tablespoon olive oil and serve at once, passing more Parmesan.

TO MAKE IT VEGETARIAN: Omit the bacon and season the vegetables in step 4 with a dash of soy sauce (omitting the additional salt).

Rustic Linguine with Summer Herbs and Olives

When it comes to the use of fresh herbs, my mom shows no restraint. In fact, she uses them by the fistful unlike anyone I know. I envy the skill with which she puts together her improvised garden blends—this pasta is inspired by her passion. Oil allows the flavors to blossom here, so use the best-quality olive oil you can afford. If you like, shave a bit of Parmesan or *Pecorino Romano* cheese on top. Accompany with your favorite salad greens or with a plate of vine-ripened tomatoes, salted a bit to release their juices and drizzled with olive oil for good measure. And if you are in a leisurely mood, you can make your own linguine (as suggested in the recipe for Homemade Spelt Fettuccine, page 159).

SERVES 4

HERB AND OLIVE MIXTURE

1 cup Kalamata or other good-quality black olives, pitted and coarsely chopped

¹/₂ cup finely chopped fresh flat-leaf parsley

¹/₂ cup finely chopped fresh mint

1 tablespoon finely chopped fresh thyme

2 tablespoons drained nonpareil capers

1 to 2 cloves garlic, minced

1 teaspoon minced fresh red Thai chile (optional)

¹/₄ cup extra-virgin olive oil

Fine sea salt

PASTA

Fine sea salt

³/₄ pound whole wheat linguine or spaghetti

1 First, prepare the herb and olive mixture. Place the olives, herbs, capers, garlic, chile, and olive oil in a medium bowl and toss to combine. Salt to taste (keeping in mind that olives and capers might be salty enough). Allow the mixture to sit at room temperature for at least 15 minutes and up to 2 hours, stirring a couple of times, for the flavors to come together.

2 Bring a large pot of water to a rolling boil. Add salt as you see fit and then the pasta, stirring a few times. Return to a boil with the lid on; uncover and cook at a gentle boil until the pasta is al dente, according to the package directions.

3 To finish, drain the pasta and return it to the pot or to a large serving bowl, reserving ¹/₂ cup of the cooking liquid. Add the herb and olive mixture together with a scant ¹/₄ cup of the reserved cooking liquid. Toss vigorously to combine for about 1 minute, adding a tad more cooking liquid to loosen the pasta as needed. Serve at once.

TO GET A HEAD START: The herb and olive mixture, as in step 1, can be prepared 1 day ahead. Chill, covered. Remove it from the fridge when you start to boil the pasta water to take the chill out. I normally don't buy already pitted olives as the pit helps them retain flavor, but if you're in a hurry, please do.

TO LIGHTEN IT UP: You can reduce the amount of olive oil to 2 tablespoons and increase the pasta liquid a bit. But I am a believer in the transformative power of olive oil. So when I feel a need for restraint, I eat a little less pasta—and more salad—rather than cut back on the delicious and satisfying aroma of olive oil.

Spicy Spaghetti with Caramelized Onions, Anchovies, and Tuna

This pasta is one of my pantry-staple favorites. A great last-minute dish, it comes together in the time it takes the pasta to cook. Sweet caramelized onions and tuna balance the salty anchovies and briny capers, a simple everyday feast and a beautiful flavor match for hearty whole wheat pasta. Don't hesitate to use pungent anchovies—they add intense savory richness, and finicky eaters won't be able to see them as they melt into the sauce. I use tuna only as an accent here. By all means, open two cans if you like more fish on your fork. I prefer oil-packed to water-packed tuna for its richer flavor, and—naturally for a transplant from Greece—I always reach for fish packed in olive oil. **SERVES 4**

PASTA

Fine sea salt

3/4 pound whole wheat spaghetti

CARAMELIZED ONIONS
AND TUNA

1 tablespoon extra-virgin olive oil

1 (2-ounce) can oil-packed anchovy fillets, drained, 1 tablespoon of the oil reserved, fillets chopped (about 2 1/2 tablespoons)

1 pound red onions (about 2 medium), thinly sliced into rings

1/4 teaspoon fine sea salt

1 cup chopped green onions (about 7), dark green parts reserved and chopped finely

2 cloves garlic, sliced

1/4 to 1/2 teaspoon red pepper flakes

1 (6-ounce) can oil-packed tuna, drained

1/2 cup oil-packed black olives, pitted and chopped

3 tablespoons drained nonpareil capers, plus 2 tablespoons of their marinating liquid

1   Bring a large pot of water to a rolling boil. Add salt as you see fit and then the pasta, stirring a few times. Return to a boil with the lid on; uncover and cook at a gentle boil until the pasta is al dente, according to the package directions.

2   While the pasta is cooking, make the caramelized onions and tuna. Heat the olive and anchovy oils in a large skillet over medium-high heat until shimmering. Add the onion and salt. Cook, stirring frequently, until the onion starts to caramelize and turn brown at the edges, about 5 minutes. Reduce the heat to medium. Add the green onions, garlic, and 1/4 teaspoon or more red pepper flakes, to your taste; cook 1 minute, stirring. Move the vegetables to the sides and add the anchovies to the center of the skillet. Cook, pressing on the fillets with a wooden spoon, until they disintegrate, about 1 minute. Add the tuna, the olives, and the capers with their liquid; gently stir to combine and cook until just heated through, about 2 minutes. Taste for salt, and adjust seasoning.

3   To finish, drain the pasta and return it to the pot or to a large serving bowl, reserving 3/4 cup of the cooking liquid. Add the onion-tuna mixture together with a scant 1/2 cup of the reserved cooking liquid. Toss to combine for about 1 minute, adding a tad more cooking liquid to loosen the pasta if needed. Serve right away, sprinkled with the finely chopped green onion tops.

Creamy Rotelle with Basil Yogurt and Mozzarella

The allure of this speedy pasta is in its mouthwatering simplicity. Assembled in a flash, it is a cross between comforting pasta and lavish summer salad, deliciously creamy without any cream, especially when combined with Homemade Spelt Fettuccine (page 159). Combining thick Greek-style yogurt with regular yogurt gives this pasta just the right fullness. Enjoy this as a *primo piato* in the Italian tradition, followed by fish, chicken, or steak; or as a light summer meal with a plate of ripe tomatoes, black olives, and a drizzle of olive oil. SERVES 4 TO 6

....

PASTA

Fine sea salt

3/4 pound whole wheat rotelle, fusilli, or other short-cut whole grain pasta

BASIL YOGURT

1 cup plain whole-milk Greek-style yogurt

1 cup plain whole-milk yogurt

2 cloves garlic, minced

2 tablespoons extra-virgin olive oil

1 1/2 tablespoons red wine vinegar

1 to 2 teaspoons minced fresh hot green chile such as serrano

1/2 teaspoon fine sea salt

1/2 teaspoon freshly ground black pepper

4 ounces fresh mozzarella cheese, cut into 1/2-inch cubes

3/4 cup loosely packed chopped fresh basil leaves

1 Bring a large pot of water to a rolling boil. Add salt as you see fit and then the pasta, stirring a few times. Return to a boil with the lid on; uncover and cook at a gentle boil until the pasta is al dente, according to the package directions.

2 While the water is coming to a boil, make the basil yogurt. Combine both kinds of yogurt, garlic, 1 tablespoon of the olive oil, and the vinegar, chile, salt, and pepper in a medium bowl. Add the mozzarella and 1/2 cup of the basil leaves. Taste for salt, pepper, and vinegar and adjust. Set aside for the flavors to meld while the pasta is cooking.

3 To finish, drain the pasta, briefly rinse under cold water, and return to the pot or to a large serving bowl. Pour the basil yogurt over the pasta and toss to combine. Drizzle with the remaining 1 tablespoon olive oil and garnish with the remaining 1/4 cup basil. Serve at once.

TO LIGHTEN IT UP: You can replace both kinds of yogurt with lowfat varieties (do not use nonfat), but these can be a bit more tangy, so start by adding only 1 tablespoon of vinegar and adjust if needed.

Spaghetti with Roasted Chestnuts, Hazelnuts, and Sage

The assertive ingredients in this pasta cry out for fat, and lots of it—hard to justify in these health-aware times. A good Italian cook would use at least 1 stick of butter or 1/2 cup of olive oil to give this rustic whole grain composition a comforting slurp. In my search for a tasty alternative, I ended up soaking the crunchy topping in cooking liquid, or I created so dry and healthy a pasta that even a good splash of olive oil at the table didn't help. What I have learned: it's better not to drain the pasta too well—there is a reason chefs use tongs or wire-mesh strainers! And it is best to let the pasta sit for a minute or two, tossing and adding cooking liquid until it has absorbed enough to allow the second dose of oil to coat and flavor it. *Perfetto!* Serve as a first course the Italian way or as a meal by itself, accompanied by a simple dark-leaf salad. SERVES 4

PASTA

Fine sea salt

3/4 pound whole wheat spaghetti

CHESTNUT TOPPING

4 tablespoons extra-virgin olive oil, plus more to drizzle

16 whole fresh sage leaves, stemmed, rinsed, and patted dry

20 roasted or steamed whole peeled chestnuts, sliced 1/4 inch thick (1 slightly heaped cup)

1/2 cup coarsely chopped hazelnuts (2 ounces)

1/4 cup whole wheat panko bread crumbs

1 tablespoon minced garlic (about 3 cloves)

1/2 teaspoon fine sea salt

1/4 cup finely grated Parmesan cheese (1/2 ounce), plus extra for serving

1   Bring a large pot of water to a rolling boil. Add salt as you see fit and then the pasta, stirring a few times. Return to a boil with the lid on; uncover and cook at a gentle boil until the pasta is just short of al dente, according to the package directions.

2   While the pasta is cooking, make the chestnut topping. Line a plate with paper towels. Heat 2 tablespoons of the olive oil in a large skillet over medium-high heat until it shimmers. Add the sage leaves—they should sizzle when they hit the oil—and fry them until the sizzle subsides, about 1 minute. Using tongs or a spatula, transfer the leaves to the paper towel-lined plate. Decrease the heat to medium and stir in the chestnuts and hazelnuts (they may splatter!). Cook, stirring occasionally, until the nuts turn golden brown, 3 to 5 minutes. Decrease the heat if the nuts start to burn. Add the bread crumbs, garlic, and salt; cook until the garlic turns fragrant, about 1 minute. Remove from the heat and partially cover, if the pasta is not ready.

3   To finish, drain the pasta (but do not shake off the water), reserving 3/4 cup of the cooking liquid. Return the pasta to the pot. Add a scant 1/2 cup of the cooking liquid and toss vigorously for 1 to 2 minutes; add more cooking liquid by the tablespoon until the pasta does not absorb more. Toss with the remaining 2 tablespoons olive oil and transfer the pasta to a large serving bowl. Spoon on the chestnut topping, sprinkle with the cheese, and garnish with the sage leaves. Serve at once with more Parmesan on the side, and drizzle with more olive oil at the table if you like.

RAVISHING FETTUCCINE

Why on earth waste your time making your own fresh pasta? Try it once—and you might never ask again. What Italians call *pasta fresca* is exquisite, even more so when using whole grain flours, which add sublime aroma and an enticing toothiness. Feeling and working a pasta dough is a deeply satisfying experience, and, most important: it is lots of fun.

Watch your kitchen (and yourself) get covered in flour. Get a workout kneading by hand. Feel the dough change texture, from stiff to malleable and, when ready, smooth and silky. Learn to master rolling out the dough and cutting it into wide strips. Admire the long slabs of paper-thin dough you succeed in rolling out, if not on the first try, maybe on the third or fourth. Marvel at the rustic, uneven pasta, hanging to dry on wooden broomsticks or spread out on large baking sheets. To me, this is the art of life.

It takes me straight back to kindergarten in a way—when you forget about everything around you and just play. And all of this fun before you have even started eating!

Oh, before I forget: Whole grain pasta bears little or no resemblance to regular white fresh pasta, which can be divine in its own right. Whether you use buckwheat, spelt, hard wheat, or even rye or other grains, this pasta will look rustic, and it will have a chewy texture.

If you are new to whole grains, I suggest you make your first pasta with whole spelt flour instead of the heartier whole wheat flour. Spelt is mild, delightfully so. Plus the dough is more malleable and easier to work with. I always use eggs and oil when making pasta with whole grain flours; these two ingredients, while optional when working with all-purpose flour, make for a more appealing and supple dough.

Ideally, you should roll out your dough on a large wooden work surface. I use an old-fashioned noodle board from Germany, with edges to lock it in place on top of my kitchen counter. The rough surface will imprint itself on the pasta, making it better able to carry the sauce. A typical pastry board, while smaller than my noodle board, should suffice. But any work surface will do. Another helpful tool: a bench scraper (see "Equipment," page 29) to scrape and move sticky dough.

Kneading is the most enjoyable workout I know. It can be tiresome, but don't despair. You can spread the kneading time out, and do it in two or even three installments. If I get tired, I take a short break, cover my dough with a turned-over bowl, and come back to it later. This rest is not only good for me, but also for the whole grain dough—it helps the bran to absorb any liquid, resulting in finer pasta.

I love working by hand and have always rolled and cut my pasta manually. I have never owned a pasta machine—too many nuts, bolts, and levers. Or so I thought. For this book, I asked my friend Alessandra, who was raised in Italy, to come to the rescue. The result of our first chaotic laughter- and flour-filled evening was a supreme pasta meal. Alessandra's no-nonsense approach to making this Italian staple was enlightening. And now, I have to admit, I'm ready for my own pasta machine.

Homemade Spelt Fettuccine

Pasta-making takes a bit of time, but much of it is inactive, as the dough has to relax and dry before you cook it. You can work ahead if you like (see "to get a head start," on page 161). Active time is about 1 hour—not bad for a culinary revelation. One note regarding the flour: the more finely milled it is, the silkier the dough and the less water it will need. I provide instructions for a hand-cranked pasta rolling machine and for making it by hand. This recipe also allows you to hand-cut thinner linguine, but for them you need bring a bit of patience (which I most often lack).

This recipe makes more fettuccine than you will need for the recipes in this book, but I thought you might enjoy the extra. One of my favorite ways of eating homemade spelt pasta is with butter and salt. *Buon appetito*! **MAKES 16 OUNCES OF FRESH PASTA, TO SERVE 4 TO 6**

2¹/₂ cups whole spelt flour (10 ounces), plus extra for rolling and for the work surface

¹/₄ teaspoon fine sea salt

2 large eggs, at room temperature

2 tablespoons extra-virgin olive oil

3 to 7 tablespoons water

> SEE MEASURING
> WHOLE GRAIN FLOUR,
> PAGE 28

1 **BY HAND**: Make a mound of flour on your work surface. Sprinkle the salt across and create a well in the center. Using a fork, thoroughly combine both eggs, the olive oil, and 3 tablespoons of the water in a 2-cup liquid cup measure. Add the mixture to the well. Using your fingers or a fork and a circular motion, start to incorporate flour from the edges and the bottom of the crater into the egg mixture. Don't move too vigorously so as not to break the rim of the crater. Continue incorporating flour from the sides until a chunky dough starts to form, and then use your hands to incorporate the remaining flour. Drizzle with a bit more water until you can form a soft ball of dough. Use a bench scraper to help you along if the dough sticks to the surface.

   BY MACHINE: Place the whole spelt flour and the salt in the bowl of a food processor. Process for 30 seconds. Using a fork, thoroughly combine both eggs, the olive oil, and 3 tablespoons of the water in a 2-cup liquid cup measure. With the processor running, add the egg mixture through the feed tube and process just until a ball of dough forms, about 10 seconds. If no ball forms, drizzle in a bit more water by the teaspoonful until it does.

2 Knead the dough on a lightly floured work surface for 8 to 10 minutes (3 to 5 minutes for machine-made). If the dough is a tad too dry, moisten your hands; if it is sticky, dust your hands and the dough with flour. As you knead, the texture of the dough will change. While spelt flour is relatively malleable early on, the dough should become elastic, shiny, smooth, and ever-so-slightly tacky. This is when you should stop the kneading.

3 Place a glass or earthenware bowl over the dough, or wrap it in plastic wrap. Let sit at room temperature for at least ¹/₂ hour and up to 1 hour. After that, be sure to check its beautiful transformation: the dough will be soft and malleable—no wonder this step is called relaxing the dough.

CONTINUED, PAGE 160

4 Lightly flour 2 baking sheets, and dust your work surface with flour. Unwrap or uncover the dough and cut into 4 pieces. Remove 1 piece at a time and keep the others covered or wrapped.

BY HAND: Flatten each piece into a small rectangle, about 6 by 2 1/2 inches. Using a lightly floured rolling pin, start rolling the dough from the center outward and sideways, rotating often. Also, flip it over and continue rolling. You are aiming for an 11- or 12-inch square, about 1 millimeter thick. Mine are never the same size—it really doesn't matter. Be sure to keep your work surface and your rolling pin continuously yet very lightly floured. A dusting will be enough, but it has to be reapplied as you move and work the dough. If the dough resists and starts to spring back, set the piece aside, covered with a dish towel, and work on the next piece.

To cut into fettuccine, work with 1 piece at a time on a lightly floured work surface. Place the dough square in front of you and dust it with flour. In the following steps, be sure you thoroughly dust all surfaces with flour, otherwise your pasta strands will stick together. Fold both sides toward the center and then fold over again to close like a book; fold in half once more, never forgetting to dust all touching surfaces. You will now have a long piece with eight layers of dough. Using a sharp knife, cut the dough crosswise into 1/2-inch-wide pieces. You can also cut 1/4-inch-thick linguine, but this takes time, as you need to unroll double the amount of strips.

BY MACHINE: Dust the roller of the machine and each piece of dough with flour as you start to work with it, and then as needed. Flatten the piece into a small rectangle, about 6 by 2 1/2 inches, and pass it through the widest setting of your pasta machine. Fold the dough into thirds (the short sides toward the center) and pass once more through the machine sideways (with the open edge). Fold again and repeat, and then run the piece through one more time on the widest setting—or, as my friend Alessandra says, "until the pasta feels elastic." She was totally relaxed about this, and so should you be. Now keep passing ever–longer sheets of pasta through the machine while decreasing the setting one notch until you reach the second-to-last setting. As a novice you might even stop one before that and enjoy a slightly thicker pasta for the first time.

Help, my pasta sheets are too long! Our sheets varied widely: some had a length of 27 inches by 3 1/2 inches, some 37 inches, and some even 55 inches—you will need help for cranking here! In any case, as Alessandra says, "Just cut them in half crosswise, and continue working with each half."

To cut into fettuccine, be sure to have the work surface and both sides of the long pasta sheets thoroughly dusted with flour to prevent sticking. Work with 1 sheet at a time (not longer than 15 to 20 inches). Gently roll up the pasta from 1 short end to the other, in 2-inch folds. Using a sharp knife, cut the resulting package crosswise into 1/2-inch-wide pieces. You can also cut 1/4-inch-thick linguine, but this takes time, as you need to cut and unroll double the number of strips.

I forgot to flour the sheet. Look at this sticky mass! It can't be untangled. Alessandra says, "No problem, just put it back through the machine."

5 Immediately unfurl or carefully unroll the fettuccine and spread the strands on the prepared baking sheets, or hang them on a pasta rack. Repeat with the remaining 3 parts of dough. Allow the pasta to dry at room temperature for at least 30 minutes and up to 1 hour.

How do I know my pasta is ready to be cooked? Alessandra says, "Just feel the dough with a finger. It should not be sticky anymore."

6 Bring a large pot of water to a rolling boil. Add salt to taste and the fresh fettuccine, gently stirring them with a wooden spoon so they don't stick together. Once the water returns to a boil, cook the pasta until al dente, 2 to 4 minutes. Test the pasta for doneness as soon as the pieces float to the top—the cooking time for handmade pasta varies. Drain and serve at once, on preheated plates if you like.

What to do with all the tangled and less-than-perfectly-shaped pasta pieces? Alessandra says, "Don't throw them away. Just cook them. In a good sauce, no one will notice anyway."

TO GET A HEAD START: You can make the dough, up through step 3, as much as 1 day ahead. Chill, tightly wrapped in plastic wrap. Allow to come to room temperature before proceeding with the recipe, about 15 minutes. Or freeze the dough for up to 1 month. Defrost in the refrigerator (you might need a bit more flour when you work with previously frozen dough).

Fresh pasta, up through step 5, can be made ahead and frozen after drying. I place the whole baking sheets with the pasta in the freezer until the pasta is firm, at least 30 minutes. Then I store portions in ziplock bags, as needed, up to 1 month. Boil frozen pasta straight from the freezer (do not defrost).

Conchiglie with Lamb and Minted Yogurt

Lamb's robust flavors make it a natural partner for character-strong whole wheat pasta. Topped with pan-roasted pine nuts and aromatic browned butter, this pasta is enveloped in minted yogurt, a classic flavor pairing that brightens the dish. This sensual feast comes together fast enough even for a busy weeknight. Serve with sautéed snow peas or spinach and a glass of red wine, and relax. **SERVES 4**

....

PASTA

Fine sea salt

1/2 pound whole wheat pasta shells (conchiglie), or other small whole grain tube-shaped pasta

MINTED YOGURT AND BROWNED BUTTER WITH PINE NUTS

1 1/2 cups plain whole-milk yogurt

1/4 cup packed fresh mint leaves, finely chopped

2 cloves garlic, minced

Fine sea salt

2 tablespoons unsalted butter

1/4 cup pine nuts

LAMB, AND TO FINISH

1 tablespoon extra-virgin olive oil

1 tablespoon whole cumin seeds

1/2 cup minced shallots (about 2 medium)

2 cloves garlic, minced

1/2 teaspoon fine sea salt

3/4 pound ground lamb

1/4 cup water

1/4 cup packed fresh mint leaves, finely chopped

1/4 teaspoon Aleppo pepper (see page 117) or dried red chile flakes

1/4 teaspoon freshly ground black pepper

1 Bring a large pot of water to a rolling boil. Add salt as you see fit and then the pasta, stirring a few times. Return to a boil with the lid on; uncover and cook at a gentle boil until the pasta is al dente, according to the package directions.

2 While the water is coming to a boil, prepare the minted yogurt. Place the yogurt, mint, and garlic in a small bowl and stir to combine; season with salt to taste. Set aside.

3 Meanwhile, prepare the browned butter with pine nuts. Melt the butter in a large skillet over medium heat. Add the pine nuts and cook, stirring frequently, until the butter emits a nutty aroma and the nuts turn golden brown, 4 to 5 minutes. Using a rubber spatula, scrape the nuts and butter into a small bowl.

4 A few minutes before adding the pasta to the boiling water, prepare the lamb. Add the olive oil to the skillet you used for browning the butter, and heat over medium heat until shimmering. Add the cumin seeds and cook, stirring, until they turn fragrant, about 30 seconds. Add the shallots, garlic, and 1/4 teaspoon of the salt and cook until the shallots soften, 1 to 2 minutes. Increase the heat to medium-high and add half the ground lamb. Cook, stirring occasionally and breaking up large clumps, until no traces of pink remain and the meat is nicely browned, 5 to 7 minutes. Push the cooked lamb to the sides of the pan, add the remaining lamb to the center, and repeat. Add the water (so the lamb doesn't dry out) and the mint. Stir in the Aleppo pepper, pepper, and remaining 1/4 teaspoon salt; remove from the heat. Taste for salt and pepper and adjust; set aside and cover, with the lid slightly askew.

5 To finish, drain the pasta and transfer it to a large serving bowl. Pour the minted yogurt over the pasta and toss to combine. Spoon the lamb on top, followed by the browned butter with the pine nuts; toss and serve at once.

TO LIGHTEN IT UP: Omit the browned butter and toast the pine nuts without any fat (see page 37). Plus, you can drain (and discard) the fat from the skillet before adding the water at the end of step 4.

Farro: Ancient and Ambrosial

In this day and age, when humble grains are enjoying a chewy comeback on restaurant menus after the lean low-carb years, farro has become the ultimate trendy side dish. No other grain berry has been able to swim along on this current, to ride this tremendous wave of success. Neither rye, nor barley, nor wheat kernels has garnered this much celebrity status on our plates, so far. What is a lover of all whole grains to do? Happily ride along, for a simple reason: farro indeed deserves its stardom.

As I was not raised in Italy, this ancient grain entered my kitchen fairly late, only about ten years ago. Yet when it landed on my palate, it made a lasting impression, leaving me longing for more. I hadn't paid much attention when I grabbed the first farro product of my life in a natural supermarket in Munich. It was an unobtrusive package of spaghetti made from whole grain farro. This pasta caught my eye because of its color. Rather than dark brown like many of its hearty cousins, these spaghetti strands had a dainty reddish hue that made me curious. I don't remember how I prepared the pasta that night, but I do remember the consequences of this meal: years of adding half a dozen packages of pasta to the already heavy load of foods that crossed the Atlantic with me each time I returned to the United States.

From all the whole grain pasta in my pantry, my newly discovered farro spaghetti stood out. It had a delectable mild flavor, with an ever-so-elegant starchiness, and was nicely chewy in a perfect al dente way. In short, this pasta had the right mouthfeel. But first and foremost I remember detecting my favorite childhood spice: a precious hint of cinnamon. I was hooked, and I have since learned that others share my belief that farro makes the best pasta.

The deliciousness of farro pasta has, of course, to do with the grain it is made from. Italians typically lump three ancient grains of the wheat family together when they use the term *farro* (see also page 16). Most often, the farro cultivated in Italy is emmer. So it is no surprise that the flavor of the grain is faintly reminiscent of wheat, yet its chewiness is more graceful. Unlike wheat, farro kernels have a plump starchiness that adds mightily to their appeal. In this characteristic, they most closely resemble barley. But while barley has a distinct and delicious earthiness, farro has a dainty yet pronounced sweetness that makes it very agreeable. It helps that farro comes to us from Italy. With our adoration for that country's ethereal cuisine, anything from Italy tastes good, doesn't it? No wonder farro has nestled onto our plates and has become the hipster of grains.

Another reason for the grain's claim to fame is its amazing versatility. Its beautiful lush kernels are a boon to comforting soups and stews (see Mediterranean Mussels with Farro and White Wine, page 112). It lends itself as a side to a juicy slab of meat such as steak or chicken, and is equally ambrosial in a warming breakfast cereal (see Creamy Farro with Honey-Roasted Grapes, page 45). Risotto made from farro, be it with mushrooms or spring-fresh asparagus, adds a new dimension to this alluring dinner favorite.

Finding the cinnamon-brown grain berries on store shelves has become much easier. But you might still find yourself in a dizzying maze trying to investigate what you actually ate, let alone whether it was a whole grain. In my pantry, my personal favorites are shifting faster than the seasons. Currently, I'm smitten by tiny dark brown *farro piccolo*, grown in the United States, delectably plump, fast cooking, and truly sublime. But then, only a few weeks ago, I salivated over larger kernels of whole grain emmer farro. And, well, not so long ago, I slurped up a stew with an Italian semipearled farro, also of the emmer variety. Do I need to say how supremely balmy it was? All of this is farro—which means in whatever form farro lands on your plate, try it.

CHAPTER 6

MODERN MAINS

Afraid to fail in the kitchen? Always expecting to dish up four-star meals? Forgotten how to make something from scratch? It's time to start experimenting. Be sure you fail, and more than once. Everything I know I have learned from trying and failing, trying and failing, and more of the same. Maybe it's because I neglect to read a recipe carefully through before I start cooking (rule no. 1 of Kitchen 101). Maybe it's because I keep thinking a little less sugar will do, or maybe it's because I talk on the phone while sautéing onions.

But don't allow anxiety to prevent you from experimenting at the stove. In my opinion, even a humble homemade meal always beats fast food. It didn't turn out perfect the first time? Just try again. The livers in the oat pilaf weren't as tender as you hoped because you got distracted? Next time you will watch them more closely. You worked the olive oil crust a bit too much? Don't worry, the sardine tart will still be delicious, because *you* made it. All one needs is a bit of practice.

I call this chapter "Modern Mains" because it is designed for contemporary lifestyles. Today, more than ever, our eating habits have changed. We enjoy smaller, inspiring meals just as much as an old-fashioned sit-down dinner with multiple courses, or a quick bite on the fly. This is why you will find here a collection of unconventional recipes to pique your curiosity. Use it as an opportunity to experiment with a wide range of whole grain dishes, but without the stress.

I invite you to use this chapter to explore these ancient grains in your twenty-first-century kitchen. Some recipes are straightforward and super-easy, such as lamb chops with a flavorful whole grain walnut-sage topping, or a Mediterranean-inspired rye risotto with smoky-sweet Spanish chorizo. Others will entice you to let loose on a leisurely day to create an unusual tart with a soft polenta crust and a tangy artichoke and cheese filling, or a mouthwatering caramelized onion quiche studded with lavender and crisped prosciutto. But whatever you try, you will not be left alone in the process, and you will find time-saving tips throughout. So go ahead and start to play in your kitchen.

Worth Waiting For

"You cook every day?" Whenever this topic comes up, I can hear the gasps of astonishment from friends and colleagues. So many of us have come to regard cooking as a time-consuming hobby, a luxury for the culinarily obsessed. As a result, I have become a bit embarrassed to admit that I do indeed cook every day. But my dinners are modest. I do not sit down to homemade pasta or an elaborate slow-braised stew every night. Most weeknights, I simply cook with whatever is on hand from my once-a-week shopping trip. If only it wouldn't take so long, right? Like most of us, I enter the kitchen after a long workday tired and famished, with a capital *F*. I have to admit that in this state of starvation, a microwaved meal or take-out has real appeal.

So why do I still cook every night? Because cooking compensates and rewards me every time I light the stove. It compensates for the wait with a delicious home-cooked meal. It rewards the time spent stirring the pot with a freshness no take-out can deliver. And, to my own surprise, it restores my energies after an exhausting day at work.

These blissful benefits can come from the simplest meal. They linger in a perfectly seared aromatic steak, served with sautéed greens and crusty bread. They emanate from a classic Roman pasta dish such as *cacio e pepe*, made from just three ingredients: good-quality olive oil, cracked roasted black pepper, and salty sheep's milk cheese. Or they can spring from an austere wine-infused mussel stew (see page 112).

Be it a quick meal on a weeknight or a slow feast for a special occasion, good food is worth the wait. Waiting helps me to appreciate the effort that goes into cooking. Some of the best food memories of my life have been painstakingly awaited: The slow-cooking German beef *Rouladen* my father would sometimes prepare with their delicate filling of savory bacon and briny cornichons, accompanied by a gravy to die for. The aromas of his signature dish would waft through our house for what seemed to a twelve-year-old like endless hours. Or a roasted chunk of Greek Easter lamb, slowly rotating to perfection on an improvised grill in a spring field in Munich. Dripping its fat into the open fire, it emitted dizzying aromas of savory herbs and succulent meat while we waited, salivating.

The most memorable meal I had during a one-year stint in India was equally hungrily awaited, a dinner at the home of our friend, Sonal. I had asked her to teach me her brilliant mini-eggplants stuffed with spicy chickpea flour, a labor-intensive delicacy. At the time, Sonal was a busy social worker. It was already 9:00 P.M. when we reached her house after shopping for ingredients. A group of friends had arrived, eagerly awaiting Sonal's cooking, yet my friend didn't rush. I'm sure she was just as starved as all of us when she came home after a long, exasperating workday. While I, increasingly famished, took notes, she went patiently through all the steps needed to clean and prepare the small shiny eggplants, to make the aromatic chickpea flour filling, and to cook the vegetables to perfection, first in a pressure cooker, and then sautéed on a bed of roasted garlic, green chiles, and cilantro leaves. The eggplants were just one part of an amazing multicourse dinner she dished up that night for her friends. Near midnight, when we finally all sat down on the floor of her apartment, as is customary, the lively group became suddenly quiet. And once I popped one of the small, supple-soft eggplant packages into my mouth, the endless wait was forgotten.

My own impatience was (and still is) at odds with my lifelong passion for whole grains. Some whole grains can be slow to put on the table. They force you to think ahead. It is thus no surprise that at times I simply don't cook "slow" whole grains such as hulled barley, Kamut, or spelt. Instead, I fall back on quick-cooking bulgur, buckwheat, couscous, or quinoa—until, one day, the memory of the delicious chew of a wheat berry, the alluring sweetness of whole oats, or the delicious tang of whole rye will haunt me, creeping into my brain during a busy day, incessantly knocking away until I get home. Then I put out some crackers, olives, and a few cubes of cheese to tide me over. And I dream up a slow home-cooked meal, a dinner worth waiting for. Then I light the stove.

Artichoke-Rosemary Tart with Polenta Crust

If you find classic tart crusts intimidating, try this super-easy polenta crust, which doesn't require a rolling pin or a baker's touch. With an aromatic artichoke filling atop a cheese-flavored polenta, this savory tart is perfect for a barbecue or a beach party, where you can also offer it as a delicious starter. Best of all, it can and *must* be prepared ahead—it takes about two hours, but much of it is plain waiting. Pour a glass of chilled rosé or prosecco and enjoy a piece with a salad of summer greens.

If using coarse stone-ground whole grain cornmeal instead of the polenta, reduce the amount of water to 1 cup, (for more on types of polenta, see page 11). Instead of frozen, you can use canned or jarred artichoke hearts, in water or in a simple oil marinade. You will need 2 cans or jars (12 to 14 ounces each; a few will be left over) and might have to cut the hearts in half. Leftover slices of this tart are great for the lunch box. Reheat in a microwave (1 to 2 minutes on high) or in a toaster oven (10 minutes). **SERVES 4 AS A MAIN COURSE, OR 8 AS A STARTER**

....

POLENTA CRUST

1^1/$_2$ cups low-sodium vegetable broth

1^1/$_4$ cups water

^{1}/$_2$ teaspoon fine sea salt

1^1/$_4$ cups polenta or corn grits

^{1}/$_2$ cup shredded Parmesan cheese (about 2^1/$_2$ ounces; use the large holes of a box grater)

1 large egg, at room temperature

^{1}/$_4$ teaspoon freshly ground black pepper

ARTICHOKE CHEESE FILLING

1 cup plain whole-milk Greek yogurt

2 large eggs

^{1}/$_2$ cup finely chopped green onions (about 3)

2 tablespoons chopped fresh flat-leaf parsley

1 tablespoon minced fresh rosemary

^{1}/$_4$ teaspoon fine sea salt

^{1}/$_4$ teaspoon freshly ground black pepper

1 (12-ounce) package frozen quartered artichoke hearts, thawed and drained

2 ounces crumbled goat cheese (about ^{1}/$_2$ cup)

^{1}/$_2$ cup shredded Parmesan cheese

1   To make the polenta crust, bring the broth and the water to a boil in a large heavy-bottomed saucepan over medium-high heat. Add the salt. Using a large whisk, slowly add the polenta in a thin stream, and continue whisking for 30 more seconds. Decrease the heat to low and cover. Cook for 10 minutes, stirring vigorously with a wooden spoon about every 2 minutes to keep the polenta from sticking to the bottom. Remove the saucepan from the heat and let sit, covered, for 10 minutes, stirring a few times. The polenta will be fairly stiff. Stir in the cheese, egg, and pepper.

2   Grease a 10-inch ceramic tart pan with olive oil or coat with cooking spray, and place on a wire rack. Have ready a tall glass of cold water. Dip a wooden spoon into the water as needed as you spread the polenta mixture across the center of the pan, pushing it up the sides. Set aside to firm up at room temperature, about 15 minutes, and then form an even rim about ^{3}/$_4$ inch thick with your slightly moist fingers, pressing firmly. No need to fret over this—it's easy.

3   Meanwhile, position a rack in the center of the oven and preheat to 375°F.

CONTINUED, PAGE 170

4   Prepare the artichoke cheese filling. Place the yogurt, eggs, green onions, parsley, rosemary, salt, and pepper in a 2-cup liquid measure or a medium bowl and combine well with a fork. Distribute the artichoke quarters over the crust, cut sides up, forming a circle along the rim and filling the center (you might not need all the hearts). Sprinkle the goat cheese on top and gently pour the filling over the artichokes. Sprinkle with the Parmesan cheese.

5   Bake the tart until the top turns golden brown and the filling is set, about 45 minutes. Transfer the pan to a wire rack and set aside at room temperature to firm up for at least 20 minutes, 40 if you can wait. Using a sharp serrated knife, cut into slices. Serve with more freshly ground pepper on top if you like.

TO GET A HEAD START: The polenta crust, as in steps 1 and 2, can be prepared 1 day ahead, as can the entire tart. Cool to room temperature, chill for a couple of hours, and then cover with plastic wrap. Allow the tart to come to room temperature before serving, or gently reheat to warm (not hot) in a 325°F oven for about 20 minutes.

TO LIGHTEN IT UP: Use 1 cup non- or lowfat Greek yogurt in the filling instead of whole-milk yogurt.

Tomato-Rye Risotto with Cumin and Chorizo

I can't stop singing the praises of the delicious tang of whole rye berries, and if you still haven't tried them, this Mediterranean-inspired dinner will win you over. The slight sourness of rye berries is a perfect match for smoky-sweet Spanish chorizo (do not use Mexican chorizo here). Serve this "ryesotto" with oven-roasted crostini and a dollop of yogurt for a light meal, or as a toothsome side next to simple sautéed chicken breast. SERVES 3 TO 4

RYE

1¹/₂ cups water

³/₄ cup rye berries, soaked overnight and drained

RYESOTTO, AND TO FINISH

4 ounces cured Spanish chorizo, casings removed and sliced ¹/₄ inch thick

1¹/₂ cups chopped red onion (about 1 medium)

2 cloves garlic, lightly crushed

2 small bay leaves

1 teaspoon whole cumin seeds, or cumin powder

1 teaspoon dried oregano

¹/₈ teaspoon red pepper flakes (optional)

¹/₄ teaspoon fine sea salt

2 tablespoons tomato paste

1¹/₂ cups finely chopped fresh plum tomatoes (about 4), or 1 (14-ounce) can diced tomatoes, preferably fire-roasted

¹/₄ cup drained and chopped oil-packed sun-dried tomatoes (see page 138)

About ¹/₂ cup water

¹/₂ to 1 teaspoon sugar

Freshly ground black pepper (optional)

1   To prepare the rye, bring the water and the rye berries to a boil in a small heavy-bottomed saucepan. Decrease the heat to maintain a simmer, cover, and cook until the berries are tender but still slightly chewy, 50 to 60 minutes. Remove from the heat, cover, and let sit for 10 to 15 minutes, if you have time. Drain any remaining liquid.

2   While the rye is steaming, start making the ryesotto. Have a plate with paper towels ready. Heat a large saucepan over medium heat until hot, about 2 minutes. Add the chorizo and cook, turning once with a spatula, until the slices are lightly browned and crisp, about 3 minutes. Transfer the slices to the paper towel-lined plate. Remove the pan from the heat. If you like, drain much of the rendered fat, leaving 1 table-spoon in the saucepan (or drain all and use olive oil instead).

3   Return the saucepan to medium heat. Add the onion, garlic, bay leaves, cumin, oregano, red pepper flakes, and salt. Cook, stirring frequently (stir constantly if using cumin powder), until the onion softens and just starts to brown at the edges, about 3 minutes. Add the tomato paste and cook, stirring, until it darkens, about 1 minute.

4   Stir in the tomatoes, sun-dried tomatoes, rye berries, and chorizo. Add water if needed, up to ¹/₂ cup (depending on the tomatoes you use), to get a slightly saucelike consistency similar to a risotto. Bring to a boil, stirring. Decrease the heat to maintain a simmer, cover, and cook until the flavors come together, 10 to 15 minutes.

5   To finish, add ¹/₂ teaspoon sugar. Taste for sugar and salt and adjust, adding a few twirls of pepper if you like, and serve.

TO GET A HEAD START: Make the rye berries, as in step 1, ahead (see page 23).

TO VARY IT: Use about 2 cups cooked whole wheat berries for a change (see page 25).

TO LIGHTEN IT: Use 2 ounces chorizo to add just enough of its smoky-rich flavor.

TO MAKE IT VEGETARIAN: Omit the chorizo. In step 3, use 1 tablespoon olive oil to sauté the vegetables. Sprinkle the dish with ¹/₄ cup crumbled feta cheese if you like.

Easy Whole Wheat and Olive Oil Tart Shell

This is one of my favorite go-to crusts for savory quiches and tarts. If you want to trick your family into eating more whole grains, be sure to use white whole wheat flour. Olive oil makes the dough easy to work with—perfect if you are intimidated by the process of making a crust. There's no need to fiddle with a rolling pin because the dough is simply pressed by hand into the tart pan. This is the crust to use for the Caramelized Onion Quiche with Lavender and Crisped Prosciutto (page 184) and for the Sardine Tart with Sweet Bell Peppers and Currants (page 174). Don't be surprised if little white dots appear across the crust when you chill it. These are just undissolved crystals of fine sea salt; they won't affect the outcome.

MAKES 1 PARTIALLY OR FULLY BAKED 9¹/₂- TO 10-INCH TART SHELL

³/₄ cup white whole wheat or regular whole wheat flour (3 ¹/₄ ounces)

³/₄ cup whole wheat pastry flour (3 ounces)

¹/₂ teaspoon baking powder

¹/₂ teaspoon fine sea salt

¹/₃ cup extra-virgin olive oil

¹/₃ cup chilled whole or lowfat milk

SEE MEASURING WHOLE GRAIN FLOUR, PAGE 28

1 Lightly grease a 9¹/₂- or 10-inch tart pan with olive oil. Use a metal tart pan with a removable bottom or a ceramic tart pan, according to the recipe instructions.

2 **TO MAKE THE DOUGH IN THE FOOD PROCESSOR:** Place the white whole wheat and whole wheat pastry flours, the baking powder, and the salt in the bowl and process to combine, about 10 seconds. Pour the olive oil and milk into a liquid 2-cup measure and beat with a fork until thoroughly combined. Pour the liquid over the dry ingredients and pulse, in 1-second intervals, just until a soft ball of dough forms, 3 to 5 pulses.

   TO MAKE THE DOUGH BY HAND: Whisk together the white whole wheat and whole wheat pastry flours, the baking powder, and the salt in a medium bowl and make a well in the center. Pour the olive oil and the milk into a liquid 2-cup measure and beat with a fork until thoroughly combined. Pour the mixture into the well. Using a dough whisk or a fork, stir from the center, gradually incorporating the flour from the sides until a soft, lumpy dough just comes together.

3 Scrape the lumpy dough into the tart pan. Press it gently but firmly into the pan (it will look raggedy), using the bottom of a cup measure to even it out and pressing it up the sides to create a 1-inch rim. Be sure to patch up any tears with your fingers. Prick the crust all over with a fork and chill, uncovered, for 1 hour, or overnight covered with plastic wrap.

4 Position a rack in the center of the oven and preheat to 375°F. Set the tart pan on a large rimless baking sheet for easier handling. Place a piece of parchment paper on the crust and fill it with pie weights or dried beans.

5 To partially bake the crust, carefully place the sheet with the tart pan in the oven (it can slide!) and bake until the crust just starts to pull away from the sides, 10 to 12 minutes. Remove from the oven, and carefully slide the tart pan onto a wire rack. Remove the parchment paper with the pie weights. Allow the crust to cool to room temperature before filling.

To fully bake the crust, carefully place the sheet with the tart pan in the oven and bake for 10 minutes. Remove the parchment paper with the pie weights and continue baking until the crust has pulled away from the sides, the center is dry to the touch, and the edges just begin to brown, 15 to 17 more minutes. Remove from the oven, and carefully slide the tart pan onto a wire rack. Allow the crust to cool to room temperature before filling.

TO GET A HEAD START: You can partially or fully bake the crust 1 day ahead (or freeze up to 1 month). Store at room temperature under a cake dome, or loosely covered with plastic wrap.

TO VARY IT: Add 1 teaspoon ground cumin or coriander to the flour mixture in step 2 for an aromatic twist.

HOW TO UNMOLD A TART

Wearing oven mitts, carefully center the tart pan on top of a 28-ounce can; the outer ring will drop. The tart can now be served with the bottom part still underneath. If you like (I never bother), you can slide the tart onto a serving plate by running a long spatula between the bottom of the pan and the crust and then transferring it to the plate.

Sardine Tart with Sweet Bell Peppers and Currants

Marrying sardines with yellow and red bell peppers, currants, and olives makes for an opulent fusion of sweet, salty and briny flavors. I don't use many cans in my cooking, but here they are a great time saver. If you make the olive oil crust ahead, this is on the table fast. Pair the tart with a salad of leafy greens such as a mesclun mix or butter lettuce, to be followed by Greek Yogurt Ice Cream (page 198) for dessert or, on a more festive occasion, Riesling Zabaglione over Red Currants (page 200). When you serve a crowd, this is a magnificent appetizer with a glass of white wine. SERVES 3 OR 4 AS A MAIN COURSE, OR 8 AS A STARTER

BELL PEPPER FILLING

1 or 2 lemons

1 tablespoon extra-virgin olive oil

1 cup red bell peppers, cut into 1/4-inch dice (about 1/2 medium)

1 cup yellow bell peppers, cut into 1/4-inch dice (about 1/2 medium)

1 1/2 cups thinly sliced leeks, white and light green parts (about 1 medium)

1/4 teaspoon fine sea salt

1/2 cup pitted and chopped oil-packed black olives (about 20 olives)

1/2 cup dried currants

1/4 teaspoon freshly ground black pepper

1/2 teaspoon sugar

TO FINISH

Easy Whole Wheat and Olive Oil Tart Shell (page 172), preferably with cumin, fully baked, using a 9 1/2-inch metal tart pan with removable bottom

1 cup plain whole-milk or lowfat Greek yogurt

2 (3.75-ounce) cans sardines, preferably oil-packed, drained

Extra-virgin olive oil, for brushing

1/4 cup crumbled mild feta cheese, preferably sheep's milk

1 To make the filling, prepare the bell pepper filling. Finely grate the lemons until you have 1 tablespoon zest. Press 1 lemon until you have 2 tablespoons juice (reserve the remaining lemon for another use).

2 Heat the olive oil in a medium skillet over medium to medium-high heat until shimmering. Add the bell peppers, leeks, and salt. Cook, stirring frequently, until the vegetables soften, about 5 minutes. Stir in the olives, currants, lemon juice, zest, and pepper; cook, stirring, until the juice has evaporated, about 2 minutes. Remove the pan from the heat. Stir in the sugar. Taste for salt and pepper and adjust (I like this quite peppery), but keeping in mind that you will add salty feta cheese.

3 To finish, place a rack about 6 inches below the broiler and preheat for about 5 minutes. Place the tart pan with the crust on a large rimless baking sheet for easier handling. Using the back of a spoon, spread the yogurt across the bottom of the tart. Spoon the filling into the crust (it will be quite full). Arrange the sardines, forming a star, in the center, and brush them and the rim of the crust with olive oil. Sprinkle the tart with the cheese.

4 Carefully place the sheet with the tart pan in the oven (it can slide!) and broil just until the sardines are heated through, about 5 minutes. Watch closely so as not to burn the rim of the crust. Remove from the oven, and carefully slide the tart pan onto a wire rack to cool for a few minutes. Unmold (see sidebar, page 173) and cut into wedges. Serve warm.

TO MAKE IT A FEAST: Use 1 cup mascarpone for a decadently rich and creamy touch instead of the Greek yogurt.

Lamb Chops with Walnut-Sage Crust

Topping ordinary lamb chops with a vibrant herb and walnut crust is easy, and transforms them into a weeknight feast. I serve them with ever-so-lightly-buttered mounds of polenta and a glass of red wine.
SERVES 4

....

1/2 cup toasted walnut pieces (see page 37)

1/3 cup whole wheat panko bread crumbs

1/3 cup lightly packed flat-leaf parsley leaves

6 medium-size sage leaves, stemmed

1 or 2 cloves garlic, peeled

1 tablespoon plus 2 teaspoons extra-virgin olive oil, more for rubbing

1/4 teaspoon fine sea salt

1/4 teaspoon freshly ground black pepper

4 lamb loin chops, each about 1 1/2 inches thick (about 1 1/4 pounds total weight)

1 Position a rack in the center of the oven and preheat to 450°F.

2 Place the walnuts, bread crumbs, parsley, sage, garlic, 2 teaspoons of the olive oil, salt, and pepper in the bowl of a food processor fitted with the metal blade. Process until the mixture resembles bread crumbs, about 15 seconds.

3 Pat the lamb chops dry, rub both sides with a bit of olive oil, and season with salt. Divide the walnut mixture among the chops, pressing an even layer on the top of each.

4 Heat the remaining 1 tablespoon olive oil in a 10-inch ovenproof skillet, preferably cast-iron, over medium-high heat until shimmering. Add the lamb chops, crust side up, and cook until they are nicely browned on the bottom, 2 to 3 minutes.

5 Transfer the skillet to the oven and roast the chops until an instant-read thermometer inserted into the thickest part registers 130°F for medium-rare, about 10 minutes, or to desired doneness. Let sit for 5 minutes before serving.

TO VARY IT: You can use 4 boneless pork loin chops, about 3/4 inch thick (about 1 1/4 pounds total weight). In step 4, they will need to reach an internal temperature of 145°F, about 5 to 6 minutes. Let sit for 2 minutes before serving.

Spelt Crust Pizza with Fennel, Prosciutto, and Apples

If a pizza crust seems daunting and time-consuming to make, try this easy spelt dough, which is moistened with ricotta cheese and aromatic linseed oil. This rustic dinner is stunning to behold—thinly sliced apples and fennel sit on a tangy sour cream layer and are topped with lightly crisped prosciutto. The crust is inspired by classic German dough with Quark, a delicious fresh cheese, which keeps baked goods fresh. While your dough rests, preheat the oven and prepare the toppings—voilà, dinner! Great also as a party appetizer in the early fall with a glass of rosé or dry white wine, or with a chilled lager in the summer.

Use a mandoline to slice apples and fennel about ⅛ inch thick. If you don't have one, try to slice them as thinly as possible to get flavorful brown edges. If you don't own a pizza stone, preheat an inverted baking sheet for 30 minutes as described in step 3. Place the dough on a piece of parchment paper, carefully slide the paper with the dough right onto the baking sheet, and bake. While the crust will not be as crisp, it will still be delicious. **MAKES 2 PIZZAS, TO SERVE 4 TO 6 AS A MAIN COURSE, OR 8 AS A STARTER**

....

SPELT CRUST

2 cups whole grain spelt flour
   (8 ounces)

2 teaspoons baking powder

¾ teaspoon fine sea salt

½ teaspoon sugar

1 cup whole-milk ricotta cheese

¼ cup whole milk

2 tablespoons linseed oil or
   extra-virgin olive oil

1 large egg

Coarse cornmeal, if using a
   pizza peel

TOPPINGS

4 or 5 green onions

1 cup sour cream

¼ cup drained nonpareil capers

¾ teaspoon freshly ground black pepper

1 Granny Smith apple, halved, cored,
   and sliced very thinly

1 fennel bulb, halved lengthwise, cored,
   and sliced very thinly

4 ounces thinly sliced prosciutto, cut crosswise
   into ½-inch-wide strips

Linseed or extra-virgin olive oil, for brushing

1 First, make the dough. **TO PREPARE THE DOUGH BY HAND:** Whisk together the spelt flour, baking powder, salt, and sugar in a large bowl. Make a well in the center. In a small bowl, combine the ricotta, milk, linseed oil, and the egg and beat with a fork until smooth. Pour the ricotta mixture into the well. Combine with a dough whisk (see page 30) or a fork, stirring from the center and gradually incorporating the flour from the sides until a fairly moist dough comes together.

TO PREPARE THE DOUGH BY FOOD PROCESSOR: Place the spelt flour, baking powder, salt, and sugar in the bowl and process for about 10 seconds. In a small bowl, combine the ricotta, milk, linseed oil, and the egg and beat with a fork until smooth. Pour the ricotta mixture across the top of the flour mixture and pulse, in 1-second intervals, just until a ball forms, 5 to 10 pulses. The dough will be fairly moist.

> **SEE MEASURING WHOLE GRAIN FLOUR, PAGE 28**

CONTINUED, PAGE 178

SPELT CRUST PIZZA WITH FENNEL,
PROSCIUTTO, AND APPLES, CONTINUED
FROM PAGE 176

DO YOU NEED A BAKING STONE AND A PIZZA PEEL?

If you love crusty pizza, breads, and flat breads, a baking stone is well worth having. There is simply no better way to get an appealing crisp crust in a home oven, as the porous stone absorbs moisture from the dough. Be sure to preheat the stone for at least 30 minutes, better up to 60 minutes. Another useful tool: a pizza peel. It makes transferring a piece of wobbly dough to the oven so much easier and safer. Here is how it works: Sprinkle coarse cornmeal over the peel and place the dough on it, topping it to suit your taste. Open the oven door and give the peel a gentle thrust with your wrist. This is all it needs to catapult the pizza onto the preheated stone. It sounds much harder than it is. Afraid of dropping the pizza on the floor? Just relax and try. If the dough does not budge and seems stuck to the peel, close the oven door (so as not to lose too much heat), use a dough scraper to loosen the pizza around the edges and underneath, and try again.

2   Transfer the dough to a well-floured work surface. Lightly flour your hands and briefly knead 5 to 7 turns to get a smooth yet slightly tacky dough. Wrap the dough in plastic wrap and let sit at room temperature for 30 to 45 minutes to allow the bran in the flour to soften.

3   Meanwhile, place a baking stone on a rack on the bottom shelf and preheat oven to 425°F. Liberally sprinkle a pizza peel with coarse cornmeal. Finely chop the white and light green parts of the green onions until you have $1/2$ cup. Combine them with the sour cream, capers, and $1/4$ teaspoon of the pepper in a small bowl. Finely chop the dark green parts as well (about $1/4$ cup) and set aside for garnish.

4   Unwrap the dough, transfer to a lightly floured work surface and cut into 2 pieces. Keep 1 piece covered with plastic wrap. Lightly flour your hands and briefly knead the other until smooth, 7 to 10 turns. Using a rolling pin, roll the dough into an elongated pizza, 11 by 8 inches and about $1/4$ inch thick. Do this in stages, occasionally turning the dough over and rolling it out further, lightly flouring your work surface and the rolling pin each time. Place the dough on the pizza peel. Spread half of the sour cream topping across, leaving a $1/2$-inch border. Cover with half of the apple slices, top with half of the fennel slices, and sprinkle with half of the prosciutto. Brush the border with oil.

5   Slide the dough onto the baking stone and bake until the fennel just starts to brown at the edges and the rim turns golden brown and starts to crisp—it should yield when pressed with a finger—about 15 minutes. Use a large spatula to lift the edges of the pizza so you can slide the peel underneath; carefully transfer the pizza to a wooden board. Sprinkle with half of the reserved green onions and $1/4$ teaspoon of the pepper. Cut with a sharp knife and serve at once. Repeat with the second pizza.

TO GET A HEAD START: The dough, as in steps 1 and 2, can be prepared 1 day ahead. Chill, wrapped in plastic wrap. Remove the dough from the fridge and unwrap; flatten it slightly, and allow to come room temperature while you prep the ingredients and preheat the oven, about 1 hour.

TO LIGHTEN IT UP: Feel free to use part-skim ricotta, lowfat milk, and lowfat sour cream, but do not use nonfat.

178   ANCIENT GRAINS FOR MODERN MEALS

Roast Chicken with Orange, Lavender, and Thyme

The simple beauty of a juicy roast chicken sparks a primordial craving in many people, myself included—that is why you find it in this cookbook. There are no whole grains in this recipe (except any grains the chicken was raised on). I make up for this by including whole grain pairings to whet your appetite. When busy, I serve tangy Orange and Lemon Couscous (page 100) with the bird. Otherwise, I make the Barley with Crisped Prosciutto and Truffle Oil (page 104) and combine it with the lemon variation of this recipe below.

Remember to plan ahead: the chicken needs to chill with an herbal salt coating for at least 4 hours—the longer the better—for crisp skin and flavorful meat. If you don't have a broiler pan and a V-rack, crumple a long piece of aluminum foil (about 6 feet), twist it firmly into a long snake, and roll it up into a coil. Set the coil in the center of a baking sheet, and place the chicken on top. Bake as directed, increasing the oven temperature to 475°F. SERVES 4

1 large orange

2 1/4 teaspoons fine sea salt

1 tablespoon finely chopped fresh thyme, or 1 teaspoon dried thyme

1 teaspoon dried lavender buds

1/2 teaspoon freshly ground black pepper

1 (3 1/2- to 4-pound) chicken, preferably organic, giblets removed

1 to 2 tablespoons extra-virgin olive oil

1 First, make the herbal salt. Finely grate the zest of the orange. Cut the orange in half and reserve one half for another use. Cut the other half into 2 pieces and set aside. Combine the zest, 2 teaspoons of the salt, the thyme, lavender, and pepper in a small bowl. Set the herbal salt aside.

2 Place a V-rack atop a broiler drip pan with its slotted cover. Pat the chicken dry and trim any excess fat. Rub some of the herbal salt over the skin and inside the cavity. Using your fingers, gently loosen the skin from the breast meat and both thighs to create pockets so you can spread some of the herbal salt there as well. Put the 2 orange quarters inside the cavity and close it with kitchen twine. Place the chicken in the V-rack and transfer the contraption to the fridge. Chill, uncovered, for at least 4 hours and up to 24 hours.

3 About 2 hours before you would like to eat, position a rack in the center of the oven and preheat to 450°F. Remove the chicken from the fridge and set aside for 30 minutes. Before you place the chicken in the oven, rub the olive oil across the skin and sprinkle with the remaining 1/4 teaspoon salt. Place the chicken in the V-rack, breast side up. Tie the legs together with kitchen twine and tuck the wing tips under the body.

4 Roast the chicken for 25 minutes. Remove and turn it breast side down, using sturdy tongs. Continue roasting until an instant-read thermometer, inserted into the thickest part of the thigh, registers between 165°F and 170°F, about 20 to 25 more minutes, depending on the size. Loosely tent the chicken with aluminum foil and let it rest for 15 to 25 minutes before carving and serving.

TO VARY IT: Use the finely grated zest of 1 lemon instead of the orange zest, and place half a lemon inside the cavity.

Oat Pilaf with Chicken Livers, Marsala, and Sage

Comforting classics such as risottos and pilafs (or pilaus) are typically made with different kinds of rice. But whole grains such as farro or barley are delicious stand-ins. Here you can try one of my favorites, toasty-sweet whole oat berries, better known by their raspy name "oat groats." Allow about an hour from start to finish for this pilaf to come together; it's worth the wait. Serve with sautéed chard or collard greens. Avoid crowding the pan when cooking chicken livers. They will steam and not brown, which means a lot less flavor. SERVES 4

....

OAT PILAF

1 tablespoon extra-virgin olive oil

1¹/₂ cups chopped red onion (about 1 medium)

1 (2-inch) stick cinnamon

1 bay leaf

¹/₄ teaspoon fine sea salt

1¹/₂ cups whole oat berries (groats)

2 cups low-sodium chicken broth

¹/₂ cup finely chopped soft dried apricots, preferably Turkish

1 tablespoon sweet Marsala wine

CHICKEN LIVERS, AND TO FINISH

2 tablespoons extra-virgin olive oil, or more as needed

1 pound chicken livers, trimmed, patted dry, and cut into pieces (about 1¹/₂ inch square)

Fine sea salt and freshly ground black pepper

1 tablespoon plus 3 teaspoons finely chopped fresh sage

¹/₄ cup sweet Marsala wine

¹/₄ cup low-sodium chicken broth

1 tablespoon unsalted butter

2 pinches cayenne pepper

1 To make the oat pilaf, heat the olive oil in a 4-quart heavy-bottomed saucepan over medium heat until shimmering. Add the onion, cinnamon stick, bay leaf, and salt and cook, stirring frequently, until the onion starts to turn golden brown at the edges, about 8 minutes. Add the oats and cook, stirring, until the kernels become shiny and start to crackle, 1 to 2 minutes. Add the broth (it might splatter!) and bring to a boil, scraping the bottom to release any browned bits. Decrease the heat to maintain a simmer, cover, and cook until the liquid is absorbed and the oats are tender but still slightly chewy, 40 to 45 minutes. Remove and discard the cinnamon stick and bay leaf.

2 While the oat pilaf simmers, place the apricots in a small bowl and drizzle with the Marsala wine. Set aside, stirring once or twice.

3 To make the chicken livers, start when the oats are almost done. Heat the olive oil in a large skillet over medium heat until it shimmers. Add half the chicken livers and season them with salt and pepper. Cook until the livers are nicely browned on the bottom, about 3 minutes, covering the pan with a splatter guard or partially covering with a lid. Using tongs, turn the livers and cook until browned but still pink in the center (cut into one to check), 2 to 3 more minutes. Transfer the livers to a plate and repeat with the second batch, adding a bit more oil if the pan gets dry. Stir in 1 tablespoon and 1 teaspoon of the sage. Add the Marsala wine and the chicken broth, together with the first batch of liver and any juices. Simmer, uncovered, for 1 to 2 minutes to thicken the sauce slightly, scraping the bottom of the pan to release any browned bits. Add the butter and wait until it has melted, and then taste the sauce for salt and pepper and adjust.

4 While the sauce simmers, stir the Marsala-infused apricots with their liquid into the oats. Season with the cayenne. Taste for salt and adjust.

5 To finish, spoon the livers with a bit of the sauce over the oat pilaf. Sprinkle with the remaining 2 teaspoons sage and serve at once, with more black pepper on the side if you like.

TO GET A HEAD START: The oat pilaf, as in step 1, can be made up to 3 days ahead—it will, however, lose a bit of its nice chewiness. Gently rewarm over medium heat, loosening the clumped oats with a wooden spoon and stirring a few times, and adding a scant $1/2$ cup of water or broth before proceeding as described in step 4.

TO MAKE IT VEGETARIAN: Omit the chicken livers and the sage and use vegetable broth (instead of chicken broth). Dice 1 large red bell pepper. Heat 1 tablespoon olive oil over medium heat. Cook the bell pepper together with 1 teaspoon cumin powder until the bell pepper is crisp-tender, about 3 minutes. Season with salt to taste, and stir into the cooked oat pilaf. Garnish with $1/2$ cup chopped toasted hazelnuts (see page 37).

Saffron Risotto with White-Wine Clams and Peas

Despite my tireless pursuit of starches, I have found making brown rice risotto prohibitively time-consuming. While the rewards are out of this world, I prefer to stay in this world and eat something else—except maybe every three years or so. That is, until I tried it one night with parboiled short-grain brown rice. I combine it with a quick-cooking trick, adding lots of liquid at the start, which reduces the many stirs a good risotto requires. This recipe is inspired by the classic Italian combination of rice and peas, which the Venetians call *risi e bisi*. A hint of cream and butter intensifies the faint sweetness of brown rice. I have topped it here with clams for good measure, but it would be just as delicious on its own.

In this risotto, I don't use the clam juice, as its gray color dulls the bright orange hue of the dish. And never rinse rice being used for risotto, as doing so will wash out the starch. It is the starch that contributes the heavenly creaminess of a classic Italian risotto. SERVES 4

RISOTTO

2 1/2 cups low-sodium chicken broth or vegetable broth

1 piece of Parmesan cheese rind, a 1 by 2-inch chunk (optional)

1/4 teaspoon fine sea salt

2 pounds littleneck clams (about 25 clams)

1 tablespoon extra-virgin olive oil

1/3 cup minced shallot (about 1 medium)

1 clove garlic, lightly crushed

1/2 teaspoon saffron threads

About 4 cups parboiled short-grain brown rice (1 1/2 cups uncooked; see page 26)

1 cup dry white wine, such as Pinot Grigio

TO FINISH

7 ounces frozen peas (do not thaw; about 1 1/2 cups)

2 tablespoons heavy whipping cream

1 ounce or more finely grated Parmesan cheese (about 1/2 cup)

1 1/2 teaspoons unsalted butter

1/4 teaspoon or more freshly ground white pepper

1/4 teaspoon fine sea salt

2 tablespoons finely chopped flat-leaf parsley

1 First, prepare the broth for the risotto. Bring the broth to a boil in a medium saucepan. Add the cheese rind and stir in the salt. Cover and decrease the heat to maintain a simmer while you make the risotto. Have a 2-cup liquid measure ready.

2 Clean the clams. Discard any chipped, broken, or open clams and soak the rest in a large bowl of cold water for about 20 minutes. This enables the clams to clear out sand and salt from inside their shells.

3 Meanwhile, make the risotto. Heat the olive oil in a large heavy-bottomed saucepan over medium heat until it shimmers. Add the shallot, garlic, and saffron and cook, stirring frequently, until the shallot softens, about 2 minutes. Add the rice and cook, stirring vigorously, until the kernels are coated with oil and look shiny, 1 to 2 minutes. Increase the heat to medium-high and add 3/4 cup of the wine. Cook, stirring and scraping the bottom, until the wine turns syrupy and is almost absorbed, 1 to 2 minutes.

4 Measure and add 1 1/4 cups of the broth all at once, stirring vigorously with a wooden spoon, and bring to a boil. Decrease the heat to maintain a gentle bubble, cover, and cook until much of the liquid is absorbed, 10 to 12 minutes, giving it another good stir about halfway. Add 1/2 cup more broth, stir vigorously again, cover, and cook at a gentle bubble for 5 more minutes, stirring once halfway. At this point,

test for doneness. The risotto should be slightly soupy and creamy, and the kernels tender but still slightly chewy. If not, add a bit more broth (you may not need all of it), stir, and cook for a few more minutes.

5   While the risotto cooks, finish preparing the clams. Lift them out of the bowl with your hands (don't drain them) so the sand stays at the bottom. Scrub the clams under cold running water to remove any sand and grit on the outside. To cook the clams, bring the remaining $^1/_4$ cup wine just to a boil in a large Dutch oven or heavy-bottomed pot over medium-high heat. Add the clams, ideally in a single layer; cover and steam until they open, 3 to 5 minutes, shaking the pot once halfway. Transfer the clams using a slotted spoon to a large plate, and discard any that haven't opened. Cover the clams loosely with aluminum foil to keep them warm. (You can save the clam juices for another use.)

6   To finish, stir the peas and cream into the risotto, cover, and cook on low until the peas are crisp-tender, about 3 minutes. Stir in the cheese, butter, white pepper, and salt. Taste for salt and white pepper and adjust. Serve in deep plates and divide the clams on top of each serving (5 or 6 per plate). Garnish with a bit of parsley, grind in more white pepper if you like, and pass more Parmesan around.

Caramelized Onion Quiche with Lavender and Crisped Prosciutto

Hunting down dried lavender buds for this tart is definitely worth your while. The strong aroma of these purple blossoms, perfume sweet and pungent at once, offsets the rich sweetness of caramelized onions. Norwegian TV chef Andreas Viestad inspired the extra step of drawing out the juices from the onions for an intensely succulent filling—the longer you wait, the more juices you will get and the richer the flavor. (Watch closely, as your onions may brown more easily.) I always serve this quiche in a classic ceramic tart pan, also called a quiche pan—it moves elegantly from oven to table. You can use a 9-inch glass pie pan, but it will not hold all the onions. Serve with a simple green salad, so as not to distract from the rich flavors.

To draw juices from the onions, 1 teaspoon of salt is ideal. But if you monitor your salt intake, reduce to 1/2 teaspoon. SERVES 4 AS A MAIN COURSE, OR 6 TO 8 AS A STARTER OR BRUNCH DISH

....

CARAMELIZED ONIONS

2 1/2 pounds yellow onions (about 5 medium), cut in half through the root and sliced crosswise 1/4 inch thick (10 cups)

1 teaspoon fine sea salt

2 teaspoons packed light brown sugar

1 tablespoon extra-virgin olive oil

1 tablespoon unsalted butter (optional)

1 tablespoon white balsamic or red wine vinegar

PROSCIUTTO AND CUSTARD FILLING

2 teaspoons extra-virgin olive oil

4 ounces chopped prosciutto (about 1 cup)

2 large eggs

1/2 cup plain whole-milk Greek yogurt

1/4 cup whole or lowfat milk

1 ounce finely grated Gruyère cheese (about 1/2 cup)

1 1/2 teaspoons dried lavender buds

1 teaspoon dried thyme

1/4 teaspoon freshly ground black pepper

Easy Whole Wheat and Olive Oil Tart Shell (see page 172), made with white whole wheat flour and partially baked in a 10-inch tart pan, preferably ceramic

1 tablespoon Dijon mustard

1 To prepare the caramelized onions, put the onions in a large colander set over a large bowl and sprinkle with the salt and sugar. Toss to combine and let sit for at least 10 minutes and up to 2 hours for the juices to draw, tossing a few times. Reserve the onion juices.

2 Heat the olive oil in a large Dutch oven or a heavy-bottomed saucepan over medium heat until shimmering. Add the butter and wait until it melts and the foam almost subsides. Add the onions and cook, uncovered, stirring every 4 minutes or so until a brown sticky layer forms at the bottom and the onions start to brown at the edges, 25 to 30 minutes (decrease the heat a bit if the onions brown too fast). Add the onion juices, scrape the bottom of the pan to remove any browned bits, and cook for about 20 more minutes, stirring and scraping every minute or so, until the onions are golden and lightly caramelized. Stir in the vinegar and cook for 1 minute. Set aside to cool. You will have about 2 cups of onions.

3 Position a rack in the center of the oven and preheat to 375°F.

THE SWEETEST ONIONS

Trying is everything. When I first attempted to caramelize the onions for this recipe, they didn't really brown much, but guess what: dinner guests loved their intense sweetness and asked for more. I tried again without luck, and once more the tart was finished before I could get a second slice for myself. The third time, I finally had lovely, sweet darkened caramelized onions (slicing them thinly was the trick), but in the end I preferred the chunky sweet onions of my first "failure."

4   To prepare the prosciutto and the custard filling, heat the olive oil in a 10-inch skillet over medium heat until shimmering. Add the prosciutto and cook, stirring frequently, until crisp, 5 to 7 minutes. Transfer the prosciutto to a plate. To make the custard, lightly beat the eggs with a fork in a 2-cup liquid cup measure or in a medium bowl. Add the yogurt, milk, cheese, herbs, and pepper and combine well. Place the tart pan with the crust on a large rimless baking sheet for easier handling. Brush the crust with the mustard and sprinkle with half the prosciutto crisps. Distribute the onions across the tart bottom and pour the custard mixture evenly on top.

5   Carefully place the sheet with the tart pan in the oven (it can slide!) and bake until the top of the tart is lightly puffed and golden brown and the filling has firmed up, 45 to 50 minutes. Remove from the oven, carefully slide the tart pan onto a wire rack, and let sit for 15 minutes. Unmold (see sidebar page 173), and cut into wedges, using a sharp serrated knife. Serve warm or at room temperature, sprinkled with the remaining prosciutto.

TO GET A HEAD START: The caramelized onions, as in steps 1 and 2, can be prepared up to 5 days ahead. Chill, covered. The tart can be prepared completely 1 day ahead. Allow to cool to room temperature, cover loosely with plastic wrap, and chill. Bring to room temperature before serving, or warm in a 325°F oven for 15 to 20 minutes.

TO LIGHTEN IT UP: You can use lowfat or nonfat Greek yogurt.

TO MAKE IT VEGETARIAN: Omit the prosciutto. In step 4, add 1/4 teaspoon salt to the custard. Sprinkle the crust with 1/2 cup crumbled blue cheese (2 ounces) before adding the onions.

Greek Millet Saganaki with Shrimp and Ouzo

A saganaki is a traditional two-handled skillet in which Greeks serve aromatic one-pot dishes, typically topped with cheese. This recipe is a play on the classic shrimp and feta saganaki, to which I have added millet for a deliciously satisfying meal, finished with a dash of ouzo to infuse the shrimp with its distinctive anise flavor. A Dutch oven doubles beautifully as a serving vessel, or transfer the cooked millet to a shallow serving bowl and top with the ouzo-infused shrimp. SERVES 4

MILLET

1¹/4 cups water

3/4 cup millet

1 bay leaf

Pinch of fine sea salt

SAGANAKI

1 tablespoon extra-virgin olive oil

1 cup finely chopped yellow onion (about 1 small)

1 clove garlic, peeled and slightly crushed

1 small hot green chile, minced (optional)

1/4 teaspoon fine sea salt

2 tablespoons tomato paste

1 (28-ounce) can whole tomatoes, crushed in a bowl

1/4 teaspoon freshly ground black pepper

1/2 cup green pimiento-stuffed olives, halved if large

4 ounces coarsely crumbled Greek feta cheese (about 1 cup), preferably sheep's milk

SHRIMP, AND TO FINISH

1 pound jumbo shell-on shrimp, deveined and patted dry

Fine sea salt and freshly ground black pepper

2 tablespoons extra-virgin olive oil

1/3 cup ouzo, or other anise-flavored liqueur

1/4 cup chopped fresh flat-leaf parsley

1   To prepare the millet, bring the water, millet, bay leaf, and salt to a boil in a 2-quart saucepan. Decrease the heat to maintain a simmer, cover, and cook until the water is absorbed, about 15 minutes. Remove from the heat and let sit, covered, for 5 to 10 minutes. Uncover, remove the bay leaf, and set aside to cool.

2   Meanwhile, make the saganaki. Heat the olive oil in a large Dutch oven or large heavy-bottomed saucepan over medium heat until it shimmers. Add the onion, garlic, chile, and salt; cook, stirring frequently, until the onion softens and turns light golden, about 5 minutes. Add the tomato paste and cook, stirring, until it darkens, about 1 minute. Add the tomatoes with their juices and the pepper; bring to a boil over medium-high heat. Decrease the heat to maintain a light boil and cook, uncovered, for 3 minutes.

3   Stir in the millet and green olives. Taste for salt and pepper and adjust (keeping in mind that olives and feta cheese can be quite salty). Remove the pot from the heat, sprinkle with the feta, and cover to allow the cheese to soften.

4   To prepare the shrimp, season them with salt and pepper. Heat the olive oil in a 12-inch skillet over high heat until it shimmers. Add the shrimp. Cook, undisturbed, until the shrimp turn golden, 1 to 2 minutes, and then flip them with a spatula and cook until they are just opaque throughout, 1 to 2 more minutes, depending on the size. Add the ouzo and cook until syrupy, about 30 seconds. Using a spatula, briskly remove the shrimp from the pan and arrange on top of the millet. Sprinkle with the parsley and serve at once.

Rye: Tangy and Surprisingly Sweet

My passion for rye is firmly rooted in the German half of my upbringing, and thus inevitably connected to my late father. Mention the German word for rye bread, *Roggenbrot*, to him, and his eyes would light up—and faster than you could close the proverbial gates of the past, his childhood memories would flood the room. So strong is the allure of rye in our family, it even cast a spell on my Greek mom. One of the first things both she and I do when we return to Munich is buy a loaf of whole grain rye bread, with its characteristic coarse crumb—mine from a small organic bakery and hers, naturally, from the ovens of one of the finest bakers in town.

My mom had never seen a classic dark German rye bread in her native Greece, let alone eaten one, before arriving as a young married woman in her twenties in the former German capital of Bonn. Still, these dense and chewy loaves enchanted her for life. I'm not surprised. Allow yourself an introduction to the remarkable rye berry, and you might fall for it as much as she did.

If you have eaten a slice of rye bread in the United States, you probably have noticed the subtle tang it adds to your sandwich, as in the classic Jewish deli food pastrami on rye. Yet these grayish rye breads only hint at the peculiar nature of the grain, whose claim to fame in northern Europe is largely connected to poverty and deprivation. To me, the spell of rye is invariably linked to its use as a whole grain—this is when rye unveils its sensational character. Nowhere else is this more notable than in bread: chew long enough on a slice of whole grain rye, which you must, and wait. Don't swallow, but wait. Notice as the slight sourness of the bread morphs into a sublime subtle sweetness, releasing the natural sugars in the rye, blissfully out of this world.

This mesmerizing trait makes whole grain rye bread the perfect foil for open-faced sandwiches; savory cheeses, mild and pungent; and the hams and cold cuts for which Germany is equally renowned. Both my mom and I crave little else when we get to Munich. My favorite is the simplest of all: a thick slice of rye bread with just a slather of fresh rich butter and a sprinkle of coarse sea salt. Because German butter is richer in fat, you actually need less of it for more flavor. Another slice worth your try is one covered with the thinnest cuts of exquisite dry-cured Westphalian or Black Forest ham. As is customary, we lay it on in waves to get more bang for the bite. Add a few turns of freshly ground black pepper and welcome to cloud nine.

Rye's transformation from slightly sour to ever-so-slightly sweet is even more pronounced in another kind of German bread. This one is linked to the western region of Rhineland, where my father was raised and I was born: it is coal-colored pumpernickel bread (for a recipe, see page 77), a family obsession. Little does it resemble the soft, cottony slices you might find on U.S. supermarket shelves. To emulate the distinct sweet-and-sour personality of pumpernickel, American recipes use cocoa, molasses, espresso, buttermilk, and vinegar. Nothing could be further from its roots. Real German pumpernickel, first documented in 1450, has traditionally been made from two ingredients only, rye and water.

The passion for dark rye bread extends across northern and eastern Europe. A heavy, dark rye loaf will be served on a Russian table, and you will find recipes for many different kinds of rye bread in Scandinavian countries such as Sweden and Finland. Hardy rye has traditionally been grown there because it can sprout in cold climates. Thus ingredients such as sauerkraut, onions, leeks, potatoes, and strong cheeses are a natural fit. Robust spices such as garlic, paprika, and coriander complement its hefty flavor. And of course, don't forget aromatic caraway, whose oil-rich seeds have long been baked into hearty rye bread to aid digestion. One of my favorite uses: savory pie crusts, enhanced with a portion of rye flour, are a suitable bed for onion pies and tarts. Rye's distinct tang lends itself even to sweets, when combined with dried apricots in delicious butter cookies, for example, or in a pear crumble topped with coarsely ground rye and chopped hazelnuts.

Yet rye as a whole grain, not as a flour, is easily overlooked by even the most devoted of grain lovers. German recipes pair the whole berries with red cabbage, tangy-sweet apples, and red wine. Or they marry the sour-sweet grain with red bell peppers and raisins. For this book, I combined this northern grain with the flavors of the Mediterranean, as in Tomato-Rye Risotto with Cumin and Chorizo (see page 171) and in Leek Salad with Grilled Haloumi Cheese and Rye Berries (see page 92).

Ultimately, it was my longing for the tempting chew of German whole grain breads, especially the slow-rising rye breads of my childhood, that made me into the food writer I am today. While I desperately stuffed my suitcases to the hilt, carrying huge bread loaves across the Atlantic—much to the amusement of customs staff—they would always disappear faster than I could slice them. And then what? Before long, I was baking bread, soon to be followed by grinding my own flour in a grain mill (see "My Life with Two Grain Mills," page 148). And last but not least, I created a traditional German sourdough starter to give low-gluten rye flour its lift and a delicious flavor boost. Naturally, it is made from water and rye flour, nothing else.

CHAPTER 7

SWEET ENDINGS

Exploring after-dinner treats with whole grains introduces a culinary universe, intensely flavorful and textured. Some are creamy revelations with an intriguing bite, others are surprisingly soft and comforting creations. And sometimes you won't even know you just had whole grains for dessert. And why should you? First and foremost, dessert should be the splendid crowning of a simple or a lavish meal.

In this chapter, you will find recipes for a Greek-inspired walnut cake with barley, easily assembled when the fancy strikes. And a luscious dark chocolate cake, made with naturally sweet white whole wheat flour. Your guests can play the guessing game to pin down the secret ingredient. Or serve a plate of tiny honey-sweetened almond *cantuccini*, perfect after-dinner bites. Are you a fan of chilled rice pudding? Try a stunning purple-colored one, garnished with a rose water–date topping. Or impress your guests with an intensely fruity olive oil cake, studded with Grand Marnier–plumped figs.

I will also share a few desserts that contain no grains at all. I include them because they pair beautifully with whole grain dishes in the book; plus these desserts are effortless creations that have served me well over the years for surprise guests. And, as you already know from reading this book, I'm obsessive about whole grains only to a point.

Intoxicating Fruit

I like my food tipsy. I dash, drizzle, and splash into my pots and pans any chance I get—volatile spirits, beer, wine, you name it—for breakfast, lunch, and dinner. I don't know how it all got started. According to my mom, in the days of yore, impoverished Greek peasant women pacified their screaming progeny with ouzo, the classic anise-flavored liqueur. It wasn't because they intended to create early alcohol dependency, but it was a last resort when they badly needed to tend to their fields and the small bundles wouldn't stop crying. Desperate to get to work, they would dab a little ouzo onto a piece of cotton for the babies to suck on, putting them quickly to sleep.

Considering the passion with which my mom shares this story, I have sometimes wondered whether she used this volatile pacifier on me, her only daughter. All she admits today is that I was a "lively" child. Maybe she would call me a bit challenging. Or she mentions the day she left me in the playpen to attend to urgent household chores, placing some newspaper in the pen so I could crumble it and entertain myself. When she returned a little while later, I had, to her dismay, eaten much of the printed work. Little did she know that this would set me off toward a promising career as a journalist, and—no surprise there—as a food writer.

While I like to blame my mom for everything, I'm pretty certain that my Greek grandmother laid the foundation for my penchant for stirring spirits into my cooking. I am certain that I have looked too deeply into my *yiayia*'s famed bottle of sour cherry cordial, or *visino* liqueur. Come harvest time, she would combine fresh sour cherries from the city market with cloves, cinnamon sticks, and a healthy dose of sugar. Topped off with a good-quality brandy, she would then set the bottles in a sunny spot to ripen for about four weeks, creating an aromatic concoction like no other. Yet I was never allowed even the tiniest sip, despite the fact that I was six years old and addicted—to the heavenly smell emanating from the crystal flacon locked away in her tall living room buffet. Only adults were given a small sweet shot, on special occasions, in tiny elegant glasses, while I looked on as they oohed and aahed over the ambrosial aroma.

We, the children, were consoled with a delicious sour cherry syrup she also made from scratch every year. *Yiayia* would pour us tall glasses of the thick, dark red syrup, topped off with chilled water from the fridge, on a hot summer day. Divine, yes. But I felt deep disappointment each time, having smelled heaven already.

My *yiayia's* celestial whiff had a profound impact on me. The moment I moved away from home, I established a well-stocked liqueur cabinet in my first apartment and started pouring. A dash of orange liqueur into my first homemade chocolate truffles, a drizzle of Kirsch into a fruity dessert, and a little something into cookies and cakes. Now, to set things straight: while I may sound like a closet alcoholic, I drink little. I will sometimes have a small glass of wine with dinner, but rarely more than that. Still, I hunt for a good table wine with a passion, and my liqueur cabinet is always full. Tangy sweet limoncello, orange-infused Grand Marnier, deep purple-blue cassis, always ouzo, smooth Baileys Irish Cream. Plus sherry, Porto, and Marsala. Not to forget the vodka in my freezer, and at least two kinds of gin.

As a food writer today, I understand the powerful chemical reaction a bit of alcohol can impart to many a cooked dish. The volatile alcohol molecules carry subtle aromas to our noses, refining even the simplest of recipes and making them so much more attractive to eat.

I am thrilled that food culture in this country has changed much since my arrival in 1993. Today, my American friends do what I have always done: they deglaze a pan of mushrooms with a shot of wine, and refine a sauce with vodka or stout. And they will even try my German *Rumtopf*, literally "pot of rum," which typically consists of many layers of summer fruit covered in rum. I prepare mine in the winter on a foundation of dried fruit. My *Rumtopf* is not based on any recipe; I just use the bounty of dried fruit in my pantry. I layer prunes, apricots, apples, and figs together with a few strips of lemon or orange zest, or both, in a ceramic jar. I throw in a cinnamon stick, cloves, honey or sugar, and, of course, enough rum to cover. I leave some space for the fruit to expand, cover the jar, and let the boozy concoction sit in a cool, dark place for at least one week. Voilà, a no-fuss holiday dessert! I spoon out a few of the macerated fruits, deeply flavored and ripe with rum, and serve them over ice cream or yogurt. Or with homemade chocolate pudding—and a dollop of whipped cream, naturally.

Strazzate (*Italian Chocolate-Almond Cookies*)

These chewy, chocolaty, but not-too-sweet cookies are inspired by traditional *strazzate* from the Basilicata region of southern Italy. When I first saw a recipe in *Saveur* magazine, I knew the cookies would be even more alluring with mild spelt flour, so I rushed to create them anew. I didn't have the traditional herbal liqueur Strega, so I flavored them with Amaretto and added more almonds and chocolate chips for good measure. The next day, I dipped these Americanized *strazzate* into afternoon coffee with my Roman friend Alessandra on a 90-degree day in Boston—*perfetto!*

Keep a close eye on these cookies and do not overbake them, if you like them chewy and moist. The overnight chilling makes for a more even cookie, so it's best to make this easy dough ahead.

MAKES ABOUT 36 (2-INCH) COOKIES

....

$1^1/_2$ cups whole grain spelt flour
(6 ounces)

$1^1/_2$ cups lightly packed almond
meal ($5^1/_4$ ounces; see page 195)

1 cup packed light brown sugar

$1^1/_2$ tablespoons cocoa powder,
preferably Dutch-process

$1/_2$ teaspoon baking powder

$1/_2$ teaspoon fine sea salt

3 ounces bittersweet chocolate chips
with 60 percent cocoa content
(about $1/_2$ cup)

$1/_4$ cup coarsely chopped toasted
skin-on almonds (see page 37)

$1/_2$ cup Amaretto liqueur

$1/_3$ cup strong black coffee, at room
temperature

1 tablespoon extra-virgin olive oil

About 18 whole skin-on almonds,
halved lengthwise, or 36 additional chocolate chips

> **SEE MEASURING
> WHOLE GRAIN FLOUR,
> PAGE 28**

1   Whisk together the spelt flour, almond meal, brown sugar, cocoa powder, baking powder, and salt in a large bowl. Take care to break up any clumps of almond meal or brown sugar with your fingers. Stir in the chocolate chips and almonds. Make a well in the center. In a small bowl, whisk together the Amaretto, coffee, and olive oil. Pour the wet ingredients into the center of the dry ingredients and combine with a dough whisk (see page 30) or wooden spoon just until a soft and moist dough forms. Cover the bowl with plastic wrap and chill overnight.

2   Position a rack in the center of the oven and preheat to 350°F. Line 2 large rimless baking sheets with parchment paper. Have a small bowl with water ready.

3   Moisten your hands, pinch off truffle-size pieces (1 slightly heaped tablespoon, or $3/_4$ ounce each) and roll between your palms into smooth $1^1/_4$-inch balls. The dough will be quite sticky. Place the balls on the baking sheets, leaving 2 inches between each one. Gently press an almond half or a chocolate chip into the center of each cookie. Chill the sheets with the cookies for 15 minutes.

4   Bake, one sheet at a time, until the cookies have spread and firmed up but still yield when gently pressed with a finger, 16 to 18 minutes. Remove the cookies from the oven, but leave them on the baking sheet for 2 minutes, and then slide the parchment paper with the cookies onto a wire rack to cool comlpetely. They will continue to firm up as they cool.

TO GET A HEAD START: The dough, as in step 1, can be made up to 2 days ahead. *Strazzate* can be stored, between layers of waxed paper, in an airtight container for up to 3 days. They freeze well for at least 1 month.

Honey-Almond Cantuccini

Small almond biscotti are called *cantuccini*, or "little nooks," in the Tuscany region of Italy. These are honey-sweetened and delicately flavored with almonds in two forms—a finely ground meal and whole toasted nuts. Watch these twice-baked cookies closely, as you don't want them to brown too much and lose their fine fragrance. You will need extra almond meal for the work surface. **MAKES ABOUT 44 SMALL COOKIES**

1³/4 cups whole wheat pastry flour (7 ounces)

1 cup lightly packed almond meal (3¹/2 ounces)

¹/2 teaspoon fine sea salt

¹/2 cup coarsely chopped toasted skin-on whole almonds (see page 37)

¹/2 cup extra-virgin olive oil

¹/2 cup honey

2¹/2 teaspoons vanilla extract

2 teaspoons finely grated lemon zest

ALMOND MEAL

Almond meal is nothing other than simple ground almonds. Almond meal has become more widely available as bakers cherish its sweet, nutty fragrance. You can easily make it yourself. Place 1 cup whole skin-on almonds (4¹/2 ounces) in the bowl of a food processor fitted with the metal blade and process until finely ground, about 35 seconds. This will give you about 1¹/3 cups almond meal. Keep a close eye to avoid over processing the almonds, as they can turn quickly into an oily paste.

1 Whisk together the whole wheat pastry flour, almond meal, and salt in a large bowl, and then stir in the almonds. Make a well in the center. In a medium bowl, using a large whisk, thoroughly blend the olive oil, honey, vanilla, and lemon zest until thick and syrupy, about 1 minute. Add to the center of the dry ingredients and combine, using a rubber spatula or a wooden spoon, just until a soft dough forms. Do not over-mix. Cover the bowl with a plate and let sit at room temperature for 30 minutes.

2 Meanwhile, position a rack in the center of the oven and preheat to 300°F. Line a large rimless baking sheet with parchment paper.

3 Lightly sprinkle your work surface with almond meal. Cut the dough inside the bowl into four equal pieces. It will be soft, sticky, and malleable. Briefly knead each piece a few times to smooth and form into a log, about 7 inches long and 1¹/2 inches wide—first rolling it between your palms, and then briefly rolling on the work surface. If almond pieces protrude, gently press them in while working the dough. Add more almond meal to your work surface if needed. Repeat with the remaining dough. Place the logs on the prepared baking sheet, leaving about 2 inches in between.

4 Bake the logs until the tops show small cracks, firm up, and just start to brown, 32 to 35 minutes. Remove from the oven, and carefully slide the parchment paper with the logs onto a wire rack to cool for about 15 minutes (or use a metal spatula to transfer the logs if your baking sheet has a rim). Leave the oven on.

5 Transfer the logs to a cutting board. Using a large, sharp serrated knife, cut each log diagonally into ¹/2-inch-thick slices. Return the parchment paper to the baking sheet. Place the slices upright (not cut-side up) onto the sheet.

6 Bake until the *cantuccini* feel dry to the touch at the cut sides (not on top) and just start to brown at the edges, 15 to 17 minutes. Transfer the *cantuccini* to a wire rack to cool completely before storing.

TO GET A HEAD START: The *cantuccini* can be stored in an airtight container for 1 to 2 weeks. They freeze well for at least 1 month.

Purple Rice Pudding with Rose Water Dates

The first time I tasted rose water in a milky pudding, as a child in Turkey, I was overwhelmed by its intensity. Always the curious eater, I tried again, wondering whether I could ever like this flavor, and then again—and again and again. Rose water has this effect on you. Its concentrated, bold aroma, evoking the serenity of churches or mosques, does require some getting used to, but when you do, you will never stop longing for it. In this dessert, I infuse sweet dates with rose water's heady aroma and add them to a rice pudding made with Chinese black rice. This soft-textured rice was once eaten only by the emperors of China. Lotus Foods offers a delicious heirloom variety under the trademarked label Forbidden Rice (for sources, see page 219). It makes for a stunning dessert as it turns a deep burgundy hue when cooked. Choose firmer dates such as Deglet Noor for this dessert, as you don't want them to become mushy in the pudding. SERVES 4

....

PURPLE RICE

1¹/₄ cups water

¹/₂ cup Chinese black rice

DATE TOPPING

¹/₄ cup finely chopped pitted dates (about 6)

2 dates, pitted and cut into thin strips

3 teaspoons rose water

RICE PUDDING, AND TO FINISH

1¹/₄ cups half-and-half

2 tablespoons turbinado sugar

Pinch of fine sea salt

1 teaspoon finely grated lemon zest

1 (1-inch) piece cinnamon stick

¹/₂ teaspoon vanilla extract

1 To prepare the rice, bring the water and rice to a boil in a small heavy-bottomed saucepan. Decrease the temperature to maintain a simmer, cover, and cook until the rice is tender yet still slightly chewy, about 30 minutes. Some water will remain (do not drain).

2 While the rice is cooking, prepare the date topping. Place the chopped dates in a small bowl and drizzle with 2 teaspoons of the rose water. Add the date strips to a different small bowl and drizzle with the remaining 1 teaspoon rose water. Stir the dates in both bowls and set aside, stirring once or twice more.

3 To finish, add the half-and-half, sugar, salt, ¹/₂ teaspoon of the lemon zest, cinnamon stick, and vanilla to the rice. Return to a boil over medium-high heat, stirring several times. Decrease the heat to maintain a gentle bubble and cook, uncovered, for 15 more minutes, stirring every few minutes or so. The consistency should be creamy yet soupy— the mixture will thicken as it cools. Remove the saucepan from the heat and remove the cinnamon stick. Stir in the chopped dates and the remaining ¹/₂ teaspoon lemon zest.

4 Divide the rice pudding among small individual dessert bowls or cups. Garnish with a few of the rose water–infused date strips, and serve warm or at room temperature.

TO GET A HEAD START: The rice pudding can be made 1 day ahead. Transfer the pudding to a medium bowl and allow to cool to room temperature, stirring a few times. Cover and chill. The rice will continue to absorb liquid—you may need to add a bit of chilled milk or half-and-half just before serving to loosen it. Keep the infused date strips separate, covered with plastic wrap, and garnish the pudding just before serving.

TO LIGHTEN IT UP: Use whole milk instead of half-and-half for an everyday treat.

Greek Yogurt Ice Cream

Creamy, rich Greek yogurt is so versatile, it even makes a light and tangy ice cream—just what you need on a hot summer day. It is made in a flash (no time-consuming custard base) and, in our house, eaten almost as fast. Adding a dash of liqueur to ice cream lowers the freezing point, resulting in a smoother texture. Enjoy this treat on its own or with summer-ripened peaches and drizzled with more honey, if you like. My tester Karen topped it with grilled pineapple—fabulous! If you are in the mood for baking, serve it with Honey-Almond *Cantuccini* (page 195), or, if you're in a hurry, with store-bought ginger snaps. Yogurt ice cream will last for 1 week. **MAKES ABOUT 2 PINTS**

2 cups plain whole-milk Greek yogurt

1/2 cup heavy whipping cream

1/2 cup honey

1 tablespoon freshly squeezed lemon juice

1 tablespoon limoncello or vodka

1 Place all the ingredients in a large stainless steel bowl. Whisk until they are well blended and the honey is incorporated.

2 Cover with a lid or with plastic wrap and refrigerate the mixture for 2 hours. Freeze in an ice cream maker according to the manufacturer's instructions. (If you don't have an ice cream maker, transfer the bowl with the ice cream to the freezer. After 1 hour, beat the mixture using a handheld mixer until smooth while scraping down the sides of the bowl with a spatula. This prevents the formation of ice crystals. Return to the freezer and repeat a few more times until frozen. This will take at least 5 hours, depending on your freezer.) Remove from the freezer 15 minutes before serving.

TO LIGHTEN IT UP: Lowfat Greek yogurt works fine.

Orange-Rosemary Cookies with Olive Oil

All throughout my childhood, I had a weak spot for Greek Lenten cookies. I was smitten by their remarkable simplicity, mouthwatering and nourishing at once. These small rosemary-scented treats are inspired by Lenten cookies (hence no eggs or butter), and you'll find them as delicious as they are easy to make. My testers had a split opinion on the crunchy turbinado sugar topping. Some loved it, while others preferred a plain cookie. Eat them on their own, or serve alongside ice cream or with dessert wine. **MAKES ABOUT 30 (1½-INCH) COOKIES**

....

1 orange

1 cup white whole wheat flour (4¼ ounces)

½ cup lightly packed almond meal (1¾ ounces; see page 195)

¾ teaspoon baking powder

⅛ teaspoon fine sea salt

¼ cup extra-virgin olive oil

¼ cup packed light brown sugar

½ teaspoon minced fresh rosemary

½ teaspoon vanilla extract

2 to 3 tablespoons turbinado sugar, for topping

> SEE MEASURING WHOLE GRAIN FLOUR, PAGE 28

1   Finely grate the zest of the orange until you have 1 teaspoon. Set the zest aside, and squeeze the orange until you have ¼ cup juice. Set aside as well.

2   Whisk together the white whole wheat flour, almond meal, baking powder, and salt in a large bowl. Take care to break up any clumps of almond meal with your fingers. Make a well in the center.

In a medium bowl, vigorously whisk together the olive oil and brown sugar for about 1 minute until the sugar starts to dissolve and the color lightens, about 1 minute. Add the orange juice, zest, rosemary, and vanilla extract; whisk to combine. Pour the oil mixture into the center of the flour mixture. Combine the wet and the dry ingredients with a dough whisk (see page 30) or a wooden spoon until just incorporated. Do not overmix.

3   Place a 12 by 18-inch sheet of parchment paper on a work surface in front of you, the long side parallel to the edge of the counter. Scrape the soft, moist dough onto the bottom third of the parchment paper. Using your hands, roughly shape the dough into a 14-inch-long log about 1½ inches in diameter. Use the parchment paper to help you roll it up into a tight log. Twist the ends to secure the log. Chill in the freezer until the dough has firmed up, about 1½ hours (it will still be soft to the touch).

4   Place 1 rack in the top third of the oven and the other in the bottom third, and preheat to 350°F. Line 2 large rimless baking sheets with parchment paper. Place the turbinado sugar in a small bowl.

5   Unwrap the log and cut it with a sharp knife into slices a little less than ½-inch thick (the dough will still be soft). Gently press the top of each cookie into the turbinado sugar and place it on a prepared baking sheet, spacing at least 1 inch apart.

6   Bake both sheets at the same time, swapping them halfway, until the edges and bottoms of the cookies turn golden brown (they will still yield slightly when pressed with a finger), 16 to 18 minutes. Carefully slide the cookies with the parchment paper onto a wire rack to cool completely. They will crisp as they cool.

Riesling Zabaglione over Red Currants

Italian zabaglione, or sabayon in French, is a billowy custard, light yet deeply scented with aromatic wine. Despite its sophisticated name, it is a cinch to prepare and impressive to serve. In short, zabaglione is a host's dream. You can whip it up in an instant after your guests have cleaned their plates. Just be sure to line up your ingredients and clean and chill the fruit ahead of time (sugar them a few minutes before you start beating the eggs). Tart red currants are my first choice, but strawberries or a mix of summer berries work nicely as well. Do I need to say: no whole grains in this dessert? It pairs beautifully with the Sardine Tart with Sweet Bell Peppers and Currants (page 174) or with the Caramelized Onion Quiche with Lavender and Crisped Prosciutto (page 184). SERVES 4

RED CURRANTS

1 pound red currants, rinsed and drained

2 to 3 tablespoons turbinado or granulated sugar

ZABAGLIONE, AND TO FINISH

3 large egg yolks, at room temperature

3 ounces semidry Riesling or Sauvignon Blanc (1/4 cup plus 2 tablespoons)

3 tablespoons granulated sugar

1 tablespoon Grand Marnier or other good-quality orange-flavored liqueur

1 First, prepare the red currants. Work on top of a medium bowl: using a fork, remove the red currants from their stems with a single downward scraping motion. Combine the currants with sugar to taste, and set them aside for 15 to 30 minutes for the juices to draw.

2 To make the zabaglione, prepare a water bath: bring a large saucepan with about 1 inch of water to a lively simmer but not a vigorous boil. Whisk together the egg yolks, wine, and sugar in a large stainless steel or copper bowl and rest the bowl on the saucepan. Be sure the bottom of the bowl does not touch the water.

3 Using a handheld mixer at medium speed, beat the mixture on top of the water bath until it triples in volume and becomes glossy, 3 to 4 minutes. First it will expand and become airy, light, and foamy. After about 2 minutes it will thicken and then turn glossy and more stable—done! Be sure to scrape the bottom and sides of the bowl with the beaters so the eggs don't scramble. (You can also use a large balloon whisk, though it might take a bit longer.) Remove the bowl from the water bath and whisk in the Grand Marnier.

4 To finish, divide the red currants among serving bowls and top with the warm zabaglione. Serve at once.

FINGER-LICKING FAILURE

When I made zabaglione the first time, I missed the key moment of luscious glossiness and kept beating for another minute. As a result, the mixture collapsed and turned into a thick yellow cream. Guess what: everyone licked their bowl clean, myself included. Imperfectly delicious!

Almond-Peach Clafouti

This beautiful rustic dessert from the south of France is a breeze to make and striking to behold—perfect for last-minute dinner guests. This clafouti gives off the alluring scent of marzipan, a childhood favorite, thanks to a handful of ground almonds and a dash of Amaretto, combined with mild whole wheat pastry flour. I like my clafouti a tad creamy. Leave it in the oven a few minutes longer if you prefer yours more cakelike. Serve on its own, or with a dollop of whipped cream or vanilla ice cream.

For an attractive presentation, use an ovenproof ceramic gratin dish (1-quart volume). You will need extra almond meal for the dish. SERVES 6

1/2 cup heavy whipping cream

1/2 cup whole milk

1 tablespoon finely grated orange zest (from about 1 orange)

1 teaspoon vanilla extract

3 large eggs, at room temperature

1/3 cup granulated sugar

1/3 cup almond meal (11/4 ounces) (see page 195)

1/3 cup whole wheat pastry or whole spelt flour (13/8 ounces)

1 tablespoon Amaretto or brandy (optional)

2 cups chopped fresh peaches, cut into 1/2- to 3/4-inch pieces, about 12 ounces (thawed, drained, and chopped if using frozen slices)

Confectioners' sugar, for dusting

> **SEE MEASURING WHOLE GRAIN FLOUR, PAGE 28**

1. Position a rack in the center of the oven and preheat to 375°F. Butter a round 9-inch glass pie dish, or coat with cooking spray. Sprinkle with almond meal, tapping out any excess.

2. Whisk together the cream, milk, orange zest, and vanilla extract in a 2-cup liquid measuring cup or small bowl. In a large bowl, using a large whisk, lightly beat the eggs to blend. Gradually add the granulated sugar and whisk vigorously until slightly thickened and pale, about 1 minute. Whisk in the cream mixture, and then the almond meal until smooth. Gently stir in the whole wheat pastry flour until just combined. Stir in the liqueur. The batter will be liquid.

3. Scatter the peaches in the pan and gently pour the batter on top (the fruit will bob up).

4. Bake until the clafouti is puffed and golden brown around the edges and a knife inserted into the center comes out just about clean, about 30 minutes. Transfer the pan to a wire rack to cool for about 15 minutes. Serve warm or at room temperature, dusted with confectioners' sugar.

TO GET A HEAD START: The clafouti can be prepared about 1 hour ahead. Set aside at room temperature. Dust with confectioners' sugar when ready to serve.

TO VARY IT: Many types of fresh fruit, cut into 1/2-inch pieces, can be used instead of peaches. Fresh cherries are a classic choice. In the winter, clementines add zing. Increase the sugar by 1 to 2 tablespoons if the fruits are tart.

TO LIGHTEN IT UP: You can use 1/2 cup half-and-half instead of the cream and 1/2 cup lowfat milk instead of whole milk.

Wheat Berry Fools with Grand Marnier Figs

This is how I like to eat my wheat berries—and not just on Sundays. Softly whipped cream and naturally thick Greek yogurt make a winning combination, resulting in a lofty dessert with a snappy tartness. Soft wheat berries are my first choice here, but other leftover cooked berries from the wheat family work just as nicely, especially spelt, Kamut, or farro (for cooking instructions, see pages 24–25). Hard wheat berries add a bit too much chew for my taste. If you want to make this for children, plump the figs in freshly squeezed orange juice instead of liqueur. This concoction would be equally delicious as a decadent topping for the saffron waffles (page 51), or add it as a treat to a brunch table on the weekend. **SERVES 6 TO 8**

3/4 cup finely chopped dried figs, preferably Turkish or Greek

3 tablespoons Grand Marnier or other good-quality orange-flavored liqueur

1 cup plain whole-milk Greek yogurt

4 tablespoons honey

1 tablespoon plus 1 teaspoon freshly grated orange zest (about 2 oranges)

1/4 teaspoon ground cinnamon

1 cup cooked soft whole wheat berries

1 cup heavy whipping cream, chilled

1 Combine the figs and the liqueur in a small bowl and set aside to plump for 15 minutes, stirring once or twice, while you prep the ingredients.

2 Meanwhile, beat the yogurt with 2 tablespoons of the honey, 1 tablespoon of the orange zest, and the cinnamon in a large bowl until smooth. Stir in the wheat berries. Using a hand mixer at medium speed, whip the cream in a medium bowl until foamy. Add the remaining 2 tablespoons honey and continue whipping until soft peaks form.

3 Drain the figs, reserving their juices. Combine 2 tablespoons of the figs with the remaining 1 teaspoon zest in a small bowl and set aside for garnish. Stir the remaining figs into the bowl with the yogurt mixture. Scrape one-third of the whipped cream on top and fold in using a spatula. Fold in the remaining whipped cream in 2 additions until just incorporated. Divide among serving bowls, cover with plastic wrap, and chill for 2 hours. To serve, top each bowl with a bit of the reserved figs and their juices.

TO GET A HEAD START: The dessert can be prepared up to 4 hours ahead. Add a dash more liqueur to the figs reserved for the garnish, if necessary.

TO LIGHTEN IT UP: You can use lowfat plain Greek yogurt, if you like.

Greek Walnut-Barley Cake

Greeks love walnut cake, *karidhopita*. There are a myriad of recipes for this popular sweet. Some burst with richness from eggs and butter. Others, like this whole grain cake, are more austere, with olive oil and orange juice. The result is a subtle fruitiness and a beautiful crumb. But don't expect a moist American cake such as the Walnut Spice Breakfast Cake (page 62)—this is dry in comparison, but in a delicious crumbly way. Serve the cake for dessert, topped with vanilla ice cream or with softly whipped cream. I also slice it up for breakfast, and eat it either on its own or with a dollop of lightly sweetened Greek yogurt. **MAKES 1 (8-INCH-SQUARE CAKE) TO SERVE 10 TO 12**

1/2 cup dark raisins

2 tablespoons brandy or orange juice

2 cups white whole wheat flour (8 1/2 ounces)

1 cup whole grain barley flour (4 ounces)

1 1/4 teaspoons ground cinnamon

1/2 teaspoon ground cloves, preferably freshly ground

1/2 teaspoon baking soda

1/2 teaspoon fine sea salt

3/4 cup extra-virgin olive oil

3/4 cup freshly squeezed orange juice

3/4 cup packed light or dark brown sugar

1/2 cup chopped toasted walnuts (see page 37)

3 tablespoons turbinado or granulated sugar, for sprinkling

Confectioners' sugar, for dusting

> SEE MEASURING
> WHOLE GRAIN FLOUR,
> PAGE 28

1   Position a rack in the center of the oven and preheat to 350°F. Butter an 8-inch square glass baking dish, or coat with cooking spray. Dust with flour, shaking out any excess.

2   Combine the raisins and the brandy in a small bowl to plump, stirring once or twice while you prep the ingredients.

3   Whisk together the white whole wheat flour and barley flour, 1 teaspoon of the cinnamon, cloves, baking soda, and salt in a large bowl. Make a well in the center. Place the olive oil, orange juice, and brown sugar in a medium bowl. Beat vigorously with a large whisk until the sugar dissolves and the mixture thickens slightly and becomes opaque, about 2 minutes. Pour the olive oil mixture into the center of the dry ingredients and stir with a spatula until just combined. Do not overmix. Fold in the plumped raisins along with any liquid, and then the walnuts.

4   Scrape the batter into the prepared pan, evening out the top with a spatula. Combine the turbinado sugar with the remaining 1/4 teaspoon cinnamon in a small bowl and sprinkle over the cake. Bake until a cake tester or wooden skewer inserted into the center comes out clean, about 40 minutes.

5   Transfer the pan to a wire rack to cool for about 10 minutes. Loosen around the edges with a small sharp knife, unmold, and return the cake to the wire rack right side up to cool completely. Just before serving, dust generously with confectioners' sugar. Cut into 9 or 12 pieces.

TO GET A HEAD START: Don't hesitate to bake this cake 1 day ahead, as its flavors deepen. Store in an airtight container at room temperature.

Dark Chocolate Cake with Amaretto

Deliciously velvety and not overly sweet, this pitch-dark and scrumptious chocolate cake is assembled with such ease that you might never be tempted to buy one again. Ruth Reichl's Last-Minute Chocolate Cake, published in her book *Garlic and Sapphires*, inspired my whole grain version. Be sure to check for doneness a few minutes early. You don't want your cake tester to come out fully dry, as the residual moistness makes this a treat! I like to contrast this cake's deep flavor with a dollop of tangy crème fraîche, briefly whisked and spiked with a dash of Amaretto, just to be fair. MAKES 1 LOAF; 12 TO 16 SLICES

6 tablespoons unsalted butter
  (3 ounces)

4 ounces unsweetened chocolate,
  coarsely chopped

3/4 cup brewed strong black coffee

1/2 teaspoon instant espresso powder

1 cup white whole wheat flour
  (41/4 ounces)

1/2 teaspoon baking soda

1/4 teaspoon fine sea salt

1 large egg, at room temperature

2 tablespoons Amaretto liqueur

1 teaspoon vanilla extract

2/3 cup turbinado sugar

Confectioners' sugar, for dusting

> SEE MEASURING
> WHOLE GRAIN FLOUR,
> PAGE 28

1   Position a rack in the center of the oven and preheat to 325°F. Butter a 9 by 5-inch aluminum loaf pan or coat with cooking spray. Dust with flour, tapping out any excess.

2   Cut the butter into 4 to 5 pieces and add, together with the chocolate, coffee, and espresso powder, to a large heavy-bottomed saucepan. Heat over medium-low, stirring frequently with a wooden spoon, until the butter has almost melted, 3 to 5 minutes. Remove the pan from the heat and stir until combined. The mixture will look granular. Set aside to cool to lukewarm, 5 to 10 minutes.

3   Whisk together the white whole wheat flour, baking soda, and salt in a medium bowl. Lightly beat the egg to blend in a small bowl, and then stir in the Amaretto and vanilla extract. Once the chocolate mixture has cooled, stir in the turbinado sugar and then the egg mixture; stir to combine. The mixture will thicken slightly. Using a large whisk, add the flour mixture in 2 additions, stirring after each addition until just blended; do not overmix. Scrape the dough evenly into the loaf pan.

4   Bake until a toothpick inserted into the center of the cake comes out with a few moist crumbs attached, about 35 minutes. Place the pan on a wire rack to cool for about 10 minutes. Loosen the cake around the edges with a small sharp knife, unmold, and set it right side up on the wire rack. You can serve the cake warm, or leave it on the rack to cool completely. Just before serving, dust with confectioners' sugar and slice with a serrated knife.

TO GET A HEAD START: This cake's deep chocolate flavor improves if baked a few hours or 1 day ahead. Store in an airtight container at room temperature.

Ricotta Millet Pudding with Warm Raspberry Compote

This creamy dessert creation, reminiscent of rice pudding, is a perfect introduction to millet. In fact, it is my secret weapon for all those convinced they don't like the grain. Just don't let your guests in on the mysterious ingredient until their bowls are empty—and empty they will be, guaranteed. This dessert improves when prepared ahead, which also frees up time on the day you entertain. While the pudding is delicious on its own, the warm raspberry compote elevates this dessert from simple to festive. In a hurry? Just decorate the pudding with a few fresh berries and a dollop of whipped cream, if you like.
SERVES 6 TO 8

MILLET

1 cup water

1/2 cup millet

2/3 cup whole milk or lowfat milk

1/2 teaspoon vanilla extract

Pinch of fine sea salt

PUDDING

1 1/2 cups part-skim ricotta cheese

1/4 cup honey

1 tablespoon finely grated lemon zest

2 teaspoons freshly squeezed lemon juice

1 cup heavy whipping cream, chilled

1/4 cup sugar

RASPBERRY COMPOTE, AND TO FINISH

2 1/2 cups fresh or frozen raspberries (do not thaw if using frozen)

1/4 cup honey

1 To prepare the millet, bring the water and the millet to a boil in a small heavy-bottomed saucepan. Decrease the heat to maintain a simmer, cover, and cook until the water is absorbed, about 20 minutes. Combine the milk, vanilla extract, and salt in a small bowl and stir into the millet. Return to a simmer, cover, and cook until the liquid is absorbed, about 15 more minutes. Remove from the heat and let sit, covered, for 5 minutes. Uncover and allow to cool to room temperature, about 60 minutes (if in a hurry, spread the millet on a baking sheet).

2 Once the millet has cooled, make the pudding. Place the ricotta, honey, lemon zest, and juice in a large bowl and beat vigorously using a wooden spoon until the ingredients are incorporated. Loosen the millet with a fork, and then stir it into the ricotta mixture, breaking up any lumps.

3 In a large deep bowl, whip the cream with a handheld mixer, first on medium then on high speed, gradually adding the sugar until medium-firm peaks form. Using a rubber spatula, fold the whipped cream into the ricotta-millet mixture in 3 additions. Divide the pudding among serving bowls. Chill, covered with plastic wrap, for at least 2 hours or overnight.

4 When ready to serve, make the raspberry compote. Place the raspberries and the honey in a medium saucepan. Cook over medium-low to medium heat, gently stirring once in a while so as not to crush the berries, until the compote is hot and the berries are just warmed through, 5 to 8 minutes.

5 To finish, spoon a bit of the raspberry compote over the chilled ricotta pudding and serve at once.

TO GET A HEAD START: Make the millet, as in step 1, ahead as per the instructions on page 23.

Crème au Chocolat with Brandied Blackberries

A cross between a suave mousse au chocolat and a dense luscious ice cream, this is a mouthful of a dessert. It is as easy as 1, 2, 3, and hence one of my favorite last-minute desserts. Admittedly, it has no whole grains, but I follow my passion for good food. Just two ingredients, crème fraîche and chocolate, are gently melted together and then chilled. Given the nature of these ingredients, you will hopefully understand that the serving size is, well, moderate. In a hurry? Garnish with a dollop of whipped cream and fresh mint leaves. This pairs with—everything.

You can use dark chocolate with 70 percent cocoa content, but you have to watch closely in step 2 as it scorches more easily. Crème fraîche has become more widely available in recent years, and it is well worth seeking out for this dessert. Full-fat sour cream does work, but it's a little less velvety—be sure you get a high-quality brand (the fewer ingredients, the better). If using sour cream, prepare 1 day ahead to allow the tanginess to mellow. Also, use 3 (instead of 2) tablespoons sugar for the fruit topping.
SERVES 6

CHOCOLATE CREAM

2 cups crème fraîche (16 ounces)

6 ounces good-quality bittersweet chocolate, finely chopped (about 1¹/₄ cups)

BRANDIED BLACKBERRIES

2 cups fresh blackberries (about 6 ounces)

1¹/₂ tablespoons packed light brown sugar

1¹/₂ tablespoons brandy

1   To make the chocolate cream, place the crème fraîche and the chocolate in a large heavy-bottomed saucepan and combine well using a wooden spoon. Heat the mixture over medium-low heat, stirring gently and almost continuously, until it is smooth and the chocolate has melted, about 5 minutes. The mixture will look granular.

2   Increase the heat to medium. Stirring all the while and watching closely, bring just to a boil (bubbles should break just below the surface), 3 to 4 minutes. Immediately remove from the heat, stir a few more times, and spoon the darkened mixture into small (5-ounce) dessert cups. Allow the chocolate cream to cool to room temperature; cover loosely with plastic wrap and chill until firm, at least 2 hours or overnight. Allow to come to room temperature before serving.

3   To make the brandied blackberries, combine the ingredients in a medium bowl and let sit for 20 to 30 minutes, stirring a few times. Top each dessert with a few berries and their juices.

TO GET A HEAD START: Crème au chocolat can be made up to 2 days ahead.

TO VARY IT: Replace blackberries with raspberries.

Amaranth-Walnut Cookies with Brandy

Everyone needs a real butter cookie once in a while. I certainly do. These cookies showcase the intense nuttiness of amaranth flour. Rolling them in minuscule amaranth seeds gives them a playful touch and adds a nice crunch, but they are also delicious without. Fine sea salt retains some of its crystalline texture during baking, adding sparks of salt to contrast with the natural sweetness of the whole grain flours.

For best outcome allow the dough to chill thoroughly and firm up, ideally overnight. If the dough balls become soft while you finish them with the walnuts, as in step 4, chill the baking sheet with the cookies for 20 minutes before baking. MAKES ABOUT 32 (2-INCH) COOKIES

4 ounces toasted walnut pieces
  (about 1 slightly heaped cup;
  see page 37)

1/2 cup sugar

*3/4 cup white whole wheat flour
  (3 1/8 ounces)*

1/4 cup amaranth flour (1 ounce)

1/4 teaspoon fine sea salt

*7 tablespoons unsalted butter
  (3 1/2 ounces), softened*

*1 large egg yolk, at room
  temperature*

1 tablespoon brandy

1 teaspoon vanilla extract

*About 6 tablespoons amaranth
  seeds, for rolling (optional)*

*About 32 toasted walnut halves
  or pieces*

SEE MEASURING
WHOLE GRAIN FLOUR,
PAGE 28

1 Place the 4 ounces of walnuts and 2 tablespoons of the sugar in the bowl of a food processor fitted with the metal blade. Process until the mixture looks sandy and the nuts are finely ground, about 15 seconds.

2 Whisk together the white whole wheat flour, amaranth flour, and salt in a medium bowl. In a large bowl, beat the butter with an electric mixer at medium speed until smooth, about 30 seconds. Gradually add the remaining sugar and beat until fluffy and smooth, 1 to 2 minutes, scraping the sides with a rubber spatula as needed. Add the egg yolk, brandy, and vanilla and beat until well blended, about 30 seconds. Reduce the speed to low and beat in the nut mixture, then gradually add the flour mixture until it is just incorporated. Cover the bowl with plastic wrap and chill until the dough is firm, at least 3 hours or overnight.

3 Place a rack 1 notch below the center of the oven and preheat to 350°F. Line 2 large rimless baking sheets with parchment paper. Place the amaranth seeds in a small bowl.

4 Pinch off walnut-size pieces of the firm dough and roll them between your palms into smooth 1-inch balls. Roll each ball in amaranth seeds, gently pressing to adhere if needed, and place on the baking sheet, leaving 2 inches between pieces. Make an indentation with your thumb in the center of each ball, gently pressing it down about a third of its height, and then lightly press a walnut half into the center.

5 Bake, 1 sheet at a time, until the cookies just turn golden brown around the edges and firm up but still yield to gentle pressure, 17 to 18 minutes. Remove from the oven and carefully slide the parchment paper with the cookies onto a wire rack to cool. The cookies will crisp as they cool.

TO GET A HEAD START: The dough, including step 2, can be made up to 2 days ahead. The finished cookies will keep in an airtight container up to 3 days, or they can be frozen for up to 1 month.

Lemon-Scented Olive Oil Cake with Plumped Figs

When the holiday season gets fast-paced, this is the cake I take to the party. Intensely fruity and moist, it looks festive in a tart pan and is easy to make, even the day before. Here, the quality of figs makes all the difference. Look for Turkish or Greek figs that yield nicely to pressure (otherwise they are old and dried-out). Various dried figs absorb liquid differently, so you may or may not have any soaking liquid left.

The inspiration for this spiked holiday treat was a lemon-fig cake in *Everyday Food* by Martha Stewart. I serve my whole grain cake with orange sorbet or with softly whipped cream, beating in a dash of any remaining soaking liquid or a swig of Grand Marnier, if you like. **MAKES 1 ROUND (9¹/₂-INCH CAKE), TO SERVE 10 TO 12**

....

8 ounces finely chopped and stemmed dried figs, preferably Turkish or Greek (about 1¹/₂ cups)

3 tablespoons freshly squeezed orange juice

3 tablespoons Grand Marnier or other good-quality orange-flavored liqueur, or more orange juice

1¹/₂ cups whole wheat pastry flour (6 ounces)

³/₄ teaspoon baking powder

¹/₄ teaspoon fine sea salt

1 large egg, at room temperature

¹/₂ cup honey

¹/₂ cup extra-virgin olive oil

¹/₂ cup whole milk

1 tablespoon finely grated lemon zest

Confectioners' sugar, for dusting

1 Position a rack in the center of the oven and preheat to 350°F. Brush a 9¹/₂-inch tart pan with removable bottom with olive oil and set on a large rimless baking sheet for easier handling.

2 Combine the figs, orange juice, and Grand Marnier in a small bowl to plump for 15 to 20 minutes while you prep the ingredients, stirring once or twice in between.

3 Whisk together the whole wheat pastry flour, baking powder, and salt in a large bowl. Make a well in the center. In a medium bowl, lightly whisk the egg to blend. Gently whisk in the honey until smooth, followed by the olive oil, milk, and zest. Pour the egg mixture into the center of the dry ingredients and stir with a dough whisk (page 30) or a rubber spatula just until combined. Do not overmix. Drain the figs, if needed, and fold them into the batter. Pour the batter evenly into the pan.

4 Carefully place the sheet with the tart pan in the oven (it can slide!) and bake until the edges of the cake turn golden-brown and a cake tester or toothpick inserted into the center comes out clean, 25 to 30 minutes. Remove from the oven, and carefully slide the tart pan onto a wire rack to cool.

5 When ready to serve, remove the outer ring of the tart pan. If you like (I never do), you can slide the tart onto a serving plate by running a long spatula between the bottom of the pan and the cake and then transferring it to the plate. Sprinkle the cake lightly with confectioners' sugar and cut into 8 to 12 wedges.

TO GET A HEAD START: The cake can be baked 1 day ahead. Store in an airtight container at room temperature.

Pomegranate Yogurt Parfait with a Kick

This smooth, thick yogurt dessert comes together quickly and is eye-catching to boot—a nice ending for a dinner party. Watch the caramel-colored turbinado sugar dissolve and seep into layers of shiny white yogurt. This is for adults only, given the sassy kick of orange liqueur (you can use freshly squeezed orange juice to make this child-friendly). Pair this creamy treat with the Chicken Stew with Artichokes and Dried Apricots over Brown Rice (page 118) or the Lamb Stew with Wheat Berries in Red Wine Sauce (page 121).

Tangy-sweet pomegranate syrup, available in Middle Eastern stores (for sources, see page 219), is worth seeking out here, as it nicely cuts through the sweetness. Leftover syrup can be used to sweeten summer drinks and lemonades, or to add a fresh twist to salad dressings. To show off this dessert's dazzling looks, I use small, clear, straight-sided glasses (2$1/2$ inches in diameter and about 4 inches tall), which hold about 1 cup volume. Depending on your dessert glasses, you might need to adjust the overall amount. SERVES 6

....

4 cups plain whole milk or lowfat Greek yogurt (2 pounds)

$1/3$ cup good-quality orange liqueur such as Grand Marnier

4 teaspoons finely grated orange zest (about 2 oranges)

About $1/2$ cup turbinado sugar, depending on the size of the serving glasses

About 1 tablespoon pomegranate syrup (optional)

$3/4$ cup pomegranate seeds (from about 1 small pomegranate)

1 Beat the Greek yogurt, orange liqueur, and zest in a tall large bowl using a wooden spoon until smooth.

2 Line up 6 dessert glasses on the counter. Spoon the yogurt mixture into a 1-gallon ziplock bag and cut off a small corner, about $1/4$ inch.

3 Add about 1 teaspoon turbinado sugar (or enough to create a thin layer) to each glass, jiggling it back and forth to spread evenly across the bottom. Pipe about a $3/4$-inch layer of the yogurt mixture on top and jiggle again to distribute evenly. Sprinkle with another layer of sugar and top with yogurt; drizzle about $1/2$ teaspoon pomegranate syrup (or another layer of sugar) into each glass. Repeat with 1 more layer of yogurt, ending with a layer of sugar. Cover each glass with plastic wrap and chill for at least 2 hours to allow for the sugar to melt.

4 Just before serving, top each glass with a couple of tablespoons of pomegranate seeds.

TO GET A HEAD START: This dessert, up through step 3, can be prepared 1 day ahead. You can also seed the pomegranate ahead of time (see "How to Seed a Pomegranate," page 87) and chill separately, covered.

TO VARY IT: A few tablespoons of diced peaches, apricots, or halved seedless grapes can also top the dessert. My tester Karen enjoyed it with black raspberries.

Artisanal Fruit Bread

This intensely tart fruit bread evolved from a recipe of my German childhood friend Gisela. Her holiday loaf piqued my curiosity because it was made with whole grain rye flour only, without any sugar or eggs. The purity of the ingredients makes for a fascinating fierceness of flavors. I have baked this dense fruit and nut loaf many times since, adapting it from her tiny scribbles on a faded postcard she sent years ago.

For our modern tastes, I spike the dried fruit with Italian limoncello liqueur, which also highlights the slight tanginess of the rye flour. MAKES 1 (1¼-POUND) LOAF

....

PLUMPED FRUIT

1 to 2 lemons

10 ounces dried fruits such as figs, apricots, and cherries, chopped into ¼-inch pieces (about 2 cups)

¼ cup water

2 tablespoons limoncello or brandy, plus extra if needed

½ teaspoon vanilla extract

FRUIT BREAD

¾ cup whole grain rye flour (3 ounces)

¾ teaspoon baking powder

¼ teaspoon ground cinnamon

¼ teaspoon ground anise, preferably freshly ground

Pinch of fine sea salt

¾ cup coarsely chopped toasted hazelnuts (see page 37)

¼ cup chopped dried dates

A few whole hazelnuts, for garnish

> **SEE MEASURING WHOLE GRAIN FLOUR, PAGE 28**

1 To prepare the plumped fruit, start at least 3 hours ahead, or the night before. Finely grate the zest of the lemons until you have 2 teaspoons. Squeeze the fruit to get ¼ cup juice (reserve the leftover lemon for another use). Combine the dried figs, apricots, and cherries in a medium bowl. Add the water, lemon juice, zest, and limoncello and stir to combine. Cover with plastic wrap and let sit at room temperature for at least 3 hours or overnight, stirring once or twice in between. Drain the fruit, reserving the plumping liquid. You should have 2 tablespoons liquid. If not, add more limoncello. Stir the vanilla into the plumping liquid.

2 Line a large rimless baking sheet with parchment paper.

3 To make the fruit bread, whisk together the rye flour, baking powder, cinnamon, anise, and salt in a small bowl. Combine the plumped fruit, chopped hazelnuts, and dates in a medium bowl. Drizzle with the plumping liquid and evenly distribute the flour mixture across. Using your hands, bring the mixture together and gently knead until it is well combined and no traces of flour remain. The dough will be dense, heavy, and slightly tacky. Moisten your hands with water and form a small oblong loaf, about 6 by 4 inches (2½ inches high). Place on the prepared baking sheet. Gently press a few whole hazelnuts lengthwise across the top. Cover loosely with plastic wrap or a dish towel and allow to sit at room temperature for 20 minutes.

4 Meanwhile, position a rack in the center of the oven and preheat to 350°F.

5 Bake the loaf until the top is nicely browned and crusty when gently pressed with a finger, about 45 minutes.

6 Slide the loaf with the parchment paper onto a wire rack. Remove the parchment paper. Cool the fruit bread completely, at least 2½ hours, and then wrap in a double layer of aluminum foil. Store for at least 1 day in an old-fashioned tin or in a container with a tight-fitting lid, for flavors to meld, before cutting into slices with a long serrated knife. The bread will last in a cool, dry pantry for about 3 weeks.

Whole Wheat and Butter Tart Crust

While living in Germany, I have had so many amazing whole wheat butter crusts that I simply couldn't settle for anything other than butter when I developed this recipe. You can make crusts with half butter and half oil, but personally I would rather eat a smaller piece of tart. Adding whole wheat pastry flour to the dough makes for a more pleasing bite than if using whole wheat flour only. Use this crust for the Dark Chocolate Truffle Tart with Walnuts (page 215). It is best when the dough has had time to "relax" in the fridge before baking; so plan ahead. **MAKES 1 PARTIALLY BAKED (9½-INCH) TART CRUST**

3/4 cup white whole wheat flour (3 1/8 ounces)

1/2 cup whole wheat pastry flour (2 ounces)

1 teaspoon sugar

1/4 teaspoon fine sea salt

7 tablespoons chilled unsalted butter, cut into 1/3-inch cubes (3 1/2 ounces)

4 to 6 tablespoons ice water

> **SEE MEASURING WHOLE GRAIN FLOUR, PAGE 28**

1 Place both whole wheat flours, sugar, and salt in the bowl of a food processor and process 10 pulses to combine. Distribute the butter cubes on top and sprinkle with 3 tablespoons of the ice water. Process 8 to 10 pulses. Pinch a small amount of the dough with your fingers. It should hold together. If not, add 1 tablespoon more ice water (if very dry), or add ice water by the teaspoonful (if it just starts to hold together). Process 2 pulses each time you add water until no floury patches remain but the dough stays uniformly crumbly with tiny butter pieces. (Do not allow to form a ball.)

2 Scrape the mixture onto a lightly floured work surface. Gently press it into a flat disk about 1 inch thick, and immediately roll into an 12-inch circle, about 1/8 inch thick. Transfer the dough to a 9½-inch fluted tart pan with removable bottom and gently press into the edges. Roll the pin across the top of the pan to remove excess dough. Prick the dough about a dozen times with a fork. Chill, covered with plastic wrap, for at least 2 hours or overnight.

3 Position a rack in the center of the oven and preheat to 375°F. Set the tart pan on a large rimless baking sheet for easier handling. Place a piece of parchment paper on the crust and fill it with pie weights (or dried beans).

4 To partially bake the crust, carefully place the sheet with the tart pan in the oven (it can slide!) and bake until the crust starts to pull away from the sides, 15 to 18 minutes. Remove from the oven, and carefully slide the tart pan onto a wire rack. Remove the parchment paper with the pie weights. Allow the crust to cool to room temperature before filling.

TO GET A HEAD START: The crust can be baked 1 day ahead (or frozen up to 1 month). Store under a cake dome at room temperature, or wrapped in plastic wrap.

TO VARY IT: Add 1 teaspoon freshly grated orange zest plus 1/2 teaspoon freshly grated lemon zest for bright citrus flavor.

Dark Chocolate Truffle Tart with Walnuts

Intensely velvety and dense, this festive chocolate tart pulls out all the stops. Admittedly, this is a rich dessert (hence the small slices), but you can also feel pretty good about eating it: the crust is made entirely from whole wheat, and heart-healthy walnuts and antioxidant-rich pitch-dark chocolate enhance the honey-sweetened filling. Serve with a dollop of tangy crème fraîche or unsweetened softly whipped cream. **MAKES 1 (9½-INCH) TART, TO SERVE 12**

½ cup sugar

¼ cup whole milk

½ cup honey

6 ounces dark chocolate with 70 percent cocoa content, chopped

¼ cup (2 ounces, ½ stick) unsalted butter, cut into 8 pieces

2 tablespoons Grand Marnier or other good-quality orange-flavored liqueur

1 tablespoon freshly grated orange zest (from 1 large orange)

1 teaspoon vanilla extract

2 large eggs plus 1 egg yolk, at room temperature, lightly beaten

1 partially baked Whole Wheat and Butter Tart Crust (page 213), plain or the citrus variation

⅔ cup coarsely chopped toasted walnuts (see page 37)

12 toasted walnut halves, for garnish

1 Position a rack in the center of the oven and preheat to 350°F.

2 Warm the sugar and milk in a small heavy-bottomed saucepan over medium-low heat, stirring occasionally, until the sugar has dissolved, 4 to 5 minutes. Add the honey and cook until it has dissolved and the mixture is smooth, 1 minute or more, depending on the consistency of the honey. Set aside.

3 Place the chocolate and butter in a large metal bowl set over a saucepan containing about 1 inch of barely simmering water (the bottom of the bowl should not touch the water). Wait until melted, stirring gently with a wooden spoon, about 4 minutes. Remove the bowl from the saucepan and set the chocolate mixture aside to cool for 5 minutes. Stir the Grand Marnier, orange zest, and vanilla extract into the sugar-honey mixture. Using a large whisk and a gentle hand, add the sugar-honey mixture to the chocolate mixture, and then whisk in the eggs and yolk just until incorporated. The mixture will thicken slightly.

4 After the crust has cooled, place the tart pan on a large rimless baking sheet for easier handling. Sprinkle the crust with the chopped walnuts. Gently spoon the filling evenly into the crust as to not disturb the nuts.

5 Carefully place the sheet with the tart pan in the oven (it can slide!) and bake for 15 minutes. Remove from the oven and decorate the tart with the walnut halves by lightly pressing them around the outer rim. Continue to bake until the filling barely jiggles when the pan is moved gently, 8 to 10 more minutes (it will puff around the edges, but settle as it cools). Remove from the oven and carefully slide the tart pan onto a wire rack. Leave the tart to cool completely in the pan, about 1½ hours, before serving. The tart can sit at cool room temperature, under a cake dome, up to 4 hours.

6 When ready to serve, remove the outer ring of the tart pan. Cut the tart into 12 pieces using a sharp knife dipped into hot water and wiped clean between each cut.

TO GET A HEAD START: The tart, including the filling, can be prepared 1 day ahead. Wait until the tart has completely cooled and then chill, covered with plastic wrap. Bring to room temperature before serving.

Millet: Sweet, and Waiting to Be Served

Whenever I prepare a dish with millet for a group of dinner guests, I hide the grain. In fact, I will do anything to disguise it from plain view and to avoid dropping its name by accident. And I am pretty certain you can guess why. If I were to say, "I am serving a dessert with millet," chances are that my friends will burst out, "Isn't that bird food?"—unless they were raised in India or Africa, where versatile millet is still part of the daily diet. After years of experimenting with millet, I can proudly report back: my stealth serving technique works amazingly well. "Hidden" millet—be it in a dessert, a side, or a main dish—is a great success. Not only will everyone enjoy the grain, but I can also reveal after dinner with the grin of the Cheshire cat, "You just ate millet," and the victory is mine.

One of the most interesting features of millet is its almost comedic inflatable quality, like a cloud that keeps billowing. This amazing trait also sparked my imagination as a three-year-old when I asked my mom to read and reread the fairy tale of the Brothers Grimm, "The Sweet Porridge." In it, a poor, hungry girl is handed a magic pot by an old woman. The pot cooks sweet millet on command until prompted to stop. One day when the girl steps out, her mother starts a pot of millet—without knowing the magic word to halt the pot from overflowing with porridge. The result is a town covered in sweet millet—until the girl finally returns and puts an end to the river of starch.

While I had never seen, let alone eaten, millet as a kid in Germany, the grain was a main staple in central Europe during the Middle Ages, before being replaced by potatoes and corn from the New World. And this seed grain will indeed expand continuously in your pot, depending on how much liquid you add.

Given my lifelong passion for comforting starches, it is no surprise that millet became a favorite the moment I discovered it on a store shelf in my mid-twenties. Millet is a nourishing and fast-cooking side with infinite possibilities for leftovers. A pot of steamed millet can be on the table in as little as 20 minutes. To me, a bowl of warm, lightly salted millet, with a slice of butter melting into its mound, is a wintertime favorite.

I have also made countless savory pancakes from leftover cooked millet. My favorites are thick, large, and golden from pan-frying, and sprinkled with a good dose of cheese for a deliciously rustic treat. If you cherish the mouthfeel of a stuffed Salvadorian *pupusa*, millet cakes are your ticket. I'm in good company: even renowned chef Jean-Georges Vongerichten fell for a butter–and egg-rich millet cake, for which he credits his colleague Didier Virot.

Similar to polenta or mashed potatoes, millet can also be dished up in gratins and savory casseroles, flavored with mushrooms, onions, carrots, or any vegetables of your choice and topped with a browned crust of cheese. German millet fans feast on alluring creamy desserts, reminiscent of chilled rice pudding, lightened with the traditional fresh cheese Quark. They will stir in fresh fruit and honey and sometimes fold in whipped cream, for the occasional indulgence. You can try a version with ricotta, as in the Ricotta Millet Pudding with Warm Raspberry Compote (page 208). Or would you prefer an airy almond soufflé with the tiny grain, accompanied by strawberries and softly whipped cream?

Comforting millet landed once more on my plate with a bang when I was in India. My husband's family roots are in the western state of Gujarat. During a visit to the village where members of his extended family live, I was introduced to the staple of farmers: a plate-covering flatbread, darkish-gray in color and smothered with ghee, the tangy clarified butter. This hefty nourishing round, accompanied by little mounds of lentils and vegetables, was prepared entirely from dark millet flour and water, nothing else.

Unlike the golden millet seeds I knew from Germany and the United States, these *bajra rotlas* are made from locally grown pearl millet. They are dense and chewy, impressively sturdy, and sweet with a rich earthiness. In today's India, *bajra rotlas* are quickly losing ground, the food of poor farmers. Many Indians in the cities will gladly leave them behind for lighter whole wheat *chapatis* or puffy *naan* breads. In fact, most of our friends and acquaintances found it amusing that a Westerner took to *bajra rotlas* the way I did.

Over the years, my husband has mastered the art of *rotlo* making, yet neither his nor mine rival my mother-in-law's. Honed by decades of rolling this claylike dough, her flatbreads emerge in perfectly sized rounds of eight inches each, without fail. No cracks, no breaking. Ever. And this despite the fact that millet has no gluten and is thus hard to shape into a malleable dough.

During a visit, I once asked her to make millet *rotlas* to accompany a meal. While I simmered ginger- and spice-infused lentils and stir-fried hot, spicy beef strips, she quietly worked on a small counter behind me. Using a moistened handkerchief, she rolled the heavy unleavened dough with a light, determined hand and the speed and precision of a pasta machine. She then cooked each *rotlo* in a cast-iron skillet, skillfully sprinkling it with drops of water to prevent cracking. Pushing on the flatbread with a spatula, she coaxed it to puff and develop its signature burned spots on the bottom, all the while rolling out the next *rotlo*, assembly-line style. Our dinner was superb that night—yet what I remember best is the earthy-sweet taste of dark millet.

BROWN RICE

SOURCES

FOR WHOLE GRAINS AND WHOLE GRAIN FLOURS

Natural food stores and specialty stores carry most of the whole grains and whole grain flours used in this book. Below, I list online sources in case you can't locate the products locally. Some are mainstream mills with national reach, others are smaller operations worth exploring. The more familiar you become with whole grains, the more you might want to check out local flour mills and farms. My selection is subjective and by no means inclusive, but designed as a starting point to pique your interest.

BOB'S RED MILL

Nationally known for its commitment to old-fashioned stone milling, this company offers a huge variety of whole grains and flours, many of them organic. Through its website, the Oregon-based firm sells more than 400 products. Customer service is great, and I have yet to get a product from them that I didn't like, from whole wheat to pumpernickel flour, from different grinds of cornmeal to whole grains such as amaranth, buckwheat, barley, millet, and brown rice.

www.bobsredmill.com
toll-free: (800) 349-2173

KING ARTHUR FLOUR

America's oldest flour company (founded in Boston in 1790) is employee-owned and renowned by homemakers and professionals alike for their dedication to the quality of their products. The Vermont-based company is another top address, especially for your flour needs, from whole grain pumpernickel to spelt flour (many of them organic). And the friendly staff at their baking hotline answers any questions you might have about succeeding with scones, muffins, cakes and more. The company also sells dough whisks for blending batter.

www.kingarthurflour.com
toll-free: (800) 827-6836

ARROWHEAD MILLS

Organic farming pioneer Frank Ford founded the company in the Texas Panhandle 50 years ago in 1960. Today owned by the Hain Celestial Group, it sells many organic whole grain products, from long grain brown rice to quinoa, millet and whole oats (groats), as well as a variety of whole grain flours, from spelt to barley and cornmeal.

www.arrowheadmills.com
toll-free: (800) 434-4246

ANSON MILLS

Revered by chefs and grain lovers, this South Carolina–based milling company is as passionate about their organic grains and flours as one can be. Under its founder Glenn Roberts, Anson Mills has revived near extinct heirloom grains from before the Civil War, from corn to rice and wheat. All products are stone-milled as in the days of yore with lots of dedicated labor involved such as hand-sifting and hand scrubbing, which is also reflected in the price. The mill offers superbly textured and aromatic grits, cornmeal, and different kinds of whole grain polenta. My current favorite: their tiny whole grain farro piccolo, which is very small ancient wheat of Italian origin. It cooks fast and brings a rustic sweetness and unique plumpness to your table. Their slow-roasted farro, a firm textured and flavorful whole grain, is equally worth exploring. Yes, some of their grains and grits need time to cook. But once you've tried them, you might never look back—or at your clock for that matter. In addition to grains, the mill also sells a number of distinct character-rich flours, such as a Colonial-style whole wheat and a coarse graham flour as well as buckwheat and rye flour.

www.ansonmills.com
phone: (803) 467-4122

BLUEBIRD GRAIN FARMS

Food lovers rave, justifiably so, about the farms' organic whole grain farro, which is sold as "Emmer Farro." The farm in Washington state also offers freshly ground whole grain farro flour and the cracked grain, plus a number of other whole grain flours and grain berries such as hard red and soft white wheat berries and rye berries.

www.bluebirdgrainfarms.com
toll-free: (888) 232-0331

WILD HIVE FARM

This New York State farm offers freshly ground organic flours and whole grains such as spelt berries and soft white wheat berries. Food lovers cherish the farms' coarse stone ground extra-fancy polenta. The farm also sells whole grain rye flour and different grinds of stone-ground whole grain cornmeal.

> www.wildhivefarm.com
> phone: (845) 266-5863

FULL BELLY FARM

Bakers savor the flavor of their organic whole grain flour. It is ground to order in a stone-mill from Sonora wheat, a soft red wheat. The organic farm, located in Northern California, doesn't advertise its flour on its website because of the very limited quantity, but aficionados would say, do give it a try.

> www.fullbellyfarm.com
> toll-free: (800) 791-2110

LOTUS FOODS

Lotus Foods pursues the universe of rice with a passion. The company offers an especially delicious Chinese black rice, which the company has trademarked as Forbidden Rice, and other whole grain rice varieties from around the globe, many organic, such as brown jasmine rice or brown kalijira rice, an heirloom variety from the region of Bengal.

> www.lotusfoods.com
> toll-free: (866) 972-6879

GUSTIAMO

Sourcing high quality products from their native Italy is the mission of this New York online business, from olive oil and pasta to short grain rice for risotto and pasta. And while both their farro and their farro pasta by Latini are semipearled, these products stand out for their appealing flavor and texture. Their farro pasta is dried at low temperatures for an extended time, between 24 to 48 hours. The farro fusilli are delish.

> www.gustiamo.com
> toll-free: (877) 907-2525

ALTER ECO

The San Francisco–based company with French roots is committed to fair trade products, from olive oil to coffee, tea, sugar and rice. Here you can find three types of excellent quinoa from cooperatives in Bolivia (white, red, and black). All are very tasty, but the chewy black quinoa is out-of-this world and stunning to look at as well. Also available at Whole Foods stores.

> www.altereco-usa.com
> toll-free: (866) 972-6879

GIBBS WILD RICE

This wild rice specialist offers organic wild rice harvested from rivers and lakes in Minnesota. For busy weeknights, try their instant wild rice which cooks in 7 to 10 minutes.

> www.gibbswildrice.com
> toll-free: (800) 344-6378

HARD-TO-FIND INGREDIENTS

Most ingredients used in this book are available at well-stocked supermarkets and natural foods stores. Some of the specialty ingredients are also available at local Greek, Turkish, Middle Eastern, and Italian stores. In addition, there are now countless well-stocked online purveyors, a few of which are listed below.

Spices such as Aleppo pepper, caraway seeds, cardamom pods, coriander and cumin seeds, fennel seeds, herbes de Provence, dried lavender, dried mint, Nigella seeds, saffron, and sumac:

> Kalustyan's: toll-free (800) 352-3451
> www.kalustyans.com

> Penzeys Spices: toll-free (800) 741-7787
> www.penzeys.com

Middle Eastern ingredients such as pomegranate syrup, and rose water, can also be found at Kalustyan's (see above). The store carries spicy Indian chile relish, too.

Greek specialty foods such as feta, haloumi, *kefalotiri*, olives, olive oils, dried oregano, dried mint, saffron, dried figs, dates, and tahini can be found at

> Christos Marketplace: toll-free (866) 608-8147
> www.christosmarket.com

> Igourmet.com: toll-free (877) 446-8763
> www.igourmet.com

Spanish ingredients such as Manzanilla olives, chorizo, and saffron are available at

> La Tienda: toll-free (800) 710-4304
> www.tienda.com

Nuts and nut products, including whole roasted or presteamed chestnuts, can be found at specialty stores and many Asian markets, or at Kalustyan's (see above). Almond butter is available at Trader Joe's and natural foods stores. Jordan almonds can be found at Greek or Middle Eastern stores, or online at

> JordanAlmonds.com: phone (215) 392-4343
> www.jordanalmonds.com

Smoked trout is available at Igourmet.com (see above).

BIBLIOGRAPHY

Cookbooks surround a cookbook author the way flowers surround a gardener. From the hundreds of books in my cook's library, these select volumes have been an inspiration or a learning tool in writing this book. I have listed them here in case you want to dig further.

Bittman, Mark. *Food Matters: A Guide to Conscious Eating.* New York: Simon & Schuster, 2009.

Brown, Alton. *I'm Just Here for More Food.* New York: Stewart, Tabori & Chang, 2004.

Brüggemann, Luise. *Meine Schätze aus der Vollwertküche: Der erste Schritt zur Gesundheit.* Münster, Germany: Wolfgang Hölker, 1986.

Davidson, Alan. *The Oxford Companion to Food,* 2nd ed. Oxford: Oxford University Press, 2006.

Graham, Kevin. *Grains, Rice, and Beans.* New York: Artisan, 1995.

Greene, Bert. *The Grains Cookbook.* New York: Workman Publishing, 1988.

Greenspan, Dorie. *Baking with Julia: Based on the PBS Series Hosted by Julia Child.* New York: William Morrow, 1996.

Grunes, Barbara, and Virginia Van Vynckt. *All-American Waves of Grain.* New York: Henry Holt and Company, 1997.

Harris, Andy. *Modern Greek: 170 Contemporary Recipes from the Mediterranean.* San Francisco: Chronicle Books, 2002.

Hertzberg, Jeff, and Zoë François. *Healthy Bread in Five Minutes a Day.* New York: Thomas Dunne Books, St. Martin's Press, 2009.

Jenkins, Nancy Harmon. *The Essential Mediterranean.* New York: HarperCollins, 2003.

Karayanis, Dean, and Catherine Karayanis. *Regional Greek Cooking.* New York: Hippocrene Books, 2008.

Kochilas, Diane. *The Glorious Foods of Greece: Traditional Recipes from the Islands, Cities, and Villages.* New York: William Morrow, 2001.

———. *Meze: Small Plates to Savor and Share from the Mediterranean Table.* New York: William Morrow, 2003.

Kremezi, Aglaia. *Mediterranean Hot and Spicy.* New York: Broadway Books, 2009.

Kyriakou, Theodore, and Charles Campion. *The Real Greek at Home: Dishes from the Heart of the Greek Kitchen.* London: Mitchell Beazley, 2004.

Lahey, Jim, with Rick Flaste. *My Bread: The Revolutionary No-Work, No-Knead Method.* New York and London: W. W. Norton & Company, 2009.

Lutterbeck, Barbara, and Jürgen Christ. *Orient: Küche & Kultur.* Munich, Germany: Gräfe und Unzer, 2007.

Malouf, Greg, and Lucy Malouf. *Artichoke to Za'atar.* Berkeley and Los Angeles: University of California Press, 2006.

Mehdawy, Magda. *My Egyptian Grandmother's Kitchen: Traditional Dishes Sweet and Savory.* Cairo, Egypt: The American University in Cairo Press, 2006.

Moon, Rosemary. *High Fiber High Flavor.* Willowdale, Ontario: Firefly Books, 2000.

Muir, Jenni. *A Cook's Guide to Grains.* London: Conran Octopus, 2002.

Mushet, Cindy. *Desserts: Mediterranean Flavors, California Style.* New York: Scribner, 2000.

Oliver, Jamie. *Cook with Jamie: My Guide to Making You a Better Cook.* New York: Hyperion, 2007.

Patent, Greg. *A Baker's Odyssey: Celebrating Time-Honored Recipes from America's Rich Immigrant Heritage.* Hoboken, NJ: John Wiley & Sons, 2007.

Planck, Nina. *Real Food: What to Eat and Why.* New York: Bloomsbury, 2006.

Pollan, Michael. *Food Rules: An Eater's Manual.* New York: Penguin, 2009.

Psilakis, Michael. *How to Roast a Lamb: New Greek Classic Cooking.* New York: Little, Brown and Company, 2009.

Psilakis, Nikos, & Maria Psilakis. *Olive Oil—The Secret of Good Health: Advice on Its Correct Use.* Crete, Greece: Karmanor, undated.

Reichl, Ruth. *Garlic and Sapphires: The Secret Life of a Critic in Disguise.* New York: Penguin, 2005.

Roden, Claudia. *Arabesque: A Taste of Morocco, Turkey, & Lebanon.* New York: Alfred A. Knopf, 2005.

Rodgers, Rick. *The Baker's Dozen Cookbook.* New York: William Morrow, 2001.

Sass, Lorna. *Whole Grains Every Day, Every Way.* New York: Clarkson Potter, 2006.

Segan, Francine. *The Philosopher's Kitchen: Recipes from Ancient Greece and Rome for the Modern Cook.* New York: Random House, 2004.

Souli, Sofia. *Das Traditionelle Griechische Kochbuch.* Athens, Greece: Verlag Michalis Toubis S.A., 1989.

Steingarten, Jeffrey. *It Must've Been Something I Ate.* New York: Vintage Books, 2002.

von Bredow, Nicole. "Happy-End am Herd (Interview mit Nigella Lawson)." *Für Sie* (2004), pp. 130–132.

Willan, Anne. *The Good Cook.* New York: Stewart, Tabori & Chang, 2004.

Wittenberg, Margaret M. *New Good Food: Essential Ingredients for Cooking and Eating Well.* Berkeley: Ten Speed Press, 2007.

Wolfert, Paula. *Couscous and Other Good Food from Morocco.* New York: Quill, 1973.

——. *Mediterranean Grains and Greens.* New York: Harper Collins, 1998.

Wright, Clifford A. *A Mediterranean Feast.* New York: William Morrow, 1999.

Zaouali, Lilia. *Medieval Cuisine of the Islamic World: A Concise History with 174 Recipes,* translated by M. B. DeBevoise. Berkeley and Los Angeles: University of California Press, 2007.

INDEX

MEASUREMENT CONVERSION CHARTS

VOLUME

U.S.	Imperial	Metric
1 tablespoon	$1/2$ fl oz	15 ml
2 tablespoons	1 fl oz	30 ml
$1/4$ cup	2 fl oz	60 ml
$1/3$ cup	3 fl oz	90 ml
$1/2$ cup	4 fl oz	120 ml
$2/3$ cup	5 fl oz (1/4 pint)	150 ml
$3/4$ cup	6 fl oz	180 ml
1 cup	8 fl oz ($1/3$ pint)	240 ml
1 $1/4$ cups	10 fl oz ($1/2$ pint)	300 ml
2 cups (1 pint)	16 fl oz ($2/3$ pint)	480 ml
2 $1/2$ cups	20 fl oz (1 pint)	600 ml
1 quart	32 fl oz (1$2/3$ pint)	1 l

TEMPERATURE

Fahrenheit	Celsius/Gas Mark
250°F	120°C/gas mark $1/2$
275°F	135°C/gas mark 1
300°F	150°C/gas mark 2
325°F	160°C/gas mark 3
350°F	180 or 175°C/gas mark 4
375°F	190°C/gas mark 5
400°F	200°C/gas mark 6
425°F	220°C/gas mark 7
450°F	230°C/gas mark 8
475°F	245°C/gas mark 9
500°F	260°C

LENGTH

Inch	Metric
$1/4$ inch	6 mm
$1/2$ inch	1.25 cm
$3/4$ inch	2 cm
1 inch	2.5 cm
6 inches ($1/2$ foot)	15 cm
12 inches (1 foot)	30 cm

WEIGHT

U.S./Imperial	Metric
$1/2$ oz	15 g
1 oz	30 g
2 oz	60 g
$1/4$ lb	115 g
$1/3$ lb	150 g
$1/2$ lb	225 g
$3/4$ lb	350 g
1 lb	450 g